CIMA EXAMINATION TEXT

Intermediate Level

Paper 8

Management Accounting – Performance Management

ISBN 1 84390 248 6

British Library Cataloguing-in-Publication data

A catalogue record for this book is available from the British Library.

We are grateful to the Chartered Institute of Management Accountants for permission to reproduce past assessment material. The solutions have been prepared by The Financial Training Company.

Published by

The Financial Training Company
22J Wincombe Business Park
Shaftesbury
Dorset
SP7 9QJ

Contents

How to use this examination text

Objective

The aim of this Examination Text is a simple one: to give you the best possible chance of achieving the pass mark when you attempt the CIMA Management Accounting – Performance Management examination. To do this, we follow three main principles:

♦ The texts cover **all** areas of the syllabus with sufficient depth to ensure that you are fully prepared. However, we use our knowledge and experience to home in on key areas that have tended to crop up again and again in previous examinations and give these areas extra attention.

♦ We use our extensive experience of teaching CIMA students to assess how much the majority of students can assimilate. We do not make the mistake of overloading you with material that most students will find worthless in the examination room. Nor do we make you slog again through material that you have already learned at earlier stages.

♦ We believe that the best way to prepare for an examination is by practice. We intersperse explanatory text with frequent examples for you to try your hand at. Full solutions are provided in all cases.

Using the Examination Text

Each chapter begins with a section headed 'Exam focus'. This reflects our key objective: we are interested above all in your examination success.

We set out CIMA's own Learning Outcomes and the main structural divisions into which the chapter is organised. This gives you a clear picture of what you should be aiming to achieve as you work through the text, and guidance on the steps to follow on the way.

The main body of each chapter consists of very full explanation of all syllabus areas. We concentrate on clear explanations of what really matters. We emphasise drills — standardised approaches that you can follow for typical questions. Never again need you ask: 'Where do I begin?'

Each chapter includes practice questions. These are graded: earlier questions involve material from the earlier sections of the chapter, while in later questions we progress to include more complex examples, including exam-standard questions. To get the best from the text you should make a serious attempt to tackle all the practice questions. Only then should you refer to our suggested solutions, which are contained in the final chapter of the text.

Each chapter ends by summarising the main points that you should have digested as you worked your way through.

Key features

The text is written in an interactive style:

♦ key terms and concepts are clearly defined

♦ 'pitfalls' and 'examination tips' help you avoid commonly made mistakes and help you focus on what is required to perform well in your examination

♦ frequent practice examples throughout the chapters ensure that what you have learnt is regularly reinforced

Icons

Throughout the text we use symbols to highlight the elements referred to above.

 Key facts

 Examination tips and techniques

 Pitfalls

 Practice questions

Syllabus

Syllabus overview

Performance Management builds on the introduction to standard costing and budgeting provided by Management Accounting Fundamentals, and covers the evaluation of plans, budgets, forecasts and the introduction to the use of costing systems for planning and decision making.

While this paper will develop students' ability to apply a range of management accounting techniques, quantitative methods and resource management strategies to the business environment, students will also have to demonstrate understanding of these tools and the issues that surround their use.

Students must also appreciate the contribution made by information technology to management accounting.

Aims

This syllabus aims to test the student's ability to:

♦ apply and evaluate standard costing
♦ prepare and evaluate plans, budgets and forecasts
♦ apply and evaluate the use of costing systems for planning and decision making for a wide range of sectors, including manufacturing, retail and service.

Assessment

There will be a written paper of three hours. The paper comprises of four sections:

Section A (20 marks): Ten multiple choice questions (compulsory).
Section B (30 marks): One compulsory question.
Section C (25 marks): One question from two.
Section D (25 marks): One question from two.

Learning outcomes and syllabus content

	Chapter where covered in this textbook

8(i) Standard costing – 25%

Learning outcomes

On completion of their studies students should be able to:

♦ Explain why costing systems and standard costs must be reviewed on a regular basis	1
♦ Calculate and interpret material, labour, variable overhead, fixed overhead and sales variances	2
♦ Prepare and discuss a report which reconciles budget and actual profit using absorption and/or marginal costing principles	2, 8
♦ Prepare reports using a range of internal and external benchmarks and interpret the results	3, 7
♦ Discuss the behavioural implications of setting standard costs	3

	Chapter where covered in this textbook

Syllabus content

♦ Criticisms of standard costing	1
♦ Material price and usage; labour rate and efficiency (including idle time); variable overhead efficiency and expenditure; fixed overhead expenditure, volume, capacity and efficiency/productivity	1
♦ Total material mix and yield variances	2
♦ Total labour mix and yield variances	2
♦ Sales price and volume variances (Note: the volume variance will be calculated on a units basis using sales revenue, contribution or gross profit)	2
♦ Interpretation of variances: interrelationship, significance	2, 3
♦ Benchmarking	3
♦ Behavioural implications of setting standard costs. Note: standard process costing is not included	3

8(ii)   Budgeting – 30%

Learning outcomes

On completion of their studies students should be able to:

♦ Explain why organisations prepare plans	4
♦ Calculate future sales and costs using forecasting techniques and evaluate the results	5
♦ Explain and interpret the effect of amendments to budget/plan assumptions	4
♦ Explain why it is necessary to identify controllable and uncontrollable costs	4
♦ Evaluate performance using fixed and flexible budget reports	4
♦ Discuss alternative approaches to budgeting	4
♦ Evaluate the balanced scorecard	7
♦ Discuss the behavioural implications of planning and budgeting	4

Syllabus content

♦ Planning	4
♦ Time series and regression	5
♦ 'What-if?' analysis	4
♦ Controllable and uncontrollable costs	5
♦ Fixed and flexible budgeting	4
♦ Incremental budgeting	4
♦ Rolling budgets	4
♦ Zero-based budgeting	4
♦ Activity-based budgeting	6
♦ Balanced scorecard	7
♦ Behavioural implications	4

**Chapter where
covered in this
textbook**

8(iii)   Costing systems and decision making - 45%

Learning outcomes

On completion of their studies students should be able to:

♦ Compare and contrast value analysis and functional cost analysis	6
♦ Apply and evaluate the use of activity-based, absorption, marginal and process costing and throughput accounting in the context of planning and decision making	6, 11
♦ Explain total quality management	6
♦ Prepare and discuss cost of quality reports	6
♦ Calculate and interpret the break even point, profit target, margin of safety and contribution/sales ratio for multiple products	9
♦ Prepare break even charts and profit/volume charts for multiple products	9
♦ Discuss multiple product CVP analysis	9
♦ Calculate and interpret the profit-maximising sales mix for a company with a single resource constraint and limited freedom of action	10
♦ Apply and evaluate relevant costs and revenues	10
♦ Solve a two-plus constraint/limitation problem for two products using the graphical method and explain the results	10

Syllabus content

♦ Value and functional cost analysis	6
♦ Resource planning systems: MRPI, MRPII and ERP	6
♦ Just-in-time	6
♦ Activity-based, absorption, marginal and process (eg FIFO and AVCO) costing and throughput accounting	6, 11
♦ Cost reduction programmes	6
♦ Total quality management	6
♦ Multi-product CVP analysis including break even, margin of safety, contribution/sales ratio, break even charts, contribution, profit/volume graphs	9
♦ Relevant costs and revenues for short term decision making	10
♦ Single limiting factor analysis where a company has restricted freedom of action	10
♦ Graphical linear programming (including an explanation of shadow prices)	10

MATHEMATICAL TABLES AND FORMULAE

LOGARITHMS

	0	1	2	3	4	5	6	7	8	9	1	2	3	4	5	6	7	8	9
10	0000	0043	0086	0128	0170						4	9	13	17	21	26	30	34	38
						0212	0253	0294	0334	0374	4	8	12	16	20	24	28	32	37
11	0414	0453	0492	0531	0569						4	8	12	15	19	23	27	31	35
						0607	0645	0682	0719	0755	4	7	11	15	19	22	26	30	33
12	0792	0828	0864	0899	0934	0969					3	7	11	14	18	21	25	28	32
							1004	1038	1072	1106	3	7	10	14	17	20	24	27	31
13	1139	1173	1206	1239	1271						3	7	10	13	16	20	23	26	30
						1303	1335	1367	1399	1430	3	7	10	12	16	19	22	25	29
14	1461	1492	1523	1553							3	6	9	12	15	18	21	24	28
						1584	1614	1644	1673	1703	1732	3	6	9	12	15	17	20	23	26
15	1761	1790	1818	1847	1875	1903					3	6	9	11	14	17	20	23	26
							1931	1959	1987	2014	3	5	8	11	14	16	19	22	25
16	2041	2068	2095	2122	2148						3	5	8	11	14	16	19	22	24
						2175	2201	2227	2253	2279	3	5	8	10	13	15	18	21	23
17	2304	2330	2355	2380	2405	2430					3	5	8	10	13	15	18	20	23
							2455	2480	2504	2529	2	5	7	10	12	15	17	19	22
18	2553	2577	2601	2625	2648						2	5	7	9	12	14	16	19	21
						2672	2695	2718	2742	2765	2	5	7	9	11	14	16	18	21
19	2788	2810	2833	2856	2878						2	4	7	9	11	13	16	18	20
						2900	2923	2945	2967	2989	2	4	6	8	11	13	15	17	19
20	3010	3032	3054	3075	3096	3118	3139	3160	3181	3201	2	4	6	8	11	13	15	17	19
21	3222	3243	3263	3284	3304	3324	3345	3365	3385	3404	2	4	6	8	10	12	14	16	18
22	3424	3444	3464	3483	3502	3522	3541	3560	3579	3598	2	4	6	8	10	12	14	15	17
23	3617	3636	3655	3674	3692	3711	3729	3747	3766	3784	2	4	6	7	9	11	13	15	17
24	3802	3820	3838	3856	3874	3892	3909	3927	3945	3962	2	4	5	7	9	11	12	14	16
25	3979	3997	4014	4031	4048	4065	4082	4099	4116	4133	2	3	5	7	9	10	12	14	15
26	4150	4166	4183	4200	4216	4232	4249	4265	4281	4298	2	3	5	7	8	10	11	13	15
27	4314	4330	4346	4362	4378	4393	4409	4425	4440	4456	2	3	5	6	8	9	11	13	14
28	4472	4487	4502	4518	4533	4548	4564	4579	4594	4609	2	3	5	6	8	9	11	12	14
29	4624	4639	4654	4669	4683	4698	4713	4728	4742	4757	1	3	4	6	7	9	10	12	13
30	4771	4786	4800	4814	4829	4843	4857	4871	4886	4900	1	3	4	6	7	9	10	11	13
31	4914	4928	4942	4955	4969	4983	4997	5011	5024	5038	1	3	4	6	7	8	10	11	12
32	5051	5065	5079	5092	5105	5119	5132	5145	5159	5172	1	3	4	5	7	8	9	11	12
33	5185	5198	5211	5224	5237	5250	5263	5276	5289	5302	1	3	4	5	6	8	9	10	12
34	5315	5328	5340	5353	5366	5378	5391	5403	5416	5428	1	3	4	5	6	8	9	10	11
35	5441	5453	5465	5478	5490	5502	5514	5527	5539	5551	1	2	4	5	6	7	9	10	11
36	5563	5575	5587	5599	5611	5623	5635	5647	5658	5670	1	2	4	5	6	7	8	10	11
37	5682	5694	5705	5717	5729	5740	5752	5763	5775	5786	1	2	3	5	6	7	8	9	10
38	5798	5809	5821	5832	5843	5855	5866	5877	5888	5899	1	2	3	5	6	7	8	9	10
39	5911	5922	5933	5944	5955	5966	5977	5988	5999	6010	1	2	3	4	5	7	8	9	10
40	6021	6031	6042	6053	6064	6075	6085	6096	6107	6117	1	2	3	4	5	6	8	9	10
41	6128	6138	6149	6160	6170	6180	6191	6201	6212	6222	1	2	3	4	5	6	7	8	9
42	6232	6243	6253	6263	6274	6284	6294	6304	6314	6325	1	2	3	4	5	6	7	8	9
43	6335	6345	6355	6365	6375	6385	6395	6405	6415	6425	1	2	3	4	5	6	7	8	9
44	6435	6444	6454	6464	6474	6484	6493	6503	6513	6522	1	2	3	4	5	6	7	8	9
45	6532	6542	6551	6561	6571	6580	6590	6599	6609	6618	1	2	3	4	5	6	7	8	9
46	6628	6637	6646	6656	6665	6675	6684	6693	6702	6712	1	2	3	4	5	6	7	7	8
47	6721	6730	6739	6749	6758	6767	6776	6785	6794	6803	1	2	3	4	5	5	6	7	8
48	6812	6821	6830	6839	6848	6857	6866	6875	6884	6893	1	2	3	4	4	5	6	7	8
49	6902	6911	6920	6928	6937	6946	6955	6964	6972	6981	1	2	3	4	4	5	6	7	8

LOGARITHMS

	0	1	2	3	4	5	6	7	8	9	1	2	3	4	5	6	7	8	9
50	6990	6998	7007	7016	7024	7033	7042	7050	7059	7067	1	2	3	3	4	5	6	7	8
51	7076	7084	7093	7101	7110	7118	7126	7135	7143	7152	1	2	3	3	4	5	6	7	8
52	7160	7168	7177	7185	7193	7202	7210	7218	7226	7235	1	2	2	3	4	5	6	7	7
53	7243	7251	7259	7267	7275	7284	7292	7300	7308	7316	1	2	2	3	4	5	6	6	7
54	7324	7332	7340	7348	7356	7364	7372	7380	7388	7396	1	2	2	3	4	5	6	6	7
55	7404	7412	7419	7427	7435	7443	7451	7459	7466	7474	1	2	2	3	4	5	5	6	7
56	7482	7490	7497	7505	7513	7520	7528	7536	7543	7551	1	2	2	3	4	5	5	6	7
57	7559	7566	7574	7582	7589	7597	7604	7612	7619	7627	1	2	2	3	4	5	5	6	7
58	7634	7642	7649	7657	7664	7672	7679	7686	7694	7701	1	1	2	3	4	4	5	6	7
59	7709	7716	7723	7731	7738	7745	7752	7760	7767	7774	1	1	2	3	4	4	5	6	7
60	7782	7789	7796	7803	7810	7818	7825	7832	7839	7846	1	1	2	3	4	4	5	6	6
61	7853	7860	7868	7875	7882	7889	7896	7903	7910	7917	1	1	2	3	4	4	5	6	6
62	7924	7931	7938	7945	7952	7959	7966	7973	7980	7987	1	1	2	3	3	4	5	6	6
63	7993	8000	8007	8014	8021	8028	8035	8041	8048	8055	1	1	2	3	3	4	5	5	6
64	8062	8069	8075	8082	8089	8096	8102	8109	8116	8122	1	1	2	3	3	4	5	5	6
65	8129	8136	8142	8149	8156	8162	8169	8176	8182	8189	1	1	2	3	3	4	5	5	6
66	8195	8202	8209	8215	8222	8228	8235	8241	8248	8254	1	1	2	3	3	4	5	5	6
67	8261	8267	8274	8280	8287	8293	8299	8306	8312	8319	1	1	2	3	3	4	5	5	6
68	8325	8331	8338	8344	8351	8357	8363	8370	8376	8382	1	1	2	3	3	4	4	5	6
69	8388	8395	8401	8407	8414	8420	8426	8432	8439	8445	1	1	2	2	3	4	4	5	6
70	8451	8457	8463	8470	8476	8482	8488	8494	8500	8506	1	1	2	2	3	4	4	5	6
71	8513	8519	8525	8531	8537	8543	8549	8555	8561	8567	1	1	2	2	3	4	4	5	5
72	8573	8579	8585	8591	8597	8603	8609	8615	8621	8627	1	1	2	2	3	4	4	5	5
73	8633	8639	8645	8651	8657	8663	8669	8675	8681	8686	1	1	2	2	3	4	4	5	5
74	8692	8698	8704	8710	8716	8722	8727	8733	8739	8745	1	1	2	2	3	4	4	5	5
75	8751	8756	8762	8768	8774	8779	8785	8791	8797	8802	1	1	2	2	3	3	4	5	5
76	8808	8814	8820	8825	8831	8837	8842	8848	8854	8859	1	1	2	2	3	3	4	5	5
77	8865	8871	8876	8882	8887	8893	8899	8904	8910	8915	1	1	2	2	3	3	4	4	5
78	8921	8927	8932	8938	8943	8949	8954	8960	8965	8971	1	1	2	2	3	3	4	4	5
79	8976	8982	8987	8993	8998	9004	9009	9015	9020	9025	1	1	2	2	3	3	4	4	5
80	9031	9036	9042	9047	9053	9058	9063	9069	9074	9079	1	1	2	2	3	3	4	4	5
81	9085	9090	9096	9101	9106	9112	9117	9122	9128	9133	1	1	2	2	3	3	4	4	5
82	9138	9143	9149	9154	9159	9165	9170	9175	9180	9186	1	1	2	2	3	3	4	4	5
83	9191	9196	9201	9206	9212	9217	9222	9227	9232	9238	1	1	2	2	3	3	4	4	5
84	9243	9248	9253	9258	9263	9269	9274	9279	9284	9289	1	1	2	2	3	3	4	4	5
85	9294	9299	9304	9309	9315	9320	9325	9330	9335	9340	1	1	2	2	3	3	4	4	5
86	9345	9350	9355	9360	9365	9370	9375	9380	9385	9390	1	1	2	2	3	3	4	4	5
87	9395	9400	9405	9410	9415	9420	9425	9430	9435	9440	0	1	1	2	2	3	3	4	4
88	9445	9450	9455	9460	9465	9469	9474	9479	9484	9489	0	1	1	2	2	3	3	4	4
89	9494	9499	9504	9509	9513	9518	9523	9528	9533	9538	0	1	1	2	2	3	3	4	4
90	9542	9547	9552	9557	9562	9566	9571	9576	9581	9586	0	1	1	2	2	3	3	4	4
91	9590	9595	9600	9605	9609	9614	9619	9624	9628	9633	0	1	1	2	2	3	3	4	4
92	9628	9643	9647	9652	9657	9661	9666	9671	9675	9680	0	1	1	2	2	3	3	4	4
93	9685	9689	9694	9699	9703	9708	9713	9717	9722	9727	0	1	1	2	2	3	3	4	4
94	9731	9736	9741	9745	9750	9754	9759	9763	9768	9773	0	1	1	2	2	3	3	4	4
95	9777	9782	9786	9791	9795	9800	9805	9809	9814	9818	0	1	1	2	2	3	3	4	4
96	9823	9827	9832	9836	9841	9845	9850	9854	9859	9863	0	1	1	2	2	3	3	4	4
97	9868	9872	9877	9881	9886	9890	9894	9899	9903	9908	0	1	1	2	2	3	3	4	4
98	9912	9917	9921	9926	9930	9934	9939	9943	9948	9952	0	1	1	2	2	3	3	4	4
99	9956	9961	9965	9969	9974	9978	9983	9987	9991	9996	0	1	1	2	2	3	3	3	4

FORMULAE

Time Series

Additive Model:

$$\text{Series} = \text{Trend} + \text{Seasonal} + \text{Random}$$

Multiplicative Model:

$$\text{Series} = \text{Trend} * \text{Seasonal} * \text{Random}$$

Regression Analysis

The linear regression equation of Y on X is given by:

$$Y = a + bX \qquad \text{or} \qquad Y - \overline{Y} = b(X - \overline{X})$$

where

$$b = \frac{\text{Covariance}(XY)}{\text{Variance}(X)} = \frac{n\sum XY - (\sum X)(\sum Y)}{n\sum X^2 - (\sum X)^2}$$

and

$$a = \overline{Y} - b\overline{X}$$

or solve

$$\sum Y = na + b\sum X$$

$$\sum XY = a\sum X + b\sum X^2$$

Exponential $\qquad Y = ab^x$

Geometric $\qquad Y = aX^b$

Learning Curve

$$Y_x = aX^b$$

where Y_x is the cumulative average time per unit to produce X units; 'a' is the time required to produce the first unit of output; X is the cumulative number of units; and 'b' is the index of learning. The exponent 'b' is defined as the log of the learning curve improvement rate divided by log 2.

Meaning of CIMA's examination requirements

CIMA use precise words in the requirements of their questions. In the schedule below we reproduce the precise meanings of these words from the CIMA syllabus. You must learn these definitions and make sure that in the exam you do precisely what CIMA requires you to do.

Learning objective	Verbs used	Definition
1 Knowledge		
What you are expected to know	List	Make a list of
	State	Express, fully or clearly, the details of/facts of
	Define	Give the exact meaning of
2 Comprehension		
What you are expected to understand	Describe	Communicate the key features of
	Distinguish	Highlight the differences between
	Explain	Make clear or intelligible/state the meaning of
	Identify	Recognise, establish or select after consideration
	Illustrate	Use an example to describe or explain something
3 Application		
Can you apply your knowledge?	Apply	To put to practical use
	Calculate/compute	To ascertain or reckon mathematically
	Demonstrate	To prove with certainty or to exhibit by practical means
	Prepare	To make or get ready for use
	Reconcile	To make or prove consistent/compatible
	Solve	Find an answer to
	Tabulate	Arrange in a table
4 Analysis		
Can you analyse the detail of what you have learned?	Analyse	Examine in detail the structure of
	Categorise	Place into a defined class or division
	Compare and contrast	Show the similarities and/or differences between
	Construct	To build up or compile
	Discuss	To examine in detail by argument
	Interpret	To translate into intelligible or familiar terms
	Produce	To create or bring into existence
5 Evaluation		
Can you use your learning to evaluate, make decisions or recommendations?	Advise	To counsel, inform or notify
	Evaluate	To appraise or assess the value of
	Recommend	To advise on a course of action

Objective test questions

The objective test questions will comprise a question with four possible answers. For example,

1   What is the world's tallest mountain?

   A   Ben Nevis

   B   K2

   C   Mount Everest

   D   Mount Snowdon

You have to select the correct answer (which in the above example is of course C).

In the examination, however, the incorrect answers, called distractors, may be quite plausible and are sometimes designed if not exactly to mislead you, they may nevertheless be the result of fairly common mistakes.

The following is a suggested technique for answering these questions, but as you practise for the examination you have to work out a method which suits you.

Step 1

Read all the questions, but not necessarily the answers. Select the ones which you think are the most straightforward and do them first.

Step 2

For more awkward questions, some people prefer to work the question without reference to the answers which increases your confidence if your answer then matches one of the options. However some people prefer to view the question with the four answers as this may assist them in formulating their answer.

This is a matter of personal preference and you should perhaps practise each to see which you find most effective.

Step 3

If your answer does not match one of the options you must:

(a)   Re-read the question carefully to make sure you have not missed some important point.

(b)   Re-work your solution eliminating any mistakes.

(c)   Beware the plausible distractors but do not become paranoid. The examiner is not trying to trip you up and the answer should be a straightforward calculation from the question.

Step 4

Time allocation. As with all questions you must not overrun your time. The questions are technically worth only two marks each which is about three to four minutes per question. It is very easy to get bogged down. If you cannot get one of the right answers then move on to the next question.

Step 5

When you have finished all the questions go back to the ones you have not answered.

Keep an eye on the clock – don't overrun the time allocation.

If you really cannot do it, **have a guess.** You are not penalised for wrong answers. **Never leave any questions unanswered.**

CHAPTER 1

Standard costs and setting standards

EXAM FOCUS

Standard costing is a fundamental technique of performance measurement. You must understand the principles of standard costs and the procedures for setting them.

LEARNING OUTCOMES

This chapter covers the following Learning Outcomes of the CIMA Syllabus.

> Explain why costing systems and standard costs must be reviewed on a regular basis

In order to cover these Learning Outcomes the following topics are included.

> Methods of developing standards
> Setting standards

1 Introduction

Frequently cost accounting is carried out on an historical basis. A budget is prepared for a period, and then costs are accumulated and analysed after they have been incurred.

Comparison of budget and actual cost is then made some time after the end of the period in question.

This approach suffers from two basic problems:

(a)   any information obtained from the comparison may be too late to be effective; and

(b)   the cost headings are frequently too general to enable management to pinpoint reasons for the differences from budget.

Clearly a system is needed that provides more immediate and detailed information to management as to why budgeted performance differs from actual performance.

Standard costing provides us with such a system. It gives us a set of predetermined benchmarks for factors such as material usage per unit produced, against which actual performance can be measured constantly.

2 Methods of developing standards

2.1 The nature of standards

Whenever identical operations are performed or identical products are manufactured time and time again, it should be possible to decide in advance not merely what they are likely to cost but, more positively, what they ought to cost. In other words, it is possible to set a standard cost for each operation or product unit.

A standard cost will comprise two elements:

(a)   technical standards for the quantities of material to be used and the working time required; and

(b)   cost standards for the material prices and hourly rates that should be paid.

2.2   Standards from past records

Past data can be used to predict future costs if operating conditions are fairly constant between past and future time periods.

The main disadvantage with this method is that past data may contain inefficiencies which would then be built into the standards, thus not encouraging improvements.

2.3   Engineering standards

This involves engineers developing standards for materials, direct labour and variable overheads by studying the product and the production process, possibly with the help of time and motion studies. This method is particularly useful when managers are evaluating new products as the historical records are only of value where they can be related to operations needed to make the new product.

The main disadvantage is that engineering standards may be too tight ('ideal') as they may not allow for the behaviour of the workers or the possibility of material being difficult to use or production staff becoming tired.

3   Setting technical standards

3.1   Standard material usage

In setting material usage standards, the first stage is to define what quantity of material input is theoretically required to achieve one unit of measured output.

In most manufacturing operations the quantity or volume of product emerging will be less than the quantity of materials introduced. In machining operations, for example, this waste will be produced as a result of cutting losses (off-cuts, bar ends and swarf). This type of waste is normal to the type of operation and the usage figure would be increased by an allowance for this normal waste.

3.2   Standard time allowed

The standard or allowed time for an operation is a realistic estimate of the amount of productive time required to perform that operation based on work study methods. It is normally expressed in standard hours.

Various allowances may be added to the theoretical operating time, to take account of operator fatigue and personal needs and periodic activities such as machine-setting, clearing up, regrinding tools and on-line quality inspection. An allowance may also be made for spoilt work as indicated under material usage above, or for rectification of defects appearing in the course of processing.

4   Setting cost standards

4.1   Basic approach

When setting cost standards at a point in time, there are two basic approaches:

(a)   to use the prices or rates which are current at the time the standards are set.

This has the advantage that each standard is clearly identifiable with a known fact. On the other hand, if prices are likely to change then the standards based on them will have a limited value for planning purposes.

The standards would have to be revised in detail from time to time to ensure that they are up to date. If this is not done, then any differences between standard and actual costs are likely to be largely due to inappropriate standards; and

(b)   to use a forecast of average prices or rates over the period for which the standard is to be used.

This can postpone the need for revision, but has the disadvantages that the standard may never correspond with observed fact (so there will be a price variance on all transactions) and that the forecast may be subject to significant error.

Neither method, therefore, will be ideal for all purposes and in deciding between them it will be necessary to consider whether the cost standards are being set principally to put a consistent value on technical variances, or as a help in budgeting, or as a means of exercising cost control, or merely to simplify bookkeeping.

4.2   Material price standards

In setting material price standards, it will often be found that a particular item of material is purchased from several suppliers at slightly different prices and the question arises which price shall be adopted as standard. There are three possible approaches:

(a)   *To identify the major supplier and to use his price as the standard*

This is particularly appropriate where there is no intention of buying large quantities from the alternative suppliers, but merely to use them as a means of ensuring continuity of supply should there be any delay or failure by the principal supplier.

(b)   *To use the lower quoted price as the standard*

This method can be used if it is wished to put pressure on the buyer to obtain price reductions from other suppliers.

(c)   *To forecast the proportion of supplies to be bought from each supplier and to calculate a weighted average price as the costing standard*

This is the most satisfactory method for control purposes if the required forecast can be made with reasonable accuracy.

Another question in relation to material price standards is whether to include the cost of carriage inwards and other costs such as non-returnable packing and transit insurance. The object always will be to price incoming goods at their total delivered cost, so the costs such as those mentioned above should be included in the standards.

4.3 Standard labour rates

A decision to be made when setting standard labour rates is whether to use basic pay rates only, or to incorporate overtime premiums. The answer will depend on the nature of the overtime work and the approach to cost control adopted by management.

♦ If a normal level of overtime work can be identified and is accepted as necessary, or if overtime is planned for the company's convenience, then the relevant overtime premium payments will normally be included in the standard labour rate.

♦ If it is a management objective to reduce or eliminate overtime working, the standard rate may be restricted to basic pay.

♦ Where overtime is worked at the request of particular customers, then the related premium payments are a direct cost of the work done and would not be included in a standard rate which was applied generally to other work.

♦ Where part of employee remuneration takes the form of incentive bonuses, then it will be necessary to forecast the level of efficiency to be achieved and the bonus payments appropriate to that performance. These bonuses will then be included in the calculation of the standard rate.

4.4 Learning outcome

At this stage of the chapter we have now covered the following Learning Outcome:

> Explain why costing systems and standard costs must be reviewed on a regular basis.

5 Types of standard

5.1 Introduction

The way in which control is exercised and the interpretation and use of variances from standards will depend on the manner in which those standards are set.

5.2 Ideal standards

In some cases standards are established on the assumption that machines and employees will work with optimal efficiency at all times and that there will be no stoppages and no losses of material or services.

 Such standards would represent an **ideal** state of affairs and therefore the objectives they set are never achieved.

Managers who are responsible for the costs will hardly approve of targets which they can never reach and which, therefore, result in large adverse variances from the standards.

5.3 Attainable (expected) standards

 In other cases the standards set will be those which are reasonably attainable, consideration being given to the state of efficiency which can be achieved from the existing facilities. There is no question of assuming, as for ideal standard costs, that production resources will be used at maximum efficiency.

A positive effort is still made to achieve a high level of efficiency, but there is no question of going beyond what is attainable.

5.4   Current standards

These are standards established for use over a short period of time, related to current conditions.

Whilst the need for fairly fixed standards is clear, if they are seen to be inappropriate because of temporarily prevailing circumstances, they become demotivating and little useful management information will come from variances.

5.5   Basic standards

A basic standard is one which, having been fixed, is not generally revised with changing conditions, but remains in force for a long period of time. It may be set originally having regard to either ideal or expected conditions. Under circumstances of rapid technological change or of significant price changes, basic standards are of limited value in relation to the achievement of the benefits of the system.

There may be variations on these methods, but the aim should be to select the standard cost which is likely to be the most realistic for the business concerned. It should be remembered that standards are the yardstick against which efficiency is measured and, therefore, if they are unrealistic then the variances will be of little meaning.

6   Definitions

The following definitions can now be made:

6.1   Standard cost

A predetermined cost which is calculated from management's standards of efficient operation and the relevant necessary expenditure. It may be used as a basis for fixing selling prices, for valuing stock and work in progress, and to provide control over actual costs through the process of variance analysis.

6.2   Standard costing

The preparation and use of standard costs, their comparison with actual costs, and the analysis of variances to their causes and points of incidence.

7   Advantages and disadvantages of standard costing

7.1   Advantages

The advantages of standard costing fall into two broad categories – planning and control.

♦   **Planning**

    Predetermined standards make the preparation of forecasts and budgets much easier. If the standards are to be used for these operational decisions then they must obviously be as accurate as possible. This again means that standards should be revised on a frequent basis.

♦   **Control**

    Control is primarily exercised through the comparison of standard and actual results, and the isolation of variances. This will highlight areas of apparent efficiency and inefficiency and, as necessary, investigations as to the causes of the variance can be made. If these investigations discover the causes of the variances, then corrective action can be taken to improve efficiency in the future.

This is called 'management by exception', since it allows management to concentrate its attentions on exceptional performance (good or bad) as indicated by the variances.

♦   In addition to the above, there are subsidiary advantages such as:

(i)   If the standards are perceived to be attainable, then they will serve to motivate the employees concerned.

(ii)   A standard costing bookkeeping system can be set up that will fulfil all requirements, for both internal and external reporting.

(iii)   Recording of stock issues is simplified, as it is done at the standard price.

7.2   Disadvantages

These relate primarily to the costs incurred in setting up and maintaining the system. As indicated, standards must be revised on a regular basis to retain effectiveness. It is for this reason that standard costing is most effective for well-established and repetitive processes, so that the revisions of standards are kept to a minimum.

Practice question 1 *(The answer is in the final chapter of this book)*

Hearn Ltd

Hearn Ltd is a medium-sized company manufacturing a range of similar products to customer specification. Mr MacGeorge has recently been appointed as managing director of Hearn Ltd. Following a review of the company's administrative systems, he is considering scrapping the standard costing system and the monthly management accounting reports as part of a cost-cutting exercise intended to improve the company's currently poor profitability.

The computer-based management accounts consist of analyses of variances between actual and standard production costs with a monthly profit and loss statement showing both the monthly and the year-to-date variances against budget. Mr MacGeorge argues that the production managers do not need the variance analyses as they are well able to monitor materials usage in physical terms at the time of manufacture, and that materials costs are outside their control. He also considers that the monthly profit and loss accounts are of little use to him because they do not address his main concern of maintaining a full order book for high contribution products.

Mrs Mason, the company accountant, does not agree with Mr MacGeorge's proposals, which would involve the reduction of accounting staff by two clerks. She feels that the information provided by her department is valuable and wishes to support her case by a cost-benefit analysis.

Required

Draft a short report for Mrs Mason outlining the main features of the cost-benefit analysis she requires, and indicate what information is necessary to complete the analysis.

(10 marks)

---

8   Summary

In this chapter we have prepared the groundwork for our detailed examination of variance analysis in the chapters that follow.

Make sure that you can discuss:

♦   the methods of setting standards;
♦   the different types of standards that can be set;
♦   the purposes of a standard costing system.

Multiple choice questions (The answers are in the final chapter of this book)

1   If a process exhibits a 90% learning effect, and the first item to be produced takes 10 minutes, how long will the second item take?

    A   8 minutes
    B   8.1 minutes
    C   9 minutes
    D   10 minutes

2   What type of standard is generally believed to have the best motivating effect on employees?

    A   Ideal standard
    B   Attainable standard
    C   Current standard
    D   Basic standard

3   Which of the following is a disadvantage of introducing a standard costing system?

    A   Easier planning
    B   Better control through identification of variances
    C   Easier recording of stock movements
    D   Costs of maintaining the system

CHAPTER 2

Variance analysis

EXAM FOCUS

This chapter explains the basic variance calculations which you are expected to be able to perform in the examination to reconcile expected profits to actual profits.

LEARNING OUTCOMES

This chapter covers the following Learning Outcomes of the CIMA Syllabus.

> Calculate and interpret material, labour, variable overhead, fixed overhead and sales variances

> Prepare and discuss a report which reconciles budget and actual profit using absorption and/or marginal costing principles

In order to cover these Learning Outcomes the following topics are included.

> Cost variances

> Sales variances

> Operating statements

---

1 Cost variances

1.1 Introduction

In the previous chapter we have seen how management will develop standard costs in advance of the period under review. During the course of that period actual costs will then be compared with standard costs, and any differences isolated for investigation as to their causes. This will then enable any corrective action to be taken as soon as possible.

If we consider top level management within the firm, perhaps the board of directors, then they will want to see a clear and succinct summary of the results for a given period. In particular they will wish to see a reconciliation between budgeted profit and actual profit that highlights the factors causing the difference.

1.2 Variance analysis example

The following illustration will be used to show the computation of all necessary cost variances.

Katzman Ltd produces soap in bulk.

The standard cost per drum of soap is made up as follows:

Raw materials	100 kg costing £2 per kg
Labour	12 hours costing £3 per hour
Variable production overheads	12 hours costing £2.50 per hour

Fixed production costs per month are budgeted at £90,000. For April 20X8, budgeted production was 7,500 drums.

The actual costs incurred in the month were:

Raw materials (900,000 kg purchased)	£1,755,000
Labour (110,000 hours paid, 102,000 hours worked)	£341,000
Variable production overheads	£280,000
Fixed production costs	£86,000

During April 7,800 drums of soap were actually produced. There were no raw materials stocks at the start or end of the period.

1.3 Solution

Standard cost card

When standards have been set for individual operations or items of material, they can be combined to give the standard costs for products, components or other units of output.

An example of a simple standard cost card is shown below.

STANDARD COST CARD						Part/Product/Assembly No		
Description							Batch quantity:	
LABOUR							Amendments	
Op No	Details	Machine	Set-up time	Allowed hours	Pay rate	Amount £	Date...	Date...
					Total	X		
MATERIAL								
Part No	Description			Qty	Price			
					Total	X		
				TOTAL DIRECT COST		X		
				ADD OVERHEADS		X		
				TOTAL STANDARD COST		X		

The standard cost card for a drum of soap would appear as below:

	£
Raw materials (100 kg × £2)	200
Labour (12 hours × £3)	36
Variable production overheads (12 hours × £2.50)	30
Fixed production overheads (12 hours × £1)	12
	——
Standard cost per drum	278
	——

The only figure requiring explanation here is the hourly fixed production overhead rate.

Based on our budgeted output, we planned to produce 7,500 drums, each taking 12 hours. Thus, budgeted hours are (7,500 × 12) = 90,000.

This gives us a standard fixed overhead absorption rate per hour of $\dfrac{£90,000}{90,000}$ = £1/hour

Notice here that we have assumed two things:

♦   We are operating a total absorption costing system, so that all production costs are absorbed into units produced; and

♦   The basis for absorbing fixed overheads is labour hours. Despite the advent of Activity Based Costing (see later in this text), this is the most commonly used absorption basis in practice, and should be used unless there is any clear indication to the contrary.

A simplistic comparison

Let us now compare budgeted total costs with actual costs incurred.

	Budgeted cost £	Actual cost £	Variance £	
Direct materials	1,500,000	1,755,000	255,000	A
Labour	270,000	341,000	71,000	A
Variable production overheads	225,000	280,000	55,000	A
Fixed production overheads	90,000	86,000	4,000	F
	2,085,000	2,462,000	377,000	A

(A = Adverse, F = Favourable)

The budgeted costs have been obtained by simply multiplying out the standard costs per drum by 7,500 budgeted production (except for fixed costs of course, which are independent of output level over a given range).

Why is this a simplistic comparison?

Quite simply because the budget and actual costs are not directly comparable. The budgeted activity level was 7,500 drums, but 7,800 were actually produced.

Since the standard costs are unit costs, it would be much more useful to management to compare actual costs of producing 7,800 drums with the standard costs of producing that same quantity.

1.4   Raw material variances

Let us now begin our detailed analysis of the difference between budgeted and actual cost, by looking at raw materials.

Total cost variance

To produce 7,800 drums we should have used (7,800 × 100 kg) = 780,000 kg.

	£
This would have cost, at standard prices (780,000 × £2)	1,560,000
Actual cost of producing 7,800 drums	1,755,000
Total cost variance (adverse)	195,000

The budgeted level of 7,500 drums is irrelevant here, since we must compute the standard cost for **actual** production.

Notice two things:

♦ The variance is adverse, because it has cost us more to produce 7,800 drums than the standard allowed.

♦ Although this total cost variance is of some use to management, it does not tell us to what extent the variance is due to using more material than standard, or to paying too much per kg. In other words, we cannot as yet establish responsibility for the variance.

Materials price variance

We actually purchased 900,000 kg

	£
At standard price per kg, this should have cost (900,000 × £2)	1,800,000
At actual price per kg, cost	1,755,000
Price variance (favourable)	45,000

Therefore despite an adverse total cost variance, there is a favourable price variance of £45,000.

This means that the actual price per kg purchased must have been less than standard. We can compute the actual price as follows:

$$\frac{\text{Actual cost}}{\text{Quantity purchased}} = \frac{£1,755,000}{900,000} = £1.95 / \text{kg}$$

Thus, for every kg we purchased, we actually paid £0.05 less than the standard price. Clearly, since this is a cost saving, it gives rise to a favourable variance.

Materials usage variance

We actually produced 7,800 drums.

	kg
At standard usage, this should have used (7,800 × 100)	780,000
We actually used	900,000
Usage variance, in kg	120,000

This over-usage is valued at the standard price per kg.

Thus, the usage variance = 120,000 × £2 = £240,000 Adverse

Clearly, the variance is adverse, since the additional usage above standard incurs extra cost.

Reconciliation

We can summarise the above computations as follows:

	kg	£	
Actual quantity purchased at actual prices (actual cost)	900,000	1,755,000	
Direct materials price variance	–	45,000	F
Actual quantity purchased at standard prices	900,000	1,800,000	
Direct materials usage variance	120,000	240,000	A
Standard quantity that should have been used at standard prices (standard cost)	780,000	1,560,000	

This tabulation is the method that we will use to compute the variances.

 Note that since there are two elements making up the cost, then we sub-divide the total variance by keeping one element constant, whilst comparing standard with actual for the other.

Thus, what we have really done is the following:

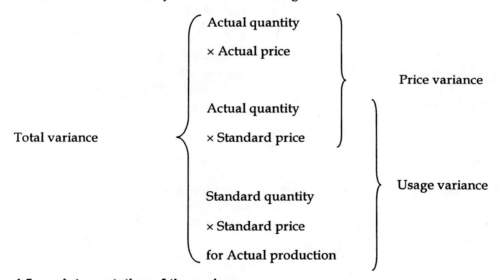

Total variance

Actual quantity
× Actual price

Actual quantity
× Standard price

Standard quantity
× Standard price
for Actual production

Price variance

Usage variance

1.5   *Interpretation of the variances*

The variances computed above act as error signals to management. They in no way explain why we have used more material than the standard allowed, or why we have succeeded in purchasing material more cheaply than the standard price.

If management decided that these exceptional performances (compared to budget) demanded explanation, then investigation would have to be carried out as to their causes. This would enable responsibility for the variance to be identified, and management could then take any corrective action considered necessary.

Some possible causes of the variances are listed below.

Price variance

♦ Purchase of a cheaper substitute than the material per the standard cost and specification. Such an action may be a deliberate policy of the buying department (and therefore controllable), or may result from uncontrollable external factors such as market shortages.

♦ Bulk buying leading to discounts that the standard had not envisaged.

♦ Market factors leading to a lower price than anticipated (this would apply for example where raw materials depend upon random factors such as the weather affecting harvests).

♦ Using different suppliers from normal.

♦ The standard may have been set at a 'mid-year' price, anticipating future price rises. Thus we would expect favourable variances initially.

Usage variance

♦ Sub-standard raw materials. Notice the possibility here of interdependence between the variances. If the favourable price variance is due to buying a cheaper substitute, this may well cause operating inefficiencies leading to an adverse usage variance. Thus, in allocating responsibility for the variances, after investigation we may hold the purchasing manager responsible for the usage variance!

♦ Mechanical breakdown leading to spoilage of raw materials.

♦ The standard itself could be too tight (is it an ideal standard that is unattainable in practice?).

♦ Measurement errors. For example, if there are raw materials closing stocks that have not been recorded, this would overstate actual usage for the current period, but underestimate usage in the next period. Widely fluctuating variances from period to period may be indicative of such errors.

♦ Operating inefficiencies.

1.6 Raw materials stocks

In our example, we said that there were no stocks of raw materials at the period end. Where there are stocks, then we would normally carry forward these stocks at standard cost. This means that the price variance is computed as early as possible, based on quantities purchased rather than quantities used.

Consider the following.

Standard usage	=	2 kg of X per unit
Standard price	=	£5 per kg

Actual purchases were 500 kg, costing £2,550.

Closing stocks were 100 kg.

192 units were actually produced.

The variances would be computed as follows:

	kg	£	
Actual purchases at actual price	500	2,550	Price variance £50A
Actual purchases at standard price	500	2,500	
Stock at standard cost	100	500	
Actual quantity used at standard price	400	2,000	Usage variance £80A
Standard quantity at standard price			
(Standard cost of actual production) (192 × 2kg)	384	1,920	

Practice questions 1 - 6 *(The answers are in the final chapter of this book)*

1   At this stage we cannot examine a full-length written question as it might appear in the examination, since we must as yet restrict ourselves to an examination of materials variances only. The following question is therefore not to be taken as representative of the type of question that may come up in the examination.

Calculate the material variances for each of the following:

(a)   Opening stock   100 kg
       Purchased during the period   3,000 kg, cost £6,200
       Standard   2 kg per unit at £2 per kg
       Original budget   2,000 units
       Production   1,600 units
       Sales   1,400 units
       Closing stock   200 kg   **(3 marks)**

(b)   Purchased during the period   6,000 kg, cost £2,400
       Standard   3 kg per unit at £0.50 per kg
       Production   2,000 units
       Opening stock   Nil
       Closing stock   400 kg   **(3 marks)**

(Total: 6 marks)

Multiple choice questions

The following information (for questions 2 and 3) relates to a month's production of a particular product:

	Budget	*Actual*
Units produced	1,440	1,392.0
Input of material Q (litres)	3,600	3,758.4
Cost of material Q purchases (£)	61,200	62,013.6

There were no raw materials stock at the beginning or end of the period.

2   What is the usage variance for material Q?

A	£1,879.2	favourable
B	£2,692.8	adverse
C	£4,593.6	adverse
D	£4,732.8	adverse

3   What is the price variance for material Q?

A	£1,879.2	favourable
B	£2,692.8	adverse
C	£2,853.6	adverse
D	£4,593.6	adverse

4   Product X has a standard cost of £25, £5 of which relates to direct materials. Budgeted production for the month was 1,600 units.

During the month 1,500 units of X were produced, and £8,000 of materials were purchased. There was no opening stock of materials but closing stock, which is valued at standard cost, amounted to £1,000.

What is the total variance for materials?

A	£500	adverse
B	£1,000	favourable
C	£500	favourable
D	£Nil	

5   During month one 120,000 kg of material Y were purchased for £1.20 per kg.

Material Y is used in the production of product A, and the standard usage per unit is 2.5 kg.

Production of product A in month 1 was 40,000 units, of which 35,000 were sold and 5,000 remained in closing stock.

The opening stock of material Y was 10,000 kg, but there were only 5,000 kg in closing stock. Stock is always valued at standard cost.

If the usage variance for the month was £32,500 adverse, what is the price variance for material Y?

A	£12,000	favourable
B	£12,500	favourable
C	£116,000	favourable
D	£40,000	adverse

6   The following data relates to manufacture of component M227 in period seven.

> Standard cost per unit: 10 kg of material Q at 75p per kg.
> Opening stock of Q 200 kg at actual cost of £170.
> Issued to work in progress 1,500 kg.
> Purchased 1,800 kg at actual cost of £1,170.
> 162 components were produced in the period.
> Raw materials stocks are valued at standard prices.

What is the raw material price variance for period seven?

A	£150	favourable
B	£180	adverse
C	£170	favourable
D	£180	favourable

2   Labour variances

2.1   Total labour cost variance

Referring back to the original example, you will see that the standard for labour per drum of soap is 12 hours at £3 per hour.

The actual results were:

Hours paid	110,000	costing £341,000
Hours worked	102,000	
Actual production	7,800 drums	

Total labour cost variance

To produce 7,800 drums we should have taken (7,800 × 12 hours) = 93,600 hours

	£
This would have cost, at the standard rate, (93,600 × £3)	280,800
The actual cost of production	341,000
Total cost variance (adverse)	60,200

Note that, just as for materials variances:

♦   The variance is adverse because the actual labour cost exceeds the standard cost for actual production.

♦   The budgeted production level of 7,500 drums is again irrelevant.

♦   Again, we would obtain more useful management information if we could analyse the total cost variance further into the rate of pay, efficiency and idle time components.

2.2   Rate of pay variance

We actually paid for 110,000 hours.

	£
At standard rate per hour, this should have cost (110,000 × £3)	330,000
At actual rate per hour, cost	341,000
Rate variance (adverse)	11,000

This means that the actual rate of pay per hour must have been more than the standard.

The actual rate is $\dfrac{\text{Actual cost}}{\text{Hours paid}} = \dfrac{£341,000}{110,000} = £3.10/\text{hour}$

Thus, for every hour paid for, we have actually paid £0.10 more than the standard price, and so the labour rate of pay variance is adverse.

2.3 Idle time variance

Having identified the adverse rate of pay variance, we must now consider the impact of having paid for more hours than were actually worked. The inference of this is that the workforce was idle for some of the time. This idle time variance is computed as follows:

	£
Hours paid for at the standard rate (110,000 × £3)	330,000
Hours worked at the standard rate (102,000 × £3)	306,000
Idle time variance (adverse)	24,000

Note that:

- The idle time may have been caused by factors entirely beyond the workforce's control, for example machine breakdown. Again, if considered necessary, an investigation would be carried out to ascertain the reasons.

- This variance is perhaps one of the easiest of all to compute. It is simply idle hours × standard rate per hour.

- Idle time will always give rise to an adverse variance, unless some idle time is expected and included in the standard set.

2.4 Labour efficiency variance

We actually produced 7,800 drums.

	Hours
At standard efficiency, this should have taken (7,800 × 12)	93,600
We actually took	102,000
Efficiency variance, in hours (adverse)	8,400

This inefficiency is valued at the standard rate per hour.

Thus, the efficiency variance = 8,400 × £3 = £25,200 adverse.

This variance is adverse, because we have taken more hours, and therefore incurred more cost, to produce 7,800 drums than the standard allowed.

Reconciliation

We can summarise the above computations as follows:

	Hours	£
Actual hours paid at actual rate (actual cost)	110,000	341,000
Rate of pay variance	–	11,000 A
Actual hours paid at standard rate	110,000	330,000
Idle time variance	8,000	24,000 A
Actual hours worked at standard rate	102,000	306,000
Efficiency variance	8,400	25,200 A
Standard hours that should have been worked at standard rate (standard cost)	93,600	280,800

Again, we can show the above in 'shorthand' as:

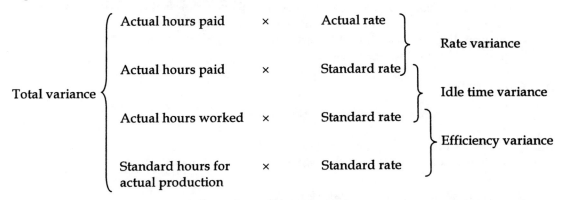

It is worth emphasising the similarity between the calculations for materials and labour variances.

In the absence of idle time they are identical, but we simply use different terminology.

In each case what we have done is:

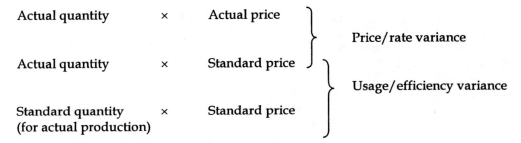

2.5   Interpretation of labour variances

Some possible causes of labour variances may be:

♦   **Rate of pay variances**

(i)   Failure to include overtime premiums in the standard, or failure to allow for pay increases during the period.

(ii)   Rush orders necessitating costly overtime working.

(iii)   Using different grades of labour compared to that budgeted for, which could of course lead to an adverse or favourable variance.

♦   **Efficiency variances**

(i)   Good quality raw materials could lead to favourable labour efficiency, or of course sub-standard materials could cause inefficiencies. Time could be lost in setting up machines after breakdowns, or rectifying poor quality output.

(ii)   The impact of a learning phenomenon that was not anticipated.

(iii)   Random fluctuations such as high morale due to the local football team's winning streak.

Although this last example is somewhat flippant, it does illustrate an important point. We are dealing here with labour – a human asset. As such its efficiency will depend greatly upon behavioural factors.

(iv)   The plan itself could be wrong! Remember that to compute the variance we compare standard labour time with actual labour time. If the standard represents an ideal time, then adverse variances are inevitable. Alternatively, if the standard is outdated due to technical innovations or revised working practices, then again we would expect to see variances.

♦   **Idle time variances**

(i)   Loss of time through machine breakdown.
(ii)   Strikes.
(iii)   Illness or other worker absenteeism.
(iv)   Failure to allocate all productive time actually spent to cost codes.

3   Variable overhead variances

3.1   Total variable overhead cost variance

Remember that variable overheads although not direct costs, do vary with the level of activity and so the computations of variances are very similar to the labour and materials variances already seen.

For our ongoing example, the standard and actual variable overhead costs were:

Standard cost per drum (12 hours at £2.50 per hour) £30
The actual cost was £280,000.

The total variable overhead cost variance to produce 7,800 drums can therefore be calculated as:

	£
At the standard rate (7,800 × 12 × £2.50)	234,000
The actual cost was	280,000
Total cost variance (adverse)	46,000

3.2   Variable overhead rate variance

(This is alternatively known as the *expenditure variance*.)

Since we are concerned here with production costs, then, unless told otherwise, we assume that variable overheads will only be incurred for hours worked. There is thus no overhead incurred for idle time.

We actually worked 102,000 hours.

	£
At standard rate per hour, this should have cost (102,000 × £2.50)	255,000
At actual rate per hour, cost	280,000
Rate, or expenditure, variance (adverse)	25,000

Again we can compute the actual rate per hour.

$$\text{Actual rate} = \frac{\text{Actual cost}}{\text{Hours worked}} = \frac{£280,000}{102,000} = £2.745/\text{hour}$$

3.3 *Variable overhead efficiency variance*

We have already said that the variable overheads are incurred per labour hour. Thus, if we work more hours than we should have done per the standard (adverse labour efficiency variance) then we will suffer a penalty because we also incur additional variable overheads.

We actually produced 7,800 drums.

	Hours
At standard efficiency, this should have taken (7,800 × 12)	93,600
We actually took	102,000
Efficiency variance, in hours (adverse)	8,400

At the standard rate per hour = 8,400 × £2.50 = £21,000 (Adverse)

Notice then, that the efficiency is exactly the same as for labour in volume terms (8,400 hours). The difference is simply that the 8,400 hours are valued at the standard variable overhead rate of £2.50 per hour, compared with £3 for labour.

Reconciliation

Again, we can summarise our computations as follows:

	Hours	*£*
Actual hours worked at actual rate (actual cost)	102,000	280,000
Rate variance	–	25,000 A
Actual hours worked at standard rate	102,000	255,000
Efficiency variance	8,400	21,000 A
Standard hours that should have been worked at standard rate (standard cost)	93,600	234,000

 Our shorthand summary would be:

Total variance
{
- Actual hours worked × Actual rate ⎫
- Actual hours worked × Standard rate ⎬ Rate variance
- Standard hours for actual production × Standard rate ⎭ Efficiency variance
}

3.4 *Choice of activity base*

In our example we have recovered variable overheads at the standard rate of £2.50 per labour hour. This infers that the incurring of variable overheads is related to labour hours worked. It is possible that variable overheads may depend on some other activity base – for example machine hours. Another alternative is that we may compute a variable overhead rate per unit, in which case there will be no efficiency variance.

Consider the following illustration:

Budget:

Variable overhead expenditure	£500
Units of production	100
Direct labour hours	250

Therefore standard labour time per unit = 2.5 hours

Actual:

Variable overhead expenditure	£600
Units produced	110
Direct labour hours	200

Compute the variable overhead variances assuming the overhead is recovered on:

♦ units produced; and
♦ labour hours worked.

Variable overhead recovered per unit

Standard variable overhead rate per unit = $\dfrac{£500}{100}$ = £5 per unit

	£
Actual production at actual rate	600
Actual production at standard rate (the allowed expenditure) = 110 × £5	550
Variable overhead rate variance (adverse)	50

Note that we cannot sub-divide this variance further.

Variable overhead recovered per hour

Standard variable overhead rate per hour = $\dfrac{£500}{250}$ = £2

	£
Actual hours at actual rate	600
Actual hours at standard rate (200 × £2)	400
Variable overhead rate variance (adverse)	200
Actual hours at standard rate	400
Standard hours at standard rate (110 × 2.5 × £2)	550
Variable overhead efficiency variance (favourable)	150

By recovering overheads per labour hour, we have really obtained a sub-division of the overall variance of £50A identified in the first computation.

Obviously in practice we should look for the recovery base that most accurately reflects the actual variable overhead behaviour.

3.5   *Interpretation of the variances*

With variable overheads the interpretation is likely to be more difficult, since the overhead rate per unit or hour is likely to be an amalgamation of many different cost elements.

Thus our first stage in ascertaining the reasons for any variance must be:

♦   a careful analysis of actual costs; and

♦   a breakdown of the standard cost into its constituent parts.

We may then investigate the material fluctuations from standard.

We must bear in mind that where we are incurring variable overheads per labour hour, the efficiency variance will be directly explained by the cause of the labour efficiency variance.

The expenditure variance may be caused by factors such as:

♦   unanticipated changes in prices for overhead cost elements;

♦   changed operating methods leading to different overhead cost patterns;

♦   outdated standards, or failure to allow for inflationary effects upon costs.

Practice questions 7 - 12 *(The answers are in the final chapter of this book)*

7   Compute variances for the following examples.

Labour

(a)	Standard	2 hours per unit at £3 per hour
	Hours paid and worked	5,000 hours, cost £14,000
	Units produced	2,800 units

(b)	Standard	3 hours per unit, £12 per unit
	Original budget	20,000 units
	Sales	17,000 units
	Production	18,000 units
	Opening stock	1,000 units
	Hours paid	50,000 hours, cost £210,000
	Hours worked	48,000 hours

Variable expenses

(c)	Standard	2 hours per unit at £0.50 per hour
	Original budget	5,000 hours
	Production	3,000 units
	Paid in period	6,300 hours, cost £3,000

(d)	Standard	3 hours per unit, £1.20 per unit
	Labour hours paid	5,000 hours
	Labour hours worked	4,700 hours
	Original budget	5,200 hours
	Cost for period	£2,000
	Units produced	1,800 units

8   'Cost variances are often found, upon investigation of causes, to be interdependent.'

Briefly explain this statement using as illustrations:

(a)   material price and usage variances;

(b)   labour rate and efficiency variances,

and comment briefly upon any possible interdependence between material cost variances and labour cost variances.

Multiple choice questions

With reference to the following data, answer questions 9 and 10.

Product X requires a standard of 4 labour hours per unit, at a standard rate of £6.50 per labour hour.

During period one 2,500 units of product X were made, and actual labour time charged to the product was 9,300 hours at a cost of £66,960.

9   What is the labour rate of pay variance?

      A   £6,510 favourable
      B   £6,510 adverse
      C   £7,000 adverse
      D   £7,000 favourable

10   What is the labour efficiency variance?

      A   £5,040 favourable
      B   £4,550 adverse
      C   £4,550 favourable
      D   £5,040 adverse

11   In July the total variance for ABC Ltd for direct labour was calculated as £250 favourable. Actual production for the month was 1,000 units, compared with budgeted production of 1,200 units.

The direct labour standard cost per unit is £25 and labour was actually paid at £5.50 per hour as opposed to the standard of £5 per hour. Assuming there was no idle time, what is the efficiency variance for the period?

      A   £2,045 favourable
      B   £2,045 adverse
      C   £2,500 adverse
      D   £2,500 favourable

12   Assuming that variable overheads are recovered over productive labour hours, which of the following is compared to actual variable overhead cost to identify the variable overhead expenditure variance?

      A   Actual hours paid × Standard variable overhead rate per hour
      B   Actual hours worked × Standard variable overhead rate per hour
      C   Budgeted hours × Standard variable overhead rate per hour
      D   Standard hours × Standard variable overhead rate per hour

4   Fixed overheads

4.1   Introduction

Remember that, in order to set a fixed overhead absorption rate per hour, we had to make an estimate of activity level in hours, as well as of the fixed cost itself.

The relevant information from the example is:

For April 20X8:

Budgeted fixed production costs	=	£90,000
Standard hours per drum	=	12 hours
Budgeted production	=	7,500 drums

The actual results were:

Labour	=	110,000 hours paid, 102,000 hours worked
Fixed production costs	=	£86,000
Production	=	7,800 drums

From these estimates we obtained the standard fixed overhead absorption rate per hour:

$$\frac{\text{Budgeted cost}}{\text{Budgeted hours}} = \frac{£90,000}{(7,500 \times 12)} = £1/\text{hour}$$

This means that, as units are produced, we will absorb £12 (12 hours at the standard of £1) per unit. Thus, there may be a variance due to the over or under absorption of fixed overheads.

For example, if actual costs were exactly as per budget of £90,000, but we actually produced 8,000 units, then we would absorb 8,000 × 12 hours × £1 = £96,000.

Thus we would have over-absorbed £6,000, due to the increased production compared to budget. Finished goods will therefore be valued at £6,000 more than actual cost, and so a favourable variance would be needed to reduce this standard cost back to actual cost. This variance is called the volume variance, and only arises because we have chosen to absorb fixed overheads into production.

4.2   Fixed overheads – total cost variance

	£
In producing 7,800 drums we have absorbed (7,800 × £12)	93,600
The actual cost was	86,000
	———
Total cost variance (favourable)	7,600
	———

4.3   Fixed overhead expenditure variance

Since fixed costs do not vary with the level of production, the expenditure variance is simply a comparison of budgeted and actual fixed costs.

	£
Actual total cost	86,000
Budgeted cost	90,000
	———
Expenditure variance (favourable)	4,000
	———

Thus we have actually incurred, regardless of activity level, £4,000 less fixed costs than budgeted. The variance is therefore favourable.

4.4 Fixed overhead volume variance

We actually produced 7,800 drums.

	£
Actual absorption (7,800 × £12)	93,600
Budgeted absorption (7,500 × £12)	90,000
Volume variance (favourable)	3,600

Remember that the variance is favourable because we have over absorbed fixed overheads. We thus require a favourable variance to compensate for this over-absorption.

We have produced 300 units more than budget, thus over-absorbing fixed overheads by 300 × the standard rate of £12 per unit ie £3,600 favourable volume variance.

4.5 Sub-division of the volume variance

The volume variance as computed above can be subdivided further to explain why the level of activity was different from budget. In other words, how did we manage to produce 300 units more than the budget of 7,500:

◆ **Capacity variance**

This compares actual hours worked with the budgeted hours, and is favourable where actual hours exceed budgeted hours since squeezing more hours out of our factory enables us to make extra units.

◆ **Efficiency variance**

This compares standard hours that should have been worked with actual hours worked, and so is the usual measure of efficiency seen already for both labour and variable overheads.

These sub-variances can be calculated as shown below:

Capacity variance

	Hours	£
Budgeted hours at the standard rate	90,000	90,000
Actual hours worked at the standard rate	102,000	102,000
Capacity variance (favourable)	12,000	12,000

Efficiency variance

	Hours	£
Actual hours worked at the standard rate	102,000	102,000
Standard hours that should have been worked at the standard rate	93,600	93,600
Efficiency variance (adverse)	8,400	8,400

(Notice that in computing the above variances we consider only hours worked and again ignore idle time.)

Reconciliation

	Hours	£
Budgeted hours at actual total cost	90,000	86,000
Expenditure variance (favourable)	–	4,000
Budgeted hours at standard cost	90,000	90,000
Capacity variance (favourable)	12,000	12,000
Actual hours at standard cost	102,000	102,000
Efficiency variance (adverse)	8,400	8,400
Standard hours at standard cost	93,600	93,600

Thus, if we absorb fixed overheads on the basis of labour hours it enables us to split the volume variance further into capacity and efficiency elements. The total cost variance must remain the same. The 'variance tree' below may help as a convenient way of remembering this.

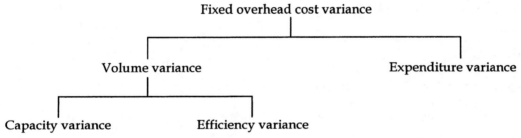

4.6   Usefulness of fixed overhead variances

The problem

We must be clear throughout the above analysis that we are dealing with a fixed cost. Refer back to the earlier sections on materials, labour and variable overheads, and you will see that there are no volume variances for these items. The volume variance arises for fixed overheads purely because of our desire to absorb fixed costs into production, and the consequent setting up of an arbitrary absorption basis such as labour hours.

Marginal costing avoids the need to absorb fixed overheads and therefore this problem with volume variances never arises.

Conflict

Thus we are really seeing a conflict between the use of standard costing for control purposes, and the use of standards for product costing. We may for example base our selling price on cost plus a fixed mark-up, in which case a production cost inclusive of fixed costs may be desired. However, for control purposes the only variance of any real significance is the expenditure variance. Since we are dealing with a fixed cost, then the cost will not change simply because we are operating at something other than budgeted output level.

Thus the volume variance is really uncontrollable, and arises due to our failure to operate at the budgeted activity level.

A partial solution

One solution to this criticism is to sub-divide the volume variance into capacity and efficiency. The capacity variance compares actual hours worked with budgeted hours that should have been worked. When actual hours exceed budgeted hours, the capacity variance is favourable, because we are making better use of our facilities than expected. In other words, we have obtained more productive hours worth of output for the same fixed cost.

If the capacity variance is of some use in terms of explaining utilisation of facilities, then how can we use the efficiency variance? The answer is that the fixed overhead efficiency variance is very different from the efficiency variances computed for labour and variable overheads. Efficient use of the latter can reduce actual cost, but fixed overhead cost cannot be affected by efficiency in the short-run. Further, there is little to be gained in terms of information to management since they are already aware of inefficiencies through the variable cost reports.

5 Comparison of budgeted and actual results

5.1 Introduction

Having computed all of the variances, we can now reconcile the budgeted and actual cost.

		£	£	£
Budgeted cost (7,800 × £278)				2,168,400
Cost variances		*Adverse*	*Favourable*	
Materials	price		45,000	
	usage	240,000		
Labour	rate of pay	11,000		
	idle time	24,000		
	efficiency	25,200		
Variable overheads	rate	25,000		
	efficiency	21,000		
Fixed overheads	expenditure		4,000	
	capacity		12,000	
	efficiency	8,400		
Net variances		354,600	61,000	293,600
Actual cost				2,462,000

5.2 Stocks of finished goods

Let us now assume that, of the 7,800 units produced, 7,200 were sold and 600 were left in closing stock.

The stock can be valued at two different amounts – actual cost or standard cost.

5.3 Stock at standard cost

We simply carry forward the balance of 600 units at the standard cost of £278 each, whilst transferring the remainder to the cost of sales account.

Finished goods account

	Units	£		Units	£
WIP	7,800	2,168,400	Cost of sales	7,200	2,001,600
			Balance c/f	600	166,800
	7,800	2,168,400		7,800	2,168,400

Under this method the variances would be written off in full against profits for the period (as shown in the above comparison).

5.4   Stock at actual cost

If it is desired to carry forward closing stock at actual cost, then we must convert the stock value above back to actual cost. This is done by transferring a proportion of the net cost variance into the finished goods account, rather than writing it all off against profits.

The proportion would be $\dfrac{600}{7,800}$ since of 7,800 units produced 600 are in stock and 7,200 have been sold.

The relevant accounts would appear thus:

Finished goods account

	Units	£		Units	£
Work in progress	7,800	2,168,400	Cost of sales	7,200	2,001,600
Variances control	–	22,585	Balance c/f	600	189,385
	7,800	2,190,985		7,800	2,190,985

Variances control account

	£		£
Balance b/f	293,600	Finished goods	
(net cost variance)		(600/7,800 × 293,600)	22,585
		Costing profit and loss	
		(7,200/7,800 × 293,600)	271,015
	293,600		293,600

Finished goods stock should now be valued at actual cost, since what we have effectively done is to 'add back' to the standard cost the proportion of adverse variance that relates to the items in stock.

The actual cost incurred in total was £2,462,000, to produce 7,800 items.

Thus, at actual cost, finished goods stock will be valued at $\dfrac{600}{7,800} \times £2,462,000 = £189,385$

5.5   Interpretation of results

We have seen that valuing stock at standard or actual cost will give two different results. The impact of this is that, since closing stock is valued differently, then under the two methods reported profit would also be different.

Thus:

	£	£
Stock at standard cost		
Actual cost of production	2,462,000	
Less: Closing stock	166,800	
Cost of sales		2,295,200
Stock at actual cost		
Actual cost of production	2,462,000	
Less: Closing stock	189,385	
Cost of sales		2,272,615
Net effect on profit		22,585

In this case, because the cost variances are adverse, then stock at actual cost has a higher value than stock at standard cost. Consequently valuing stock at actual cost gives:

♦   A higher closing stock figure;

♦   A lower cost of sales figure; and

♦   A higher profit figure.

Points to note from the above are:

♦   The result will only be a timing difference – after all this period's closing stock will form next period's opening stock.

♦   Both alternatives are used in practice.

♦   What we are effectively doing is deciding whether or not to capitalise part of the variances and carry them forward. There is an argument that says, if cost variances arise from factors peculiar to a particular period, then they should be written off in full in that period, since the profit figure will be distorted if this is not done. Thus we are really considering whether the cause of the variances is a normal business occurrence, and if it is then we may well decide to pro-rate them over cost of goods sold and closing stock.

♦   Note that if the net production variance was favourable, then actual cost would be lower than standard cost. Thus valuing stocks at standard cost would lead to a higher reported profit figure.

 In the absence of instructions to the contrary, always value stocks at standard cost in examination questions, since this avoids the need to pro-rate the variances.

6   Non-production cost variances

It is just as important to control non-productive costs such as administration and selling and distribution costs as it is to control and monitor production costs.

Standard selling and distribution costs will be found by a careful study of the costs involved such as packaging time, carriage charges and sales commission. The unit costs could also include a share of sales overheads such as advertising costs. Consequently the analysis of the difference between budgeted and actual sales and distribution cost may again include some costs that vary per unit (sold), and some that are fixed. None of these costs would be included in the cost of stocks, as they are non-product costs, although we may perhaps wish to carry forward certain costs such as packaging costs.

Administration costs are more likely to be fixed, and so a simple expenditure variance may be all that is required here to explain the difference between budget and actual.

We will not develop this area further; suffice to say that the principles applied to our analysis of product cost variances would be applied in the same way to an analysis of non-product costs.

Practice questions 13 - 19 *(The answers are in the final chapter of this book)*

13   Compute fixed overhead variances for the following examples:

      (a)

Standard	4 hours per unit
Budgeted production	2,000 units
Budgeted cost	£4,000
Labour hours paid	8,400 hours
Labour hours worked	7,800 hours
Actual cost for period	£4,150
Actual production	1,900 units

      (b)

Budgeted cost	£3,000
Budgeted production	2,000 units at 2 hours per unit
Actual cost	£2,800
Labour hours paid	4,100 hours
Labour hours worked	3,900 hours
Production	2,200 units

Multiple choice questions

With reference to the following information answer questions 14, 15 and 16.

Stan operates a standard absorption costing system, and absorbs fixed production overheads per productive labour hours. The following data pertains to operating period two.

    Budget:

Fixed overhead	£9,000
Output	200 units
Production hours 500 hours	

    Actual:

Fixed overhead	£9,800
Output	185 units
Hours paid	620 hours
Hours worked	600 hours

14   The fixed overhead volume variance is:

    A   £675   adverse
    B   £675   favourable
    C   £1,800   favourable
    D   £2,475   adverse

15   The fixed overhead capacity variance is:

    A   £675   adverse
    B   £675   favourable
    C   £1,800   favourable
    D   £2,475   adverse

16   The fixed overhead efficiency variance is:

    A   £675   adverse
    B   £675   favourable
    C   £1,800   favourable
    D   £2,475   adverse

17   The capacity (or capacity usage) ratio is calculated as

    A   budgeted production hours ÷ actual production hours
    B   actual production hours ÷ standard production hours
    C   budgeted production hours ÷ standard production hours
    D   actual production hours ÷ budgeted production hours

18   Where fixed overheads are absorbed per labour hour, the correct computation (in hours) of the fixed overhead volume variance is given by

    A   actual hours worked compared with budgeted hours
    B   actual hours worked compared with standard hours for actual production
    C   budgeted hours compared with standard hours for actual production
    D   budgeted hours compared with actual hours paid

19   Ollie is preparing his financial statements for his first year of trading. He has a standard absorption costing system, but is uncertain as to how to value closing stock of finished goods.

    His results for the year were:

Production	10,000 units
Actual production costs incurred	£230,000
Sales	9,500 units at £30 each
Opening stocks	Nil

    There was no work in progress.

    The total of the production cost variances for the period was £16,000 adverse.

    The reported profit figures, with stock valued at actual cost or standard cost, would be:

		Closing stock at		
		Actual cost		*Standard cost*
A	Profits of	£66,500	OR	£65,700
B	Profits of	£66,500	OR	£67,300
C	Profits of	£65,700	OR	£66,500
D	Profits of	£7,300	OR	£66,500

7 Sales variances

7.1 Introduction

Just as for budgeted costs, so the budgeted revenue will be made up of two factors, namely the standard selling price and the budgeted sales quantity.

Consequently the sales variance will be a combination of selling more or less units than budgeted at a selling price of more or less than standard.

Let us develop our ongoing example.

Katzman Ltd had budgeted to sell all 7,500 units produced at a standard selling price of £450 per unit.

As we have already seen, 7,200 were actually sold, and the selling price was £480.

Impact on turnover

	£
Budgeted turnover (7,500 × £450)	3,375,000
Actual turnover (7,200 × £480)	3,456,000
Sales variance (favourable)	81,000

The variance is clearly favourable, since we have obtained more revenue than budgeted for.

Again, we can split the total variance into volume and price elements.

7.2 Volume variance

	£
Budgeted quantity at standard selling price (7,500 × £450)	3,375,000
Actual quantity sold at standard selling price (7,200 × £450)	3,240,000
Sales turnover volume variance (adverse)	135,000

This is telling us that we have sold 300 units less than budgeted, which at standard price resulted in a reduction in turnover of £135,000.

7.3 Price variance

	£
Actual quantity sold at standard selling price (7,200 × £450)	3,240,000
Actual quantity sold at actual selling price (7,200 × £480)	3,456,000
Price variance (favourable)	216,000

The price variance is favourable, since for each unit actually sold we have obtained £30 more revenue than the budgeted selling price.

7.4 Interpretation of the variances

Price variance

Some possible causes of the price variance could be:

♦ Unplanned increase in selling prices, possibly caused by increased costs that management have decided to pass on to customers in the form of increased selling price.

♦ Deliberate policy to increase prices, since management feel more profits could be obtained from a higher price but lower volume of sales.

♦ Responses to the actions of competitors.

Volume variance

Some possible causes of the volume variance could be:

♦ Reduction in demand caused by the increased selling price.

♦ Failure to satisfy demand due to production difficulties (perhaps unlikely given that there are goods in stock at the period end. Note, however, that this does not conclusively prove that there were no 'stock-outs' during the period).

♦ Unexpected fall in demand due to external factors such as competitors' price cutting, or a trade recession.

♦ The budgeted sales volume itself may be an over-estimate. We will have based the budget primarily on the sales department's predictions of sales. These may be overstated as sales reps are by nature optimists!

7.5 Impact on profit

As we have already suggested, it would be useful if we could summarise our results in the form of a statement that reconciles budgeted and actual profits. To do this, all variances must be computed in terms of their impact upon **profit**. The cost variances as previously computed will clearly have a direct effect upon the profit figure. To date, however, we have only computed the sales variances in terms of their effect upon **turnover**. The crucial point is that if we sell one unit more than budget, we also incur one extra unit's worth of cost of sales as well.

Hence we must compute the sales variances using the profit margin.

7.6 Volume margin variance

We have actually sold 300 units less than budgeted.

The standard profit margin is (£450 – £278) = £172

The sales margin volume variance is therefore 300 × £172 = **£51,600 adverse**

The impact of the reduction in sales of 300 units on budgeted profit is therefore £51,600.

7.7 Price margin variance

 The crucial point to note here is that we are assessing the impact of selling price in isolation. We therefore assume that the unit costs remain constant at the standard cost of £278. (The fact that actual costs are different from standard has already been examined in the cost variance analyses.)

The variance can be computed as:

	£
Actual quantity sold at standard profit margin 7,200 × £172	1,238,400
Actual quantity sold at 'actual' profit margin 7,200 × (£480 − £278)	1,454,400
Price margin variance (favourable)	216,000

The 'actual' margin used is simply actual selling price less standard costs. Note that the actual costs are irrelevant for this purpose.

Note that the same result has already been obtained above by using revenue only.

However this method allows us to summarise the sales margin variances as follows:

	Units	£
Budgeted sales at standard profit margin (£172)	7,500	1,290,000
Sales margin volume variance (adverse)	300	51,600
Actual sales at standard profit margin (£172)	7,200	1,238,400
Sales margin price variance (favourable)	–	216,000
Actual sales at 'actual' profit margin (£202)	7,200	1,454,400

8   The operating statement

Having computed all the variances, we are now in a position to prepare a concise reconciliation of budgeted and actual profit. This is known as an operating statement.

Firstly let us compute the profit figures that we wish to reconcile.

Budgeted sales (units)		7,500
Standard profit margin (per unit)		£172
Budgeted profit		£1,290,000

Actual profit

	£	£
Sales revenue (7,200 × £480)		3,456,000
Costs (for 7,800 units):		
Raw materials	1,755,000	
Labour	341,000	
Variable overheads	280,000	
Fixed overheads	86,000	
	2,462,000	
Less: Finished goods stock, valued at standard cost (600 units)	166,800	
		2,295,200
Actual profit		1,160,800

The operating statement would present all the variances we have computed as follows.

Katzman Ltd

Operating statement for April 20X8

		Adverse £	Favourable £	£
Budgeted profit				1,290,000
Sales margin variances:				
	Price		216,000	
	Volume	51,600		
				164,400
				1,454,400
Cost variances:				
Materials	price		45,000	
	usage	240,000		
Labour	rate of pay	11,000		
	idle time	24,000		
	efficiency	25,200		
Variable overheads	rate	25,000		
	efficiency	21,000		
Variable cost variances sub-total		346,200	45,000	
Fixed overheads	expenditure		4,000	
	capacity		12,000	
	efficiency	8,400		
Net variances		354,600	61,000	(293,600)
Actual profit				1,160,800

You should memorise the layout of the operating statement above, and use it whenever a reconciliation of two profit figures via the variances is required.

9 Marginal costing

9.1 Introduction

The above example was based on total absorption costing. If we operate a marginal costing system, stock will be valued at variable cost of production only, and all fixed costs will be written off in the period concerned.

This will affect the calculation of variances and the operating statement as follows:

◆ the operating statement will commence with budgeted contribution, rather than budgeted profit;

◆ the only fixed overheads variance will be the expenditure variance. There can be no volume variances, as we make no attempt to absorb fixed overheads into production;

◆ sales margin variances need to be recalculated in terms of standard contribution, rather than standard profit; and

♦   stock should be valued at standard marginal cost, rather than standard total absorption cost.

9.2   *Marginal costing example*

The following example repeats the figures from Katzman Ltd but now we will assume that Katzman operates a marginal costing system.

Standard cost card per drum of soap:

	£
Raw materials (100 kg × £2)	200
Labour (12 hours × £3)	36
Variable overheads (12 hours × £2.50)	30
Standard marginal cost per drum	266

Budgeted fixed overheads for the period were £90,000. Budgeted production and sales were 7,500 units at a standard selling price of £450.

Actual costs incurred in the period were:

	£
Raw materials (900,000 kg purchased and used)	1,755,000
Labour (110,000 hours paid, 102,000 hours worked)	341,000
Variable overheads	280,000
Fixed overheads	86,000

7,800 drums of soap were produced, and 7,200 were sold at a selling price of £480 per unit. Stock is to be valued at standard marginal cost.

9.3   *Computation of variances*

Variable cost variances

These are exactly as computed previously, and so the computations will not be repeated here.

9.4   *Fixed overhead variances*

The only variance will be the expenditure variance. This is simply a comparison of budgeted and actual fixed cost.

	£
Budgeted fixed cost	90,000
Actual fixed cost	86,000
Fixed overhead expenditure variance (favourable)	4,000

9.5   *Sales variances*

We must now compute the sales variances in terms of their impact upon budgeted contribution.

♦   **Price variance**

We saw that the sales price variance was the same regardless of whether computed in terms of turnover or profit. It is not too surprising then to find that the price variance has exactly the same impact on budgeted contribution.

We can show the calculations as follows:

	£	£
Standard contribution per unit		
Standard selling price	450	
Standard variable cost	266	
		184
'Actual' contribution per unit		
Actual selling price	480	
Standard variable cost	266	
		214

	£
Actual sales at the standard contribution per unit (7,200 × £184)	1,324,800
Actual sales at the 'actual' contribution per unit (7,200 × £214)	1,540,800
Price variance (favourable)	216,000

For simplicity, since it gives us the same answer we can compute the price variance based on selling prices rather than contribution margins.

- ♦ **Volume variance**

We must now compute the volume variance at the standard contribution margin per unit.

	£
Budgeted sales at the standard contribution margin (7,500 × £184)	1,380,000
Actual sales at standard contribution margin (7,200 × £184)	1,324,800
Volume variance (adverse)	55,200

9.6 Marginal costing operating statement

	Adverse £	Favourable £	£
Budgeted contribution			1,380,000
Sales margin variances			
Price		216,000	
Volume	55,200		
			160,800
			1,540,800
Variable cost variances, in summary (as before)	346,200	45,000	(301,200)
Actual contribution			1,239,600
Fixed overheads			
Budgeted	90,000		
Expenditure variance (favourable)	4,000		
Actual			86,000
Actual profit			1,153,600

9.7   Reconciliation of profits

You may recall that the profit reported under the total absorption basis was different from the profit above.

		£
Profit under total absorption costing		1,160,800
Profit under marginal costing		1,153,600
Difference		7,200

The difference is caused by the different valuations of finished goods stocks.

	£
Closing stock valued at standard total absorption cost (600 × £278)	166,800
Closing stock valued at standard marginal cost (600 × £266)	159,600
	7,200

Thus, under total absorption costing we have capitalised £7,200 of fixed overhead and carried it forward into the next period. However, under marginal costing we have written off the whole of the fixed overhead incurred against profits for the period.

Finally, bear in mind that we could value stock at actual marginal cost, which would give rise to yet another different reported profit figure.

10   The stock adjustment

10.1   When a stock adjustment is needed

If stocks are valued at actual cost, rather than standard cost, in the actual profit and loss account, a 'stock adjustment' must be made in the operating statement.

Return to the earlier operating statement. This has an actual profit of £1,160,800 at the bottom, which you can see includes stocks at standard (total absorption) cost.

Had stocks been valued at actual (total absorption) cost, they would have been stated at

$\dfrac{600}{7,800} \times £2,462,000 = £189,385$. (This valuation pro-rates part of the cost variances to stock.)

This would change the profit figure:

	£	£
Current profit		1,160,800
Stock at standard cost	166,800	
Stock at actual cost	189,385	
Add back		22,585
Actual profit with stock at actual cost		1,183,385

But our operating statement shows actual profit of £1,160,800. To reconcile back to the true reported figure, an adjustment is added to the bottom of the operating statement. (The top part of the statement is exactly the same as before.)

	£	£
Actual profit, with stock at standard (as before)		1,160,800
Stock adjustment		
Stock at standard cost	166,800	
Stock at actual cost	189,385	
		22,585
Actual profit per the profit and loss account (stock at actual)		1,183,385

A similar adjustment would be made under a marginal costing system, if stock were valued at actual marginal cost in the actual profit and loss account.

Remember:

(1)   Stock can be valued at standard or actual, marginal or total absorption cost.

(2)   A stock adjustment is only needed if stock is valued at actual cost (either marginal or total absorption) in the actual profit and loss account.

10.2   Learning outcome

At this stage of the chapter we have covered the following Learning Outcome:

> Prepare and discuss a report which reconciles budget and actual profit using absorption and/or marginal costing principles.

Practice questions 20 - 29 *(The answers are in the final chapter of this book)*

20   Phasors Ltd manufacture a toy gun which is sold direct to a retail organisation under a long term contract. The budget for the month of June 20X7 was as follows:

	Per unit £	Per month £
Sales – 14,400 units at standard price	1.38	19,872
Standard cost of sales		
Materials (576 kg @ £6 per kg)	0.24	3,456
Direct wages: (30 employees : 40 hour week : £1.44 per hour)	0.48	6,912
Variable expenses (£0.54 per hour)	0.18	2,592
Fixed expenses (£0.72 per hour)	0.24	3,456
	1.14	16,416
Budgeted profit	0.24	3,456

The trading and profit and loss account for the month, prepared in conventional form, showed the following position:

	£		£
Materials purchased:		Sales – 13,200 units	
560kg @ £6.24	3,494.40	at £1.38	18,216.00
Wages	7,296.00		
Variable expenses	2,400.00		
Fixed expenses	3,840.00		
	17,030.40		
Net profit	1,185.60		
	18,216.00		18,216.00

There were no opening or closing stocks or work-in-progress. The month's actual production (all of which was sold) was achieved in 36 hours per week, although the standard 40 hour week was paid for.

Required

(a)   Calculate the variances.

(b)   Prepare an operating statement for the month based on standard absorption costing showing the breakdown, into the appropriate variances, of the difference between the standard profit and the actual profit.

21   Joachim Joiners starts business on 1.1.X3 and produces a budget for the first year as follows:

	Standard cost card £	Budget £000
(Production 5,000 units)		
Materials (2 kg @ £2.50 per kg)	5	25
Labour and variable production overheads (1 hour @ £7 per hour)	7	35
Fixed production overhead (1 hour @ £8 per hour)	8	40
	20	100
Less: Closing stock (1,000 units @ £20)		20
		80
Variable selling costs	4	16
Fixed selling costs	2	8
	26	104
Profit (on sales of 4,000 units)	4	16
Sales	30	120

At the end of the year the following summarised profit and loss account is produced:

	£000	£000
Sales revenue (4,400 units)		150
Costs (production 4,800 units)		
Materials (12,500 kg @ £2 per kg)	25	
Labour and variable production overheads (5,500 hours)	39	
Fixed production overheads	21	
	85	
Less: Closing stock (400 units @ £20)	(8)	
	77	
Variable selling costs	20	
Fixed selling costs	9	
		106
Actual profit		44

Required

(a)   Produce an operating statement for the year reconciling budgeted and actual profit.

(b)   Calculate the actual closing stock and profit figures using:

(i)   standard direct costing;

(ii)   total absorption costing, pro-rating cost variances; and

(iii)   direct costing, pro-rating cost variances.

(c)   Suggest a further stock valuation that might be produced if SSAP 9 is followed with regard to the treatment of fixed production overheads.

Multiple choice questions

22   The following data relating to a product are available for April:

Budget:

Selling price per unit	£100
Variable cost per unit	£60
Sales	21,000 units

Actual for April:

Sales	21,000 units
Sales price variance	£84,000 (favourable)
Fixed costs	£580,000
Fixed cost expenditure variance	£20,000 (favourable)
Variable cost per unit	£60

What was the budgeted profit for April?

A   £344,000
B   £280,000
C   £260,000
D   £240,000

23   The budget and actual unit costs and selling prices for Blotto for January 20X8 were:

	Budget £	Actual £
Sales price	12	13
Production cost	8	10

To compute the sales margin volume variance we multiply the difference between budgeted and actual sales volume by:

A   £1
B   £2
C   £3
D   £4

With reference to the following data, answer questions 24 and 25 below.

Peter produces and sells a single product, the Piper.

The budget for period one was:

Budgeted output and sales	5,000 units
Standard selling price per unit	£8
Standard cost per unit	£6

The actual results for the period were:

Actual output	5,500 units
Actual sales	4,800 units
Actual selling price per unit	£8.50
Actual cost per unit	£6.30

24   The sales margin volume variance is:

A   £400   adverse
B   £440   adverse
C   £500   adverse
D   £1,600   adverse

25   The sales margin price variance is:

A   £960   favourable
B   £2,400   favourable
C   £2,500   favourable
D   £2,750   favourable

26   Axe Ltd makes three types of carpet in 30 metre rolls. The budgeted and actual results for 20X8 are as follows:

	Type 1	Type 2	Type 3	Total
Budget:				
Sales (units)	1,000	1,000	2,000	4,000
Turnover	£1,000,000	£2,000,000	£3,000,000	£6,000,000
Actual:				
Sales (units)	900	1,100	2,000	4,000
Selling price per unit	£1,050	£2,200	£1,400	

What is the total sales price variance for 20X8?

A   £185,000   adverse
B   £65,000   favourable
C   £75,000   favourable
D   £154,000   favourable

27   Pear Products uses a standard costing system. Results for the last period show a favourable sales price variance of £4,000 and an adverse sales margin volume variance of £5,500.

The actual gross profit (actual sales less actual production cost) was £137,000. The production variances, all written off against profit in the period, were £2,000 adverse. There were no opening or closing stocks.

What is the budgeted gross profit?

A   £133,500
B   £136,500
C   £137,500
D   £140,500

28   When production exceeds sales, marginal costing, when compared to total absorption costing

A   always produces more profit
B   always produces less profit
C   sometimes produces more profit, sometimes less profit
D   always produces the same profit

29   Foxtrot wishes to report the highest profit figure in its first year of trading. He operates a standard costing system, but is uncertain as to how to value closing stock.

Results for the period were:

Actual production	10,000 units
Actual sales	8,000 units

Total costs incurred were:

Variable	£70,000
Fixed	£30,000

Standard costs per unit were:

Variable	£6
Fixed	£5

Which of the following methods of stock valuation should Foxtrot choose to obtain his objective?

A   Standard marginal cost
B   Actual marginal cost
C   Standard total absorption cost
D   Actual total absorption cost

11   Mix and yield variances

11.1   Materials mix and yield variances

Consider a process dear to many students' hearts – brewing. Beer is manufactured from a mixture of barley, malt, hops, sugar, water, and other substances. When preparing the standards for such a process the precise quantity of each ingredient would be specified in what is called the standard mix.

It may well then happen in practice, by design or by accident, that the actual input mix differs from the standard mix specified. This difference can be quantified by comparing the actual mix at standard prices with the standard mix that should have been used at the standard prices. This represents the mix variance.

We are also likely to see in practice a difference between the output we expected to obtain from the materials input and the actual output obtained. The yield variance is a measure of this.

11.2   Labour mix and yield variances

It is also possible to calculate labour mix and yield variances in a similar way to calculating materials mix and yield variances. Employees may be organised into teams, where a standard team has a certain number of junior, medium and senior employees. Where the actual mix of employees is different from the standard mix, the labour usage variance can be analysed into its mix and yield components.

11.3   Example

In the first stage of a particular process the following standards apply:

Input materials			£
X	30	kg @ £5 per kg	150
Y	25	kg @ £6 per kg	150
Z	45	kg @ £4 per kg	180
Standard input	100	kg @ £4.80 per kg	480
Normal loss	4		-
Standard output	96	kg @ £5 per kg	480

During March the following materials were introduced into the process:

Input materials			£
X	310	kg @ £5.20 per kg	1,612
Y	270	kg @ £5.80 per kg	1,566
Z	420	kg @ £4.10 per kg	1,722
	1,000	kg	4,900

Actual production was 968 kg.

11.4   Solution – price variance

The price variance is simply the sum of the individual price variances.

			£	£
Actual quantities at actual prices:				
X	310 × £5.20		1,612	
Y	270 × £5.80		1,566	
Z	420 × £4.10		1,722	
				4,900
Actual quantities at standard prices:				
X	310 × £5		1,550	
Y	270 × £6		1,620	
Z	420 × £4		1,680	
				4,850
Materials price variance (adverse)				50

We can see from the above that the net variance of £50 is a combination of adverse variances (actual price higher than standard) for materials X and Z and a favourable variance for material Y. It is in fact simply the sum of the three individual price variances.

11.5   Solution – mix variance

The mix variance is the monetary value representing the difference between:

♦   the standard price of the standard mixture; and
♦   the standard price of the actual mixture.

We are therefore saying, given that we actually used 1,000 kg, what would it have cost in the standard mix at standard prices, compared with the cost of the actual mix used at standard prices.

 Notice that the mix variance implicitly assumes that we can vary the mix by substituting one input material for another.

The calculation is as follows:

				£	£
				£	£
Actual quantity used in the actual mixture at standard prices:					
X		310	× £5	1,550	
Y		270	× £6	1,620	
Z		420	× £4	1,680	
		1,000			4,850

			£	£

Actual quantity used in the standard mixture at standard prices:

X (30/100)	300	× £5	1,500	
Y (25/100)	250	× £6	1,500	
Z (45/100)	450	× £4	1,800	
	1,000	× £4.80		4,800

Mix variance (adverse) 50

Notice three things from the above tabulation:

♦ The variance is adverse because the actual mixture used cost £50 more than the same total quantity would have cost in the standard mixture.

♦ There is in fact no need to split the total quantity into the individual elements within the standard mix. We know from the standard cost card that 1 kg of the standard mix costs £4.80. (This is a weighted average cost per kg that takes account of the unit costs of X, Y and Z and the relative proportion of each in the standard mix.) We now have 1,000 kg of standard mix, so at standard prices this must cost £4,800.

♦ The substitution effects can be seen if we examine the individual quantities in the tabulation. In the actual mix we have used 10kg more of X (310 – 300), 20 kg more of Y (270 – 250), and therefore 30 kg less of Z (420 – 450), than the standard allowed. Since Z is the cheapest material, we are effectively substituting dearer materials for cheaper ones, hence giving us the adverse mix variance.

11.6   Solution – yield variance

The standard says that for an input of 100 kg of materials we would expect to produce 96 kg of output. The loss could be due to factors such as evaporation or incomplete conversion of raw materials to finished goods.

Thus the expected yield from our process is 96% of input.

However, in practice the actual yield will almost certainly vary for successive input batches, even though the same quantity, quality and mixture of materials input is used.

The materials yield variance expresses in monetary terms the difference between the expected (or standard) yield from a standard input mixture, and the actual yield obtained from that mixture.

The calculation is as follows:

	kg
The standard yield from 1,000 kg inputs is 1,000 × 96%	960
The actual yield obtained was	968
Favourable yield variance	8

Valuing this at the standard cost per kg of **output** gives:

Yield variance = 8 kg × £5 = £40 favourable

11.7　Summary and interpretation

We can summarise the variances as below:

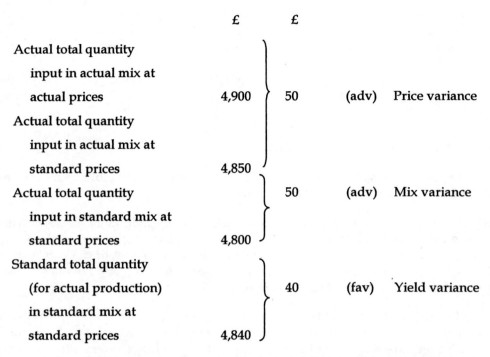

	£	£		
Actual total quantity input in actual mix at actual prices	4,900	50	(adv)	Price variance
Actual total quantity input in actual mix at standard prices	4,850			
Actual total quantity input in standard mix at standard prices	4,800	50	(adv)	Mix variance
Standard total quantity (for actual production) in standard mix at standard prices	4,840	40	(fav)	Yield variance

The summary also enables us to compute the total materials cost variance, which is simply the difference between actual cost (actual quantity in the actual mix at actual prices) and standard cost (standard quantity in the standard mix at standard prices).

Therefore materials cost variance = £4,900 – £4,840 = £60 adverse

What we have done is to analyse the total cost variance into price, mix, and yield components.

The usual interpretation is that the mix and yield variances are a sub-division of our 'traditional' usage variance.

The usage variance would therefore be computed as:

	£
Actual total quantity input in the actual mix at standard prices	4,850
Standard total quantity in the standard mix at standard prices	4,840
Usage variance (adverse)	10

The above analysis really pre-supposes that it is the users who are responsible for the change in mix. Thus the buyers simply purchase whatever mix the production department demands. It is perfectly possible in different circumstances for the buyer to dictate the mix – perhaps through the possibility of substituting a cheaper material for a dearer one. The computation of our variances would not change at all. However, in terms of allocating responsibility for the mix variance, we would look to the buying department rather than the production department.

When considering the yield variance we should remember that conversion efficiency does not only depend upon the quality of materials used or the actual mixture selected. Operator or machine inefficiencies may occur independently of any raw material factors. Again, therefore, as with any variance, a full investigation would be required before we could allocate responsibility and take any corrective actions.

Finally note that an inherent assumption of the mix variances calculated is that a change in mix of 'ingredients' will not produce a change in yield, efficiency or volume. This is unlikely to be the case – a fact that is apparent in the case of materials mix variances where the degree to which one material can be substituted for another is limited.

Practice questions 30 and 31 *(The answers are in the final chapter of this book)*

Multiple choice questions

30   Charlie Ltd mixes two ingredients, Delta and Edward in standard proportions of 7D:3E.

Actual consumption of Delta was 10 gallons higher than standard. There was no yield variance expected or incurred, but the company expected and incurred a normal loss of 10 gallons (no disposal value) in producing 90 gallons of finished product at a standard cost in total of £270.

There was a materials mix variance of £10 adverse.

What is the standard input cost of a gallon of Delta?

A   £1
B   £2
C   £3
D   £4

31   A materials mix variance is

A   actual cost of standard mix for actual quantity used less actual cost of actual mix for actual quantity used

B   standard cost of standard mix for standard quantity for actual production less standard cost of standard mix for actual quantity used

C   standard cost of standard mix for actual quantity used less standard cost of actual mix for actual quantity used

D   standard cost of standard mix for standard quantity for actual production less standard cost of actual mix for actual quantity used

---

11.8   Learning outcome

At this stage of the chapter we have now covered the following Learning Outcome.

Calculate and interpret material, labour, variable overhead, fixed overhead and sales variances.

12   Summary

This chapter has explained the calculation of basic variances. More advanced aspects are considered in the next chapter.

CHAPTER 3

Advanced variance analysis and interpretation

EXAM FOCUS

This chapter explains the more advanced aspects of variance analysis which you can expect to be tested in the examination. It builds on the basics of variance analysis explained earlier.

LEARNING OUTCOMES

This chapter covers the following Learning Outcomes of the CIMA Syllabus.

> Prepare reports using a range of internal and external benchmarks and interpret the results

> Discuss the behavioural implications of standard costing

In order to cover these Learning Outcomes the following topics are included.

> Investigation of variances
> Responsibility accounting

1　A new analysis of traditional variances

1.1　The purpose of variance analysis

The following reasons have been identified for performing variance analysis.

- To provide data which is relevant to management for feedback control purposes, to show where deviations from plan have arisen and to point towards areas where corrective action may be taken.

- To show which deviations from plan are controllable and which are non-controllable.

- To determine the cause of a controllable deviation from plan and to attempt to minimise any adverse effect on costs and profit.

- To value variances on a basis which is related to the level at which they are controllable.

- To provide a basis for feedforward control action.

2 Volume variances

2.1 Introduction

The examiner may split a volume variance into elements for capacity, idle time and productivity (efficiency). The following tabular approach is recommended for splitting either a sales or production volume variance.

(1)	(2)	(3)	(4)
Budgeted hours for budgeted sales/production	Actual hours less budgeted idle time	Actual hours less actual idle time	Budgeted hours for actual output/ production

Capacity variance	Idle time variance	Productivity (efficiency) variance

Using the formula we can now work through the following example. Note that in an example like this the examiner may give you the operating statement and would expect you to do the detailed calculations behind the variances shown in the statement.

2.2 Example

P Ltd uses a standard costing system to control and report upon production of its single product.

An abstract from the original standard cost card of the product is as follows.

	£	£
Selling price per unit		200
Materials (4 kgs material @ £20 per kg)	80	
Labour (6 hrs @ £7 per hr)	42	
Total variable costs		122
Contribution per unit		78

For period 3, 2,500 units were budgeted to be produced and sold but the actual production and sales were 2,850 units.

The following information was also available.

(i) At the commencement of period 3 the normal material became unobtainable and it was necessary to use an alternative. Unfortunately, 0.5 kg per unit extra was required as it was thought that the material would be more difficult to work with. The price of the alternative was expected to be £16.50 per kg.

In the event, actual usage was 12,450 kgs at £18 per kg.

(ii) Because of the difficulties expected with the alternative material, management agreed to pay the workers £8 per hour for period 3 only. During the period 18,800 hours were paid of which 400 were idle time.

The operating statement for period 3 showing operational and planning variances for P Ltd is as follows.

	£	£
Original budgeted contribution		195,000
Revision (planning) variances		
Materials price (W1)	39,375	
Materials usage (W1)	(25,000)	
	14,375	
Labour rate (W2)	(15,000)	
Labour efficiency (W2)	-	
Idle time (W2)	-	
		(15,000)
Revised budgeted contribution		194,375
Sales volume variance — due to:		
Capacity	49,242	
Productivity	(16,846)	
Idle time	(5,183)	
	27,213	
Revised standard contribution from actual sales		221,588
(2,850 × £77.75 — W3)		
Other (operational) variances		
Materials price (W4)	(18,675)	
Materials usage (W5)	6,187	
Labour rate (W6)	-	
Labour efficiency (W7)	(10,400)	
Idle time (W8)	(3,200)	
		(26,088)
Actual contribution		195,500

Required

Show the detailed workings for the planning and operational variances shown in the operating statement.

2.3 Solution

Workings: planning variances

(1)	*Materials price*	(Ex-ante SP - Ex-post SP) Ex-post SQ		
		(£20.00 - £16.50) × 2,500 × 4.5	=	£39,375 F
	Materials usage	(Ex-ante SQ - Ex-post SQ) Ex-ante SP		
		[(4 × 2,500) - (4.5 × 2,500)] × £20	=	£25,000 A
(2)	*Labour rate*	(Ex-ante SR - Ex-post SR) Ex-post SH		
		(£7 - £8) × 6 × 2,500	=	£15,000 A
	Labour efficiency	(Ex-ante SH - Ex-post SH) Ex-ante SR		
		[(6 × 2,500) - (6 × 2,500)] × £7	=	Nil
	Idle time	(Ex-ante IT - Ex-post IT) Ex-ante SR		
		(0 - 0) × £7	=	Nil

(3)   Revised budgeted contribution

		£	£
Standard price per unit			200.00
Direct materials:	(4.5 × £16.50)	74.25	
Direct labour:	(6 × £8)	48.00	
			122.25
Contribution per unit			77.75

Budgeted output = 2,500 units

Therefore budgeted contribution (revised) = 2,500 × £77.75 = £194,375

Workings: operational variances

(4)   (Ex-post SP - AP) AQ
(£16.50 - £18) × 12,450   =   £18,675   A

(5)   (Ex-post SQ - AQ) Ex-post SP
[(4.5 × 2,850) - 12,450] × £16.50   =   £6,187.5 F

(6)   (Ex-post SR - AR) AH
(£8 - £8) × 18,800   =   0

(7)   (Ex-post SH - AH) Ex-post SR
([6 × 2,850] - 18,400] × £8   =   £10,400   A

(8)   (Ex-post IT - AIT) Ex-post SR
(0 - 400) × £8   =   £3,200   A

A tabular approach is recommended for the sales volume variance.

Total sales variance = (SQ – AQ) Revised contribution

(2,500 – 2,850) 77.75 = £27,212.5 F

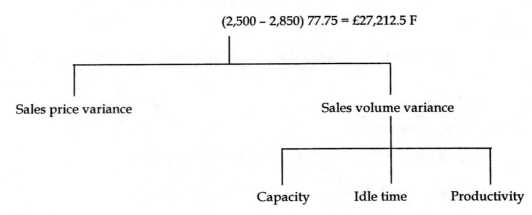

The calculations are as follows.

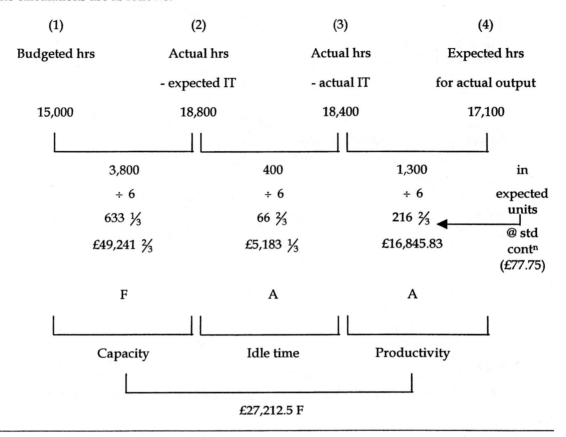

	(1)	(2)	(3)	(4)
	Budgeted hrs	Actual hrs	Actual hrs	Expected hrs
		- expected IT	- actual IT	for actual output
	15,000	18,800	18,400	17,100

3,800	400	1,300	in
÷ 6	÷ 6	÷ 6	expected units
633 ⅓	66 ⅔	216 ⅔	@ std contⁿ
£49,241 ⅔	£5,183 ⅓	£16,845.83	(£77.75)

$633 \tfrac{1}{3}$ · $66 \tfrac{2}{3}$ · $216 \tfrac{2}{3}$

$£49{,}241 \tfrac{2}{3}$ · $£5{,}183 \tfrac{1}{3}$ · £16,845.83 @ std contⁿ (£77.75)

| F | A | A |
| Capacity | Idle time | Productivity |

£27,212.5 F

Practice question 1 *(The answer is in the final chapter of this book)*

Tungach

Tungach Ltd make and sell a single product. Demand for the product exceeds the expected production capacity of Tungach Ltd. The holding of stocks of the finished product is avoided if possible because the physical nature of the product is such that it deteriorates quickly and stocks may become unsaleable.

A standard marginal cost system is in operation. Feedback reporting takes planning and operational variances into consideration.

The management accountant has produced the following operating statement for period 9.

TUNGACH LTD OPERATING STATEMENT — PERIOD 9

	£		£	
Original budgeted contribution			36,000	
Revision variances				
Material usage	9,600	(A)		
Material price	3,600	(F)		
Wage rate	1,600	(F)		
			4,400	(A)
Revised budgeted contribution			31,600	

Sales volume variance

Extra capacity	4,740.0	(F)
Productivity drop	987.5	(A)
Idle time	592.5	(A)
Stock increase	2,370.0	(A)

	790	(F)

Revised standard contribution for actual sales	32,390

Other variances

Material usage	900	(F)
Material price	3,120	(A)
Labour efficiency	1,075	(A)
Labour idle time	645	(A)
Wage rate	2,760	(A)

	6,700	(A)

Actual contribution	25,690

Additional data

(1)   The original standard contribution per product unit as determined at period 1 was as follows.

	£	£
Selling price		30
Direct material (1.5 kg at £8)	12	
Direct labour (2 hours at £4.50)	9	
		21
Contribution		9

(2)   A permanent change in the product specification was implemented from period 7 onwards. It was estimated that this change would require 20% additional material per product unit. The current efficient price of the material has settled at £7.50 per kg.

(3)   Actual direct material used during period 9 was 7,800 kg at £7.90 per kg. Any residual variances are due to operational problems.

(4)   The original standard wage rate overestimated the degree of trade union pressure during negotiations and was 20p higher than the rate subsequently agreed. Tungach Ltd made a short-term operational decision to pay the workforce at £4.60 per hour during periods 7 to 9 in an attempt to minimise the drop in efficiency likely because of the product specification change. Management succeeded in extending the production capacity during period 9 and the total labour hours paid for were 9,200 hours. These included 150 hours of idle time.

(5)

Budgeted production and sales quantity (period 9)	4,000 units
Actual sales quantity (period 9)	4,100 units
Actual production quantity (period 9)	4,400 units

(6)   Stocks of finished goods are valued at the current efficient standard cost.

Required

(a)   Prepare detailed figures showing how the material and labour variances in the operating statement have been calculated.

(b)   Prepare detailed figures showing how the sales volume variance has been calculated for each causal factor shown in the operating statement.

(c)   Prepare a report to the management of Tungach Ltd explaining the meaning and relevance of the figures given in the operating statement for period 9. The report should contain specific comments for any two of the sales volume variance causal factors and any two of the 'other variances'. The comments should suggest possible reasons for each variance, the management member likely to be answerable for each variance, and possible corrective action.

3   Measuring the significance of variances

3.1   Introduction

In exercising control it will often not be practicable to review every variance in detail for each accounting period, and attention will therefore be concentrated on those variances which have the greatest impact on the achievement of the budget plan.

One method of identifying significant variances is to express each variance as a percentage of the related budget allowance or standard value. Those showing the highest percentage deviation would then be given the most urgent attention.

This method, however, could result in lack of attention to variances which, although representing a small percentage of the standard value, nevertheless involve significant sums of money. Both percentages and money should be looked at in deciding where the priorities for control actually lie.

It is important that both favourable and unfavourable variances are reviewed, since both represent deviations from a predetermined plan.

3.2   Fluctuating variances

It will sometimes happen that the variances of a particular period are not representative of a general trend. Items like stationery costs can fluctuate widely from month to month, dependent on the amount of stationery that has been invoiced. Sometimes the accountant will make estimated adjustments to either the budget or the actual figures in an attempt to give a better picture of the underlying trend but this is not a completely satisfactory way of dealing with the matter. The simplest way of getting the month's figures into context is to show also the accumulated cost for the year to date. High cost and low cost periods will then be revealed but will balance out in the cumulative figures.

A development of the above idea is to report also each period what is the manager's latest forecast compared with the annual budget. It will then be possible to see whether variances from budget currently being reported are likely to continue to accumulate during the remainder of the year, or whether they will be offset by later opposite variances. Although this technique of forecasting is dependent on managers' subjective assessments, it is a good way of ensuring that the correct control action gets taken on the current figures.

3.3   Example

An example of a report incorporating forecast figures for the year as a whole is given overleaf.

You might like to spend a few minutes considering what this report tells you about the business. For example:

(a)   Sales, which had obviously been below budget on the first six periods of the year, are significantly in excess of budget on period 7 (reducing the cumulative shortfall to £80,000), and are now expected to exceed the budget for the year as a whole.

(b)   Direct costs are naturally higher when sales are higher. The percentage of direct costs to sales value is not consistent, however, as the following calculations show:

	Budget	Actual
Period 7	56.0%	53.6%
Cumulative	56.0%	57.0%
Forecast	58.3%	62.1%

For the seven periods as a whole, direct costs have been in excess of the budgeted percentage and even though the budget for the twelve months provides for an increase in that percentage the forecast actual increase is still higher. Period 7 in isolation shows an anomalous result, perhaps due to some peculiarity in sales mix.

(c)   The variance on factory overhead, which is favourable over the seven periods as a whole, has become adverse in period 7 and is forecast as adverse for the year as a whole (though not at the rate experienced in period 7). Failure to budget adequately for inflationary increases is one possibility.

(d)   Administration and selling costs have a cumulative favourable variance of £40,000 against a budget of £840,000, ie 4.8%. By the end of the year a favourable variance of £173,000 (13.1% on budget) is expected. It would appear that considerable economies are planned, and have already commenced. The fact that period 7 above shows a small adverse variance is obviously not significant. Such results can emerge in administration costs, which can be influenced by random occurrences like a large purchase of stationery or a major visit overseas by the managing director.

Profit and loss account

7 Periods cumulative to .... 20 ..... (£000)

	Period 7			Cumulative			Whole year	
	Budget	Actual	Variances F or (A)	Budget	Actual	Variances F or (A)	Budget	Latest forecast
Sales	500	600	100	3,500	3,420	(80)	6,000	6,200
Direct cost of sales	280	322	(42)	1,960	1,951	9	3,500	3,850
Factory overhead	58	69	(11)	420	400	20	700	750
Administration and selling costs	122	123	(1)	840	800	40	1,320	1,147
Total costs	460	514	(54)	3,220	3,151	69	5,520	5,747
Operating profit	40	86	46	280	269	(11)	480	453
Profit: sales %	8%	14.3%	-	8%	7.9%	-	8%	7.3%

3.4   Comparing against forecasts

Some large organisations in the UK have taken a step further the idea of comparing against forecasts. Many companies employ the following comparisons:

	Comparison	Information
1	Budget v actual	What progress have we made towards achieving objectives?
2	Budget v forecast	Will we continue to progress towards achievement of objectives?
3	Budget v revised forecast	Will suggested corrective actions lead us back to achievement of objectives?
4	Latest forecast v previous	Why are the forecasts different and are circumstances getting better or worse?
5	Actual v past forecast	Why were forecasts incorrect and can they be improved?

It may not be necessary to perform each of these control comparisons every month or quarter. The actual v past forecast may only be necessary annually or less frequently.

It must be remembered that managers will need to be motivated to produce these forecasts and use them. They must be educated to recognise why and how they can use them to enable them to do a better job and not feel that they are just another means for higher level management to check on them and apply pressure.

Finally, this year's results are sometimes compared with those for the corresponding period last year. In some cases this may be helpful in establishing a trend, but it must never be forgotten that the budget is this year's plan, and it is against that plan that performance must be controlled.

4   Investigation of variances

4.1   Introduction

Variance analysis, if properly carried out, can be a useful cost-controlling and cost-saving tool. However, the traditional variance analysis seen so far is only a step towards the final goal of controlling and saving costs.

4.2   Generalised reasons for variances

It has been suggested that the causes of variances can be classified under four headings:

♦   planning errors;
♦   measurement errors;
♦   random factors;
♦   operational factors.

Under the second heading would come errors caused by inaccurate completion of time sheets or job cards, inaccurate measurement of quantities issued from stores, etc. The rectification of such errors will probably not give rise to any cost savings (though this is a generalisation). Likewise elimination of errors caused by random factors may well not save costs

Thus it is the specific operational causes of variances to which we will devote our attention and consider rectifying.

4.3 Specific reasons for variances

Examples of more specific reasons for individual variances are shown below.

Variance		*Possible causes*
Materials:	price	Bulk discounts Different suppliers Different materials Unexpected delivery costs Different buying procedures
	usage	Different quality material Theft, obsolescence, deterioration Different quality of staff Different mix of material Different batch sizes and trim loss
Labour:	rate	Different class of labour Excessive overtime Productivity bonuses National wage negotiations Union action
	efficiency	Different levels of skill Different working conditions The learning effect Lack of supervision Works to rule
	idle time	Machine breakdowns Lack of material Lack of orders Strikes (if paid) Too long over coffee breaks
Overhead:	expenditure	Change in nature of overhead Incorrect split of semi-variable costs
	capacity	Excessive idle time Increase in workforce

Variances should be investigated and attempts made to quantify the extent to which a variance is caused by one factor or another and this cost compared with the cost of correcting causes of adverse variances.

4.4 Example

An adverse materials usage variance of £50,000 arose in a month as follows:

Standard cost per kg	£10
Actual cost per kg	£12
Units produced	2,000
Standard quantity per unit	25 kg
Actual quantity used	55,000 kg
Adverse usage variance = (25 × 2,000 – 55,000) × £10 =	£50,000

On further investigation, the following is ascertained:

(a)   The actual quantity used was based on estimated stock figures. A stocktake showed that 57,000 kg were in fact used.

(b)   3,000 kg is the best estimate for what might politely be called 'shrinkage' but, in less polite circles, theft.

(c)   2,000 kg of stock were damaged by hoodlums who broke into the stores through some of the shaky panelling.

(d)   The foreman feels that existing machinery is outmoded and more efficient machinery could save 1,000 kg a month.

Additional considerations:

(a)   A security guard would cost £9,000 a year to employ and would stop 20% of all theft. Resultant dissatisfaction amongst works staff might cost £20,000 per annum.

(b)   Given the easy access to stores, vandals might be expected to break in every other month; £10,000 would make the stores vandal-proof.

(c)   New machinery would cost £720,000.

4.5   Solution

The original £50,000 usage variance could be analysed as follows:

		£
(a)	Bad measurement (57,000 – 55,000) × £10	20,000
(b)	Theft (3,000 × £10)	30,000
(c)	Damage (2,000 × £10)	20,000
(d)	Obsolete machinery (1,000 × £10)	10,000
(e)	Other factors (balance)	(30,000)
		50,000

In each case the variances should be studied and compared with the cost of rectification.

(a)   *Bad measurement* – assuming no costly decisions were made, or are likely to be made in the future, such as over-stocking, the component is of no consequence.

(b)   *Theft* – annual cost due to theft is 12 × £30,000 or £360,000; 20% of this saved would amount to £72,000 at a cost of £9,000 + £20,000, thus the security guard is worth employing.

(c)   *Damage* – annual cost due to vandalism is 6 × £20,000 or £120,000; this would presumably be avoided by spending £10,000 now; again worthwhile.

(d)   *Obsolete machinery* – annual cost of using old machines is 12 × £10,000 or £120,000; the cost of making this saving (the saving would increase as purchase prices increased or if production increased) is £720,000; the decision over this investment would require further consideration such as discounted cashflow analysis.

4.6   Simple methods of investigation

We assumed above that all variances however large or small should be investigated. However it has been noted that variances could arise due to random factors. It would be a waste of time to investigate a variance and then find that it arose purely due to random factors. Two simple methods are therefore to investigate only those variances which exceed an absolute limit, say £1,000 Fav or £750 Adv, or those which exceed a relative limit, say 10% Fav over standard or 5% Adv over standard. The assumption behind these methods is that variances over a certain level are more likely to have arisen due to operational reasons and therefore savings could be made by correcting or controlling operations.

4.7 Use of expected values

A slightly more sophisticated method, which may be more popular in examination questions than in practice, is to use expected values. As with control charts, which follow, this method can only be used where there is a repetitive production operation which is either in control (ie working properly) or out of control (ie not working properly).

Consider a company that is considering investigating a variance that arises from the use of a certain machine. From past experience it assumes the following information.

(a)   *Cost of investigation, say £2,000* – This will be made up of idle time due to production process being interrupted, as well as employing someone to dismantle the machinery.

(b)   *Cost of correction, say £1,000* – Only if the investigation uncovers a problem will this cost be incurred. It could be the cost of a new part or the cost of employing a person to repair the machinery.

(c)   *Savings made from correction, say £7,000* – This saving will only be made if the process is out of control and is the saving of future adverse variances that will now not arise as the process has been corrected.

(d)   *Probability of the process being out of control, say 0.4* – This probability can be estimated from the size of the variance based on past experience.

Where the expected saving from investigation exceeds the expected cost it is worthwhile investigating the variance.

Remember that savings and costs will only occur if the process is out of control (ie not working properly). In such a case the repair work will be undertaken that will produce the savings and costs. If the investigation shows that the process is in control (ie working) then no repairs will be made and no savings or costs will result.

(a)   Expected saving is the probability of the process being out of control times the savings made from correction.

$0.4 \times 7,000 = £2,800$

(b)   Expected cost is the cost of investigation plus the probability of the process being out of control times the cost of correction.

$2,000 + (0.4 \times 1,000) = £2,400$

(c)   The expected saving exceeds the expected costs therefore it is worthwhile investigating.

4.8 Variance control charts

When examining variances for repetitive production operations, it may be possible to employ variance control charts to try to anticipate when a particular operation or aspect of an operation is getting out of control.

There will always be some variation in the outputs of a process but the variation can be either random or systematic (having a definite cause which can be corrected). While variances lie within the acceptable range of random variation the process is under control. However, when variances exceed the limit, there must be some other cause which should be identified and dealt with.

4.9   *Control limits*

The major difficulty in using control charts is the establishing of the control limits. It involves the use of statistical techniques and the following assumptions:

(a)   The costs, or physical aspects of production, which are compared with budget are sampled from a single, homogeneous population (eg a large number of standardised units of output such as milk bottles).

(b)   The budgeted or standard cost is the arithmetic mean of the population and is therefore an attainable standard.

(c)   Where there is no systematic cause of actual deviation from standard, the variations are randomly distributed.

The implication of these assumptions is that the population of actual costs should be normally distributed about the mean of the potential costs, and standard normal distribution tables can be employed to establish confidence intervals or control limits. You will remember from your earlier studies that ±1.96 standard deviations encloses 95% of the area under the normal curve, and ± 2.58 standard deviations encloses 99%. If we know the standard deviation of the population we can therefore establish 95% and 99% control limits. The statistical analysis involved in calculating the standard deviation will not be discussed here.

A variance control chart looks as follows:

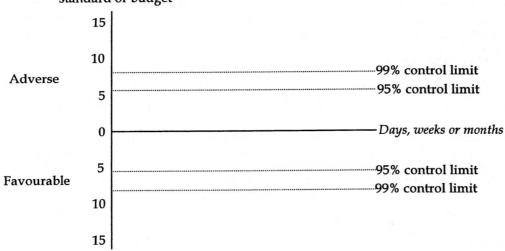

It has been assumed that the standard deviation from budget is 3% so that the control limits are:

± 1.96 × 3%	= ± 5.88%	95% limit
± 2.58 × 3%	= ± 7.74%	99% limit

The following figure shows a plot of deviations from budget which are calculated as:

$$\frac{\text{Actual} - \text{Budget}}{\text{Budget}} \times 100 = \% \text{ deviation}$$

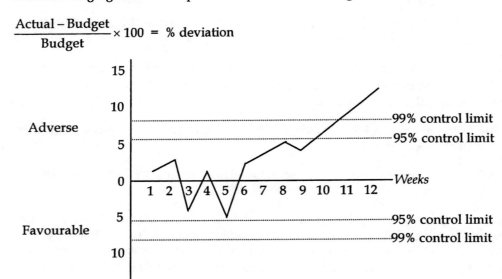

The control chart provides a pictorial presentation of two major items of information:

(a)   that in weeks 11 and 12 the cost was out of control because the deviation exceeded the 99% control limit;

(b)   if the pattern of results for weeks 6 to 10 are considered it was a reasonable prediction that the cost was going out of control because the actual deviations were consistently adverse and generally increasing.

4.10   Problems with control charts

Despite the advantages of control charts explained above and the fact that they provide 'objective' evidence of whether a cost is under control, they are not without problems.

(a)   There is the cost of establishing the control limits and regularly preparing the report.

(b)   There are problems of obtaining satisfactory data to calculate the standard deviation – material and process changes may occur which will affect the validity of the comparison of budget and actual result, and also the degree of random variation in actual costs.

(c)   Further, this degree of sophistication may be unnecessary if management are able to make satisfactory subjective judgements about whether a cost is under control or not.

(d)   Finally it will be difficult to use the technique in circumstances where the assumptions initially stated are not broadly fulfilled.

5   The cost of variance analysis

The provision of any information involves the costs of collecting the basic data, processing it, and reporting the results.   Variance analysis is no exception and, as with other forms of management information, the benefits to which it gives rise must be commensurate with the costs incurred.

Four general points may be made:

(a)   Variance analysis allows 'management by exception' and it is presumably for this purpose that a standard costing system has been introduced.

(b)   When variances are known to exist, failure to make adequate investigations, even on a random basis, will weaken the control system and thus the motivation of managers.

(c)   The amount of analysis required can sometimes be reduced by defining levels of significance below which detailed investigation is not required.

(d)   The costs of clerical work can be over-estimated. In most working days there will be some spare capacity that can be utilised without extra cost.

What has to be considered, therefore, is the amount of detail that can be incorporated usefully in variance analysis. This will fall into two categories:

(a)   Extension of formal analysis procedures by the incorporation into source documents of more detailed codings indicating causes and responsibilities. Such coding is likely to involve people outside the accounts department, who may be unwilling to give time to the task. How useful the analysis will be will depend on whether or not it is practicable to identify causes and responsibilities at the time the document is initiated.

(b)   Ex-post investigations and re-analysis of variances (possibly incorporating the distinction between planning and operational variances outlined earlier). This can involve the time of quite senior people, but the process of investigation may well be more useful from the point of view of the management of the business than any quantity of formal variance calculations.

One is concerned, as always, with costs and benefits. The benefits to be sought from the analysis of variances are:

♦   better planning and forecasting;
♦   correction of inefficiencies;
♦   positive action to improve the profitability of the business.

6   Responsibility accounting and the interdependence of variances

It is part of any system aimed at improving the performance of a business or any part of the business, that actions shall be traced to the person responsible. This may give the impression of 'laying the blame', but it is equally possible to award praise.

We have already seen that the general title for such a system is responsibility accounting; that is, a system which recognises various decision centres within a business and traces costs (and possibly revenues) to the individual managers who are primarily responsible for making decisions about the items in question.

As an example of difficulties in identifying responsibilities for variances from standards one might instance the following situation:

An opportunity arises for the buying department to obtain a consignment of a particular material at an exceptionally low price. The purchase is made; a favourable price variance is recorded and the buying department is duly praised.

Subsequently, when products are being manufactured using this type of material, significant material usage variances and labour efficiency variances are recorded, and are initially regarded as the responsibility of the department where the work is done.

Investigations, however, reveal a number of relevant facts, for example:

♦ The 'cheap' material was of poor quality, and in consequence much of it was wasted in the process of machining. The resultant material usage and labour efficiency variances should presumably be regarded as the responsibility of the buying department, to offset the favourable price variance.

♦ Due to an employee leaving it had been necessary to use an operator who was not familiar with the job. At least part of the excess usage of materials could be attributed to this cause; but whether it should be regarded as the responsibility of the operating department or of the personnel department (for failing to recruit a replacement) is still open to question. If the employee who left had been highly paid, his removal might cause a favourable wage rate variance in the period under review – an offset to the adverse efficiency variance.

♦ The tools used had been badly worn, thus causing excessive time on the job. It would be necessary to consider whether this condition was attributable to the operating department (failing to sharpen tools or to requisition replacements) or to the tools store-keeper or to the buying department (for failing to buy on time or for buying poor quality items again).

The important points to bear in mind are:

♦ that different types of variance can be interlinked by a common cause; and

♦ that the responsibility for variances in many cases cannot be identified merely by reference to the cost centre where the variance has been reported. Responsibility may be shared by several managers or may lie completely outside the cost centre where the variance has arisen.

Practice question 2 *(The answers are in the final chapter of this book)*

Newstyle Furniture Ltd

Newstyle Furniture Ltd manufacture a lounge chair by subjecting plasticised metal to a moulding process, thereby producing the chair in one piece.

From the information provided below, you are required to analyse the cost and sales variances and prepare an operating statement incorporating the result of your analysis.

Standard/Budget data

Unit variable costs:

Direct material	6 kgs at 50p per kg
Direct labour	½ hour at £6.40 per hour
Variable overhead	£2.40 per direct labour hour

Budgeted fixed overhead for the year (240 working days) £30,000

Budgeted production/sales for the year, 60,000 chairs; standard selling price per chair £10.

Actual data for period 1

Number of working days	20
Production/sales	5,200 chairs

Direct material received and used:

delivery no. 1	12,000 kg cost	£5,880
delivery no. 2	14,000 kg cost	£6,790
delivery no. 3	6,000 kg cost	£3,060

Direct labour hours worked	2,520	cost	£17,540

Variable overhead	£6,150
Fixed overhead	£2,550
Sales income	£51,300

7 Benchmarking

7.1 The meaning of benchmarking

Benchmarking is the use of other organisations' performance to evaluate your own performance.

To be effective individual organisations must agree, either directly or via their trade organisation, to make available key performance indicators.

This additional information is then used both in the setting of standards and the evaluation of actual performance.

7.2 Learning outcomes

At this stage of the chapter we have now covered the following Learning Outcomes.

Prepare reports using a range of internal and external benchmarks and interpret the results

Discuss the behavioural implications of standard costing.

8 Summary

This chapter has considered the advanced aspects of variance calculation and interpretation.

The analysis of 'traditional' variances into planning and operational variances can be useful in highlighting controllable variances to management. Variances can be monitored over a period of time by drawing up control charts, illustrating the trend of reported variances. This should enable corrective action to be taken before a process goes completely out of control.

Multiple choice questions *(The answers are in the final chapter of this book)*

1   A company has incurred an adverse variance.

There is a 40% probability that it was caused by a random factor and will not recur. There is a 60% probability that the process is out of control and that an adverse variance with a present value of £1,500 will occur.

An investigation would cost £300 and, if a problem is found, the probability of being able to correct it is 75% with a 25% probability that it cannot be corrected.

What is the expected net benefit of investigating the variance, compared with not investigating it?

A   £825
B   £600
C   £540
D   £375

2   A company is obliged to buy sub-standard materials at lower than standard price because nothing else is available.

As an indirect result of this purchase, are the materials usage variance and labour efficiency variance likely to be adverse or favourable?

	Materials usage variance	Labour efficiency variance
A	Favourable	Favourable
B	Adverse	Favourable
C	Favourable	Adverse
D	Adverse	Adverse

3   The performance report of a supervisor appears in a responsibility accounting system. Which of the following treatments of meal costs is appropriate for the supervisor of a hospital ward?

	Budget	vs	Actual
A	Expected patients × standard cost per patient		Total actual meal cost
B	Expected patients × actual cost per patient		Total actual meal cost
C	Actual patients × standard cost per patient		Total actual meal cost
D	Actual patients × actual cost per patient		Total actual meal cost

CHAPTER 4

Budgeting

EXAM FOCUS

This chapter explains the processes of budgeting which can be considered as complementary to the use of standard costing. It is a fundamental aspect of performance management.

LEARNING OUTCOMES

This chapter covers the following Learning Outcomes of the CIMA Syllabus.

>   Explain why organisations prepare plans
>   Explain and interpret the effect of amendments to budget/plan assumptions
>   Explain why it is necessary to identify controllable and uncontrollable costs
>   Evaluate performance using fixed and flexible budget reports
>   Discuss alternative approaches to budgeting
>   Discuss the behavioural implications of planning and budgeting

In order to cover these Learning Outcomes the following topics are included.

>   Planning
>   Budget preparation
>   Budgetary control
>   Motivational aspects

1 The need for planning

1.1 In a small business

All major decisions are under the control of one individual. It is possible, therefore, for him to ensure that decisions taken to deal with immediate problems are not contrary to his intentions for the business in the longer term. Under such circumstances it will not be necessary to have formal planning procedures or even plans which are written down.

1.2 In a larger business

Management responsibility is delegated. It is necessary, therefore, that there are formal procedures for pooling information and for arriving at decisions which will be in accordance with the long-term interests of the business as a whole. Hence it will be necessary to have formal plans and planning procedures.

2 The nature of planning

2.1 Introduction

Business planning can be considered under short-term and long-term aspects. However, this simple distinction may not be clear in practice because:

(a)   Decisions on current or operational projects can have long-term consequences.

(b)   The appropriate time period over which companies need to plan varies enormously. Companies marketing high fashion clothing will have a planning horizon of one or two seasons; but for heavy manufacturing companies it may be necessary to plan five or more years ahead.

2.2 Short-term aspects

A typical short-term business plan is the annual budget showing, in the same form as will eventually be used for financial and costing reports, the intended results for the year ahead. Its main concern is to lay down detailed performance targets in relation to a set of circumstances already in existence or capable of reliable forecast.

Although the budget may be shown to meet at least some short-term objectives this does not guarantee the long-term survival or profitability of the business. For example, a budget may involve the decision to sell redundant assets in the short-term, even though we may have need of those assets in the future.

2.3 Long-term aspects

 The fundamental objective of long-term planning is to provide information which will enable better decisions to be made during the current operation of the business.

Corporate planning may be defined as a procedure which aims to ensure that a company survives and improves long-term profitability by:

(a)   periodic review of the past performance of the business;
(b)   identifying the main factors in its past success;
(c)   re-consideration of the fundamental nature of the business;
(d)   reviewing the financial and other objectives of the business;
(e)   considering opportunities for improvement;
(f)   making plans for the achievement of these objectives.

These various steps will be considered in the following paragraphs but it must be borne in mind that they are interlinked and will not necessarily be carried out in rigid sequence.

3 Review of past performance

3.1 Sources of information

The accounts of a business will provide information about its past achievements in financial terms and the analysis of a series of periodic accounts will indicate the trends of profitability and the manner in which transactions have been funded.

The *cost accounts* will identify the relative profitability of different products or activities. They will also analyse the nature of expenses incurred and assist in valuing stock and work in progress.

Quantitative data will be available in addition to financial data, eg numbers of people employed by category or sales quantities of various products.

This information will reveal trends in the company's business. These trends will then need to be interpreted in the light of the various internal and external factors which had influenced them.

From the review of past performance it should be possible to identify those factors which have contributed to the past success or failure of the business.

3.2   Strengths

Most successful businesses have concentrated on doing a few things well. A business must persuade its customers that it is more beneficial for them to take the product or service which it is offering than to:

(a)   seek a competitive product or service; or

(b)   have recourse to the business's own suppliers and make the product or provide the service for themselves.

3.3   Weaknesses

To a large extent, weaknesses reflect the absence or failure of those factors which contribute to success. Among these may be:

(a)   the identification of unsatisfied market needs;

(b)   actions which have enabled the business to keep ahead of its competitors, often by technical innovation, by the success of its marketing methods, or by its pricing policy;

(c)   the effective control of costs and elimination of waste; and

(d)   the sources from which the business is financed.

3.4   Conclusion

An essential part of long-term planning is for the business to identify the activities which it is capable of performing so efficiently that the customer is willing to pay an adequate price for them. This requires identifying precisely the nature of the various parts of its business.

4   Identifying the nature of the business

4.1   Introduction

The nature of the business is not defined merely by listing its existing activities. It involves a more fundamental analysis of such features as:

(a)   the marketing skills and facilities available, and thus the size, location and type of market it is capable of serving effectively;

(b)   the distribution methods with which it is familiar, in terms of transport and sales outlets;

(c)   the technological skills available within the business; these will influence the types of product or service the business is best able to offer and also the production methods it will use.

Having reviewed the current situation, the next step is to review the business objectives which have been established in previous years to determine whether there is a need to revise them.

4.2   Reviewing the business objectives

The primary objective of most businesses will be to ensure the continuity of the business. In order to achieve this it will be necessary to ensure that risk capital will be available when required.   This means that there must be an acceptable rate of return to the proprietors or ordinary shareholders.

The *essential objective*, therefore, is *profitability*.

Other objectives will include, for example:

(a)   the sales objective;
(b)   responsibility to employees; and
(c)   public welfare.

4.3   Opportunities for improvement

The long-term objectives of a business will normally include an objective to improve the profitability of the business.   This will usually not be achievable by simply continuing to operate the existing business in the way it has been run in the past.

The long-term health of a business will depend upon its ability to exploit opportunities for:

(a)   increasing the volume of business in existing products, either in existing markets, or by entering new markets;

(b)   increasing the profitability of the business done (eg by reducing costs);

(c)   reducing the amount or the cost of the capital used;

(d)   introducing new or modified products;

(e)   some change in the nature of the business.

It will also be necessary for the organisation to examine its existing activities to see whether it should cease operating some part in order to release capital which can be used in a more profitable way.

5   The initial plan

5.1   Performance objectives

The setting of performance objectives for each part of the business is the first step in converting objectives into plans.   Each manager will then produce detailed plans for the part of the business for which he is responsible which will seek to evaluate the results achievable from both the present business and the opportunities for improvement.

5.2   Operational plans

The managers' operational plans will be converted into monetary terms and, as with short-term budgets, the following financial statements will be prepared for the business as a whole, broken down into each year of the plan:

(a)   profit and loss statement;
(b)   capital expenditure plan;
(c)   working capital requirements;
(d)   cashflow statement;
(e)   key ratios and statistical information.

The taxation implications of the planned activities will be calculated and year-end balance sheets will be prepared.

5.3   Assumptions

It will be necessary to specify the assumptions which have been made in producing the plans on such items as:

(a)   the economic environment;
(b)   general inflation;
(c)   raw materials and wage costs;
(d)   selling prices;
(e)   exchange rates – if significant for exports or overseas subsidiaries.

5.4   Results

When each manager has completed his detailed plans, it will be possible to begin assembling the results and to compare the likely pattern of profits year by year with the target figures implicit in the company's profitability objective.

5.5   Learning outcome

At this stage of the chapter we have now covered the following Learning Outcome:

Explain why organisations prepare plans.

6   Amending the initial plan

6.1   Introduction

Once the detailed plans have been completed, the results can be assembled and the yearly pattern of profits can be compared to the target figures.

6.2   What-if analysis

An illustration of one method of doing this is given in the diagram of the *profit gap* in Figure 1. The profit from the existing business, as currently carried on, is first charted and then augmented by the profits obtainable from the evaluated opportunities under main headings such as improved efficiency, product modification, the introduction of new products and the opening up of new markets.

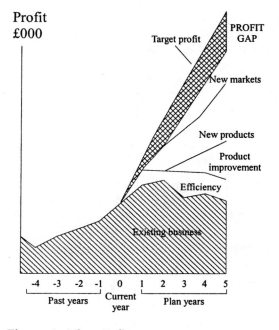

Figure 1: The profit gap

The objective of the chart is to show the extent to which the evaluated profits fall short of, or exceed, the target profit – in other words, the *profit gap*. The target profit will have been expressed in relation to a total amount of capital to be used. In seeking to revise the plans in order to close the profit gap, attention will be given both to means of increasing the profit and also to measures of reducing the capital employed.

The initial outline plans for the company must be critically examined to consider what would be the effects on them of major changes. This may be done by a series of 'what if?' questions. Some examples of these are:

What if ...

(a)   ... inflation is at double the rate we have forecast?

(b)   ... our most important customer:

   (i)   requires us to reduce our prices;
   (ii)   is lost to a competitor?

(c)   ... our competitors attack our business:

   (i)   with a new product;
   (ii)   by cutting prices?

(d)   ... we are unable to recruit the skilled labour required by the plan?

As a result of considering these possibilities at the time of producing the plan, it should be possible to adapt to them much more quickly and efficiently if they do in fact occur.

6.3   Learning outcome

At this stage of the chapter we have now covered the following Learning Outcome:

   Explain and interpret the effect of amendments to budget/plan assumptions.

6.4   Monitoring performance

The first year of the long-term plan will usually be expanded to form the annual budget. As performance against the budget is monitored, any trends which appear to be of a long-term nature must be identified. Their significance for long-term plans will be quantified and they will be taken into account during the next revision of the long-term plans.

Long-term plans will normally be revised once a year prior to the preparation of the annual budget. The effect of major changes in the economic or business environment on the plans will often be calculated during a year, but only in very exceptional circumstances will it be necessary to make changes to the plan at such times.

6.5   Summary

In developing short-term budgets and operating day-by-day controls, the management of a business must have the assurance that their activities are contributing towards the longer-term purposes of the business. This can only be achieved, in a company where management responsibilities are delegated, if there is a formal system for long- and short-term planning and control. The various stages in long-range planning have been described in this chapter and are summarised in Figure 2.

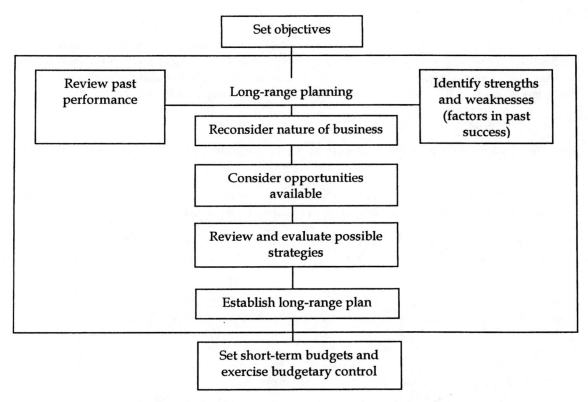

Figure 2: Stages in long-range planning

7   *The approach to budgetary control*

7.1   *Introduction*

David Otley, in the *Accountant's Digest* on 'Behavioural aspects of budgeting', suggested that 'Budgets are a means of attaining organisational control, ie the achievement of organisational objectives'. Within this context, he then went on to consider the various functions which a budget may fulfil.

7.2   *Authorisation*

A budget may act as a formal authorisation to a manager to spend a given amount on specified activities. If this is applied to an operating budget, however, it must be appreciated that over-strict enforcement would not be in the best interests of the business.

7.3   *Forecasting*

Forecasting refers to the prediction of events over which little or no control is exercised. Some parts of all budgets are, therefore, based on forecasts. Budget figures may also be used by one part of an organisation to forecast the likely impact on it of the activities of other parts.

7.4   *Communication and coordination*

Budgets communicate plans to managers responsible for carrying them out. They also ensure coordination between managers of sub-units so that each is aware of the others' requirements.

7.5   *Motivation*

Budgets are often intended to motivate managers to perform in line with organisational objectives. The problem in this area is that when budgets are made relevant and act as motivational devices, the attitude of managers using them tends to be negative. If budget variances are treated as a sign that someone is at fault, rather than as a sign of a healthy system, budgets will soon be met but they will not motivate.

7.6   Evaluation

The performance of managers and organisational units is often evaluated by reference to budgetary standards as these are quite possibly the only quantitative reference points available. The way in which performance is evaluated will be a dominating influence on how a manager behaves in the future and is therefore worthy of separate consideration.

7.7   Planning

Planning is an attempt to shape the future by a conscious attempt to affect those factors which are open to influence and control.

Prerequisites of budgetary control are the definition of **objectives** and the existence or creation of an **organisational structure** through which plans may be put into effect.

The objectives of the business will be defined in the long-term strategic plan and any short-term budget must be framed in such a way as to contribute towards the achievement of these objectives.

The budget, therefore, will incorporate its own short-term objectives, probably expressed in the form that a financial analyst would use when interpreting the final results, ie:

◆   rate of return on total capital employed;
◆   rate of profit on sales;
◆   the rate of capital turnover (ie sales: capital employed);
◆   rate of growth in sales value;
◆   liquidity and asset management ratios supporting the foregoing.

7.8   Budget centres

The organisational structure through which control will be exercised over the achievement of the budget objectives must be based on manager responsibilities.

It is only when the functions to be carried out by each manager have been defined that it becomes possible to define:

◆   the output he should achieve;
◆   the resources he can justifiably employ; and
◆   the costs he is expected to control.

The particular segments of the business for which individuals are allocated budget responsibility are known as *budget centres*.

Some budget centre managers will be responsible for profitability, either profit in relation to output or profit in relation to capital employed under their control. These centres are known as *profit centres* or *investment centres*, depending upon the amount of autonomy given.

8   The administration of budgetary control

8.1   Introduction

Two important activities relating to the preparation of budgets are:

◆   the issue of budget instructions; and
◆   the coordination of sectional budgets.

These are discussed below.

8.2   *Issue of budget instructions*

The information which must be available to enable budgets to be prepared by all managers on a consistent basis and in forms which facilitate consolidation into the master budget includes:

♦ The **organisational structure** of the business, setting out clearly the responsibilities of each manager and the limits of his authority.

♦ The **classification and coding** of the various items of income and expenditure to be covered by the budget.

◄ A statement of the **period** to be covered by the budget and of the shorter accounting periods into which it is to be subdivided (or 'phased') for purposes of control.

♦ Copies of the **forms** to be used in submitting budgets.

♦ **Instructions** on what is to be shown on the various forms and the manner in which particular items are to be calculated. Examples of practical points to be clarified are:

   (i)   whether 'sales' are to be budgeted initially on the basis of order intake or of invoiced amounts;

   (ii)   when costs are expected to increase, whether uniform percentages for particular items are to be used;

   (iii)   what rates of salary increase, if any, are to be budgeted by managers;

   (iv)   what types of cost are to be budgeted centrally and not included in departmental budgets.

♦ The **timetable** for the preparation of the budgets.

   Instructions which are to be binding on all managers must clearly be issued on the authority of the managing director or chief executive but somebody must be responsible for drafting them, explaining them when necessary and ensuring that they are being complied with as the work of budgeting progresses. The term *budget officer* may be used to describe this person but his precise status will vary from company to company.

8.3   *Coordination of budgets*

In order that an acceptable master budget can be prepared, it is necessary to ensure that the various subsidiary budgets are coordinated. The most obvious example of this is the need to ensure that the sales quantities which the sales department are forecasting are in line with the quantities which production are budgeting to produce.

Coordination of activities may be brought about in setting up a budget committee which can include the main function managers under the chairmanship of the chief executive or of the budget officer.

8.4   *Approval of budgets*

Budgets must be approved ultimately by the board of the company. The management accountant or MD will recommend approval by the Board. Before doing so, however, he will need to be satisfied that all budgets have been properly coordinated and that the budgets are in line with the company's objectives.

After being prepared, the individual budgets will therefore pass through the following stages before being finally approved by the board:

♦ Approval in principle by the manager of the function to which the budget relates.

♦ Examination by the budget controller who will ensure that the principles laid down for preparation of the budgets have been adhered to.

♦ Consideration of the budget in the light of all the other budgets by the budget committee before it recommends to the managing director that the master budget should be submitted to the board for approval.

8.5 Limiting factors on budgets

The level of activity at which a business can operate will very seldom be unlimited. Limitations may be imposed, for example, by:

♦ market demand for its products or services;
♦ the number of skilled employees available;
♦ the availability of material supplies;
♦ the space available either as a working area or for the storage of goods; and
♦ the amount of cash or credit facilities available to finance the business.

Therefore, when a manager starts to prepare a budget he should review the elements in it and identify where limiting factors (or 'governing factors') exist.

They will not all be equally significant but where one particular limitation is of major importance it may be necessary to budget for that item first and to construct the rest of the budget around it. This can happen not merely in one department but for the company as a whole, when the item concerned may be referred to as the *principal budget factor*.

It is essential to identify the principal budget factor and any other limiting factors at an early stage in the budgeting process so that management may consider whether:

♦ it is possible to overcome the limitation which they impose (eg by finding new markets for sales or by obtaining alternative supplies or substitute raw materials); or

♦ the limitations imposed must be accepted and the business's budgets must be produced within those limitations.

9 The functional budgets

9.1 Introduction

Once the limiting factors have been ascertained the company can prepare the functional budgets, for example:

♦ sales budgets;
♦ materials usage budgets;
♦ materials purchases budget;
♦ labour utilisation budget.

9.2 Sales budgets

The sales income budget is uniquely difficult to prepare because it involves forecasting the actions of people outside the business (the potential customers).

The extent to which sales forecasting is necessary will depend on the period covered by the outstanding order book and on the consistency of the conversion rate from enquiries to orders. If there is a well-filled order book for some months ahead, then less reliance will need to be placed on forecasting techniques.

Forecasts may be made in a variety of ways. The method used will depend on the nature of the business and the amount of information available, but a generalised formal procedure might be as follows:

♦   Review past years' sales for whatever period is appropriate to the company's business cycle.

♦   Analyse the time series to identify seasonal, cyclical and random fluctuations.

♦   Extrapolate from past years' figures, assuming no changes in products or prices.

♦   Adjust the projection for proposed changes which are controllable by the company, such as price alterations, changes in marketing effort, the introduction of new products and the discontinuance of existing products.

♦   Adjust for market changes due to external factors, such as government controls, action of competitors or social changes affecting demand.

♦   Check that the resultant quantities are compatible with the quantities that can be purchased or produced.

♦   Check acceptability of forecast to sectional sales managers.

♦   Check consistency of forecast with long-term corporate plans.

The forecasting method outlined above depends on the existence of a 'time series' of figures from which extrapolation can be made. It is mainly applicable to items in continuous demand. For other types of business, the sales forecast will be based on some form of market survey or on subjective estimates by people familiar with the market concerned.

9.3   Budgeting for costs

Budgeting for costs, in the same way as budgeting for sales, begins with physical facts. What physical facts they are will depend on the nature of the business but every business will employ people and most businesses will use materials of some kind.   A manufacturing business will use tools and probably machinery. Floor space will be needed, also office equipment and perhaps motor vehicles.

All these requirements will be related in some way to the output of the business (its sales) and any changes in stocks or work in progress.

In practice there are a wide range of different ways to budget for costs, for example:

♦   If standards for cost units are available, then there may be computer programs to identify the material and labour standards relative to a given output.   It then remains for departmental managers to budget for material wastage or spoilage, labour efficiency and idle time.

♦   In a business carrying out long-term contracts, cost units (contracts) may be identical with cost centres (each contract having its own controller).

♦   In some businesses it may be sufficiently accurate for the budget for direct materials cost to be an extrapolation from past total figures, without any attempt at detailed justification or analysis.

The three basic elements of cost – labour, materials and expenses – will enter into all cost budgets. The following paragraphs describe common problems encountered in budgeting for these elements.

9.4 Budgeting for numbers and costs of employees

When budgeting for people to be employed, the starting point must be an assessment of the work to be done by people with various skills and this is equally necessary for manual, clerical and managerial activities.

Having defined what work is to be done, the establishment of budgets for the employment of people falls into two main stages:

♦ planning the number of people needed; and
♦ calculating the relevant costs.

In defining the productive workload for the budget year it will be necessary to balance the requirements of the sales budget against the productive capacity available. If there is excess capacity over the year as a whole, then a decision will be needed whether to operate below full capacity or to use the excess capacity in building goods for stock or getting ahead with work in progress for the following year.

If the sales budget does not provide a steady workload month by month, then in phasing the budgets it may be decided to keep productive output constant and to balance out the short-term differences by fluctuations in work in progress or finished stockholdings.

The degree of precision possible in budgeting for numbers of people employed will depend on the type of work involved and the extent to which work measurement is possible.

9.5 Budgeting for the cost of materials

In most businesses a great variety of materials will be used. Considerable effort can be involved in preparing detailed budgets of quantities and purchase prices. Whether this effort is justified will depend on the significance of materials in relation to total costs and the extent to which effective control can be exercised.

The starting point for materials budgeting is the quantity of material to be used during the budget year, whether in direct sales or in production or for indirect use.

Just as with the budgeting of labour hours, the form of the materials usage budget will depend on the nature of the business. Where repetitive operations are carried out it will be possible, and worth the effort, to set standards for the usage of the various items of material and these standards can be associated with the production forecast to build up the total material requirements.

The purchase prices to be applied to the usage of the various items may be obtained from stock ledger records or recent purchase invoices, subject to adjustment for forecast price changes.

In budgeting for indirect materials (such as small tools, machine coolants and lubricants, fuel, cleaning materials and office stationery) the common practice is to budget merely for a total cost extrapolated from past experience. It will be important for control purposes, however, that the budget working papers contain as much detail as possible about anticipated usage, even though the individual items may not be evaluated separately.

9.6 Budgeting for other expenses

The nature of other expenses will depend on the type of business, but common categories are as follows:

♦ premises charges;
♦ costs of plant, motor vehicles and other fixed assets;
♦ communication expenses;
♦ travelling and entertaining;
♦ insurances;
♦ discretionary costs;
♦ financial policy costs;
♦ random costs.

For every type of revenue or cost it is highly desirable that a permanent budget record be prepared, giving the detailed calculations from which the budgeted amount has been derived. This will not only impose a discipline on the budget preparation but will also:

♦ facilitate the eventual explanation of any differences between budgeted and actual results; and

♦ provide a starting point for budget revisions or for the preparation of budgets in future years.

The important features of such a record are:

♦ details of the budget calculation;

♦ comparison with the actual figures for the previous year; and

♦ basis of variability, noting how the amount of the item is related to such parameters as levels of output or numbers of people employed.

9.7 Capital expenditure budget

The control of capital expenditure projects falls into five stages:

♦ budgeting;
♦ project authorisation;
♦ implementation;
♦ reporting and review; and
♦ audit of results achieved.

All short-term operating budgets are in effect abstracts from a continuously developing long-term plan. This, however, is particularly true of the capital expenditure budget because the major items included in it will not be completed within the bounds of any one budget year.

The main purpose of the capital expenditure budget, therefore, is to provide a forecast of the amount of cash likely to be needed for investment projects during the year ahead. It also indicates what items of plant, equipment, vehicles and so on will be needed for the purpose of implementing the profit and loss budget; it must therefore be submitted for approval at an early stage in the budgeting timetable.

Any capital expenditure budget would include:

♦ brief descriptive title for the project;
♦ total required expenditure;
♦ an analysis of the above over various time periods;

- ♦ where appropriate, expenditure to date on the project;
- ♦ estimates of future benefits from the project;
- ♦ investment appraisal calculations including details of assumptions made; and
- ♦ intangible benefits from the expenditure.

9.8   The master budget

The master budget for approval by the board will take the form of a budgeted profit and loss account and a forecast balance sheet as at the year-end. These will be supported by such summaries of the various functional budgets as may be required and by calculations of the key ratios which indicate conformity with the objectives for the year.

In arriving at the forecast balance sheet it will be necessary to take account of:

- ♦ The capital expenditure budget.

- ♦ Changes in stockholdings and work in progress (as calculated in connection with the budgeting of material and labour costs). If work in progress and finished stocks are valued on a 'total cost' basis, then it will be necessary to calculate overhead recovery rates.

- ♦ Changes in debtor balances. Subject to any special delays in collection, the closing debtor balances will be calculated by applying the company's normal credit terms to the phased budget of sales.

- ♦ Changes in creditor balances. In theory, the closing creditors will be calculated by applying a normal credit period to the phased budgets of material purchases, subcontracted work and any other relevant items. In practice, it may be necessary to review the budgeted cashflow before finalising a decision on the credit to be taken.

- ♦ Changes in cash balance. Initially, the closing cash balance may be taken as the balancing figure on the balance sheet, but at some stage this should be validated by building up a cash budget itemised from the other budgets. This is discussed below.

9.9   The cash budget

The purposes of the cash budget are:

- ♦ To prove that the various items of income and expenditure budgeted departmentally, and subject to the normal credit policy of the business, will result in cashflows which enable the company to pay its way at all times; in other words, to prove that it is a practical plan.

- ♦ Where the cashflow over the year as a whole is satisfactory but there are intermediate periods of difficulty in financing operations, to give a basis from which the timing of particular items can be re-planned.

- ♦ Where cash proves inadequate to finance the plan as originally envisaged, to give the financial controller an opportunity to seek sources of additional capital.

- ♦ If there is no means by which the budget can be financed as it stands, then a revised budget will have to be prepared.

- ♦ Like any other budget, to provide a basis for control during the forthcoming year.

10   Preparation of master budget example

10.1   Example

Trendy Ltd produces two products for the tourist market. The management is now planning production for the three months from 1 July 20X3. Estimates and other information relating to the three months in question are as follows:

Sales	*Product A*	*Product B*
Units	10,000	15,000
Price	£1.00	£1.20

Stocks of finished goods (units)		
30.6.X3	2,000	3,000
30.9.X3	4,000	6,000

Standard direct costs per unit		
Material X	20p	25p
Material Y	10p	10p
Labour	40p	50p

Production and purchases are to be carried out at a constant monthly rate throughout the period. Materials stocks are not to be increased or decreased.

All sales are on two months' credit.

All material purchases are on three months' credit.

Work in progress remains at a constant level.

Overdraft facilities are available up to £10,000.

Overhead expenses for three months are estimated at:

Manufacturing	£3,000
Administrative and selling	£2,000

These overhead expenses can all be assumed to be paid in cash except for £400 depreciation on fixed assets included in manufacturing overhead.

Summarised balance sheet at 30 June 20X3

	£	£
Fixed assets		
Cost		4,000
Depreciation		1,600
		2,400
Stock at standard direct cost – finished goods		
Product A (2,000 units)	1,400	
Product B (3,000 units)	2,550	
		3,950
Work in progress		
Product A	280	
Product B	510	
		790

Materials		
X	500	
Y	300	
	———	
		800
Debtors for sales of products		3,000
Balance at bank		1,000
		———
		11,940
Creditors for materials		2,500
		———
		9,440
		———
Share capital		5,000
Reserves (retained profit)		4,440
		———
		9,440
		———

Prepare the management profit and loss budget and the cash budget for the three months, and the budgeted balance sheet at 30 September 20X3. Stocks are to be valued at standard direct cost.

10.2 Solution

Trendy management profit and loss budget
for the three months ended 30 September 20X3

Product	A	B	Total £
Sales in units	10,000	15,000	
	———	———	
Sales value	£10,000	£18,000	28,000
	———	———	
Standard direct costs			
Production in units	12,000	18,000	
	———	———	
Costs	£	£	
Material X	2,400	4,500	
Material Y	1,200	1,800	
	———	———	
	3,600	6,300	
Labour	4,800	9,000	
	———	———	
	8,400	15,300	
Stock increase 2,000/3,000 units	(1,400)	(2,550)	
	———	———	
Costs of goods sold	7,000	12,750	19,750
	———	———	
Standard profit on actual sales	3,000	5,250	8,250
	———	———	
Overheads			
Manufacturing costs		2,600	
Depreciation		400	
Administrative and selling		2,000	
		———	
			5,000
Profit			3,250
			———

Cash budget – in total form

	£	£
Profit as above		3,250
Add: Retained depreciation		400
		3,650
Increase in: Stocks	3,950	
Debtors	15,667	
	19,617	
Creditors	(7,400)	
		(12,217)
Reduction in bank balance		(8,567)
Balance at bank 1.7.X3		1,000
Projected overdraft 30.9.X3		(7,567)

Cash budget – in monthly statement form

	Jul £	*Aug* £	*Sept* £	*Total* £
Receipts from debtors (see working 1)	1,500	1,500	9,333	12,333
Payments:				
Materials (see working 2)	834	833	833	2,500
Labour (see working 3)	4,600	4,600	4,600	13,800
Overhead (see working 4)	1,533	1,533	1,534	4,600
	6,967	6,966	6,967	20,900
Excess payments	(5,467)	(5,466)	2,366	(8,567)
Balance at beginning of month/period	1,000	(4,467)	(9,933)	1,000
	(4,467)	(9,933)	(7,567)	(7,567)

Bank overdraft limit throughout the period £10,000.

Note: It is assumed that sales can be taken to arise at a constant monthly rate throughout the period.

Workings

1	Receipts from debtors	£
	During the period, the debtors at 1.7.X3 will be received	3,000
	Plus $1/3$ of sales of £28,000	9,333
		12,333

2   Payments for materials

As all purchases are on three months' credit, the only payments
during the period will be in discharge of the creditors at 1.7.X3   £2,500

3   Payments for labour

Total labour cost per profit and loss account
£4,800 + £9,000   £13,800

4   Overhead

Manufacturing (less depreciation) plus administrative and selling
£2,600 + £2,000   £4,600

Budgeted balance sheet at 30 September 20X3

		£	£	£
Fixed assets				
Cost				4,000
Depreciation				2,000
				2,000
Net current assets				
Stock at standard direct cost				
Finished goods				
Product A	4,000 units		2,800	
Product B	6,000 units		5,100	
			7,900	
Work in progress				
Product A		280		
Product B		510		
			790	
Material X		500		
Material Y		300		
			800	
			9,490	
Debtors for sales of products				
Two months' credit ($2/3 \times$ £28,000)			18,667	
			28,157	
Less: Creditors for materials three months				
(3,600 + 6,300)		9,900		
Bank overdraft		7,567		
			17,467	
				10,690
				12,690
Share capital				5,000
Reserves (retained profits) (4,440 + 3,250)				7,690
				12,690

11 Budgeting for changes in prices

Unless frequent budget revisions are to be made, it is essential to take account of anticipated significant changes in prices and costs when establishing budgets. If this is not done, particularly when the costs of the various revenue and capital expenditures are increasing at different rates, then the assumptions on which it is based and accepted may prove to have been completely wrong.

The methods of incorporating price changes into budgets may be considered under three alternative circumstances:

♦ **Specific price changes**

Where specific changes in costs or in selling prices can be forecast with reasonable certainty, they should be incorporated into the budget as from the forecast date of implementation, and the phased budget figure should be adjusted accordingly.

Examples in connection with payroll costs are awards payable in accordance with published scales such as 'birthday' increases payable to junior employees.

♦ **Uncertain price changes**

Where the occurrence of cost changes is reasonably certain but the timing and amount are not, then the best possible estimate should be made and incorporated into the master budget. It may be undesirable, however, to include such estimates in the detailed budgets for departmental or product costs control since they will give rise to uncontrollable variances needing continued re-explanation.

Examples of changes of this nature are forecast wage claims negotiable with trade unions and fluctuations in commodity prices.

♦ **General inflationary changes**

Some of the effects of general price level changes may have been dealt with already as specific changes under the two preceding paragraphs and no further adjustment would then be necessary.

For items of expenditure not dealt with in this way (particularly the cost of services), an estimated rate of inflationary increase should be prescribed by the budget controller and be included in the detailed budgets of the items concerned.

12 Control against budgets

12.1 Introduction

In order that management control may be exercised, the actual results of the business will be reported period by period to the managers responsible and will be compared with the budgeted allowance. Any discrepancies will be investigated and action will be taken either to modify the budget in line with current conditions or (in most cases more desirable) to adjust future performance so that the discrepancies will be eliminated in the longer run.

12.2 Feedback

The reporting of actual results and of variances from plan is sometimes referred to as the *feedback* arising from the budgetary control system.

Feedback is the process of continuous self-adjustment of a system. It requires some predetermined standards against which to compare actual results. Any differences between the actual results and standard targets which are outside tolerance limits will indicate the need for action to be taken in an attempt to bring about consistency between actual and target.

Feedback is therefore a fundamental part of any system of control including financial control systems such as budgetary control.

12.3 Timing of feedback

Ideally feedback should take place with as little delay as possible from the occurrence of the event it reports. If there is undue delay then in the intervening period the underlying position itself may alter; there is then the danger that action correctly taken, given the information contained in the feedback report, will not be the action required by the position then existing.

12.4 Analysis of variances

The identification of variance from budget is only the first step in exercising control. So that effective action can be taken it will be necessary to identify:

- *who* was responsible for its occurrence – analysis by *responsibility*;
- *why* the variance has arisen – *analysis by cause*.

12.5 Analysis of variances by responsibility

With a well designed budgetary control system the analysis of variances by responsibility is basically simple because the organisation will have been subdivided into budget centres which represent areas of responsibility and separate operating statements will be prepared for the various budget centres.

The general title for such a system is *responsibility accounting*; that is, a system which recognises various decision centres within a business and traces the results of those decisions to the individual managers who are primarily responsible for making them. Responsibility accounting will be discussed more fully later.

12.6 Analysis of variances by cause

In dealing with the analysis of variances by cause (whether sales variances or cost variances) one will be dealing always with two aspects:

- a physical aspect – quantities of products sold or material used or hours worked, for example; and
- a pricing aspect – the selling price per unit in the case of sales; the cost price per unit in the case of materials, labour and other expenses. (The cost of labour is, of course, the rate of pay.)

In some cases it may not be possible to identify quantity changes without more effort than would be justified by any improvement in control, but in these cases it must be recognised that this weakness does exist in the control being exercised.

12.7 Flexible budgetary control

In connection with expense budgeting, the budget working sheets should include some indication of the 'basis of variability' of each item of cost.

The most common general bases of variability of costs are the volume of productive output or of sales. In some systems of budgetary control, therefore, costs are divided between those which tend to vary with the output or sales achieved, and those which tend to remain fixed regardless of the volume of output over an expected range of volumes.

This distinction having been established, it is then possible to establish for variable costs in any period an allowable level of cost *appropriate to the output actually achieved*. This new level is known as the budget allowance for that volume of output. The total variance from the original budget figure will then be divided into two parts:

♦ The difference between the original budget and the budget allowance, assumed to arise from the nature of the business. This is sometimes referred to as an *activity variance* and may be excluded from sectional control reports.

♦ The difference between the budget allowance and the actual cost incurred. This, by definition, should not have occurred and is the variance which is 'controllable' by the manager concerned.

 A system incorporating budget allowances is referred to as *flexible budgetary control*.

This idea has been seized on by writers of textbooks and setters of examination questions and converted into the concept of *flexible budgets*; in other words, at the beginning of the year there should be set out in the form of a schedule what the various cost allowances would be at various levels of output. Such an approach can be compared to a **fixed budget** with no budget allowances calculated for different possible output levels.

Flexible budgeting is not an approach you will normally find in practice, partly because an enormous number of alternative budgets would be needed to cover every possible level of activity, but mainly because management control is not a matter of automatic adjustment of figures. Every situation has to be dealt with on its own merits when it arises.

12.8   Learning outcome

At this stage of the chapter we have now covered the following Learning Outcome:

Evaluate performance using fixed and flexible budget reports.

12.9   The budget period – rolling budgets

So far we have avoided any definite statement about the length of time to be covered by a budget, though inevitably references have crept in about the budget year.

Budgets have traditionally been prepared to cover the financial year of a business because this is a natural period for reviewing progress and is associated with accounting for taxation purposes and for reporting to company shareholders.

Budgets, however, are based on forecasts and forecasts are unreliable. The actual sales and costs of the business will differ from those budgeted, ie variances will arise.

Some of these variances can be corrected by management action, but some will be due to external factors outside management control, but in either case if the variances become unacceptably large, the budget will lose credibility as an instrument of control. At this point it will be necessary to review the budget calculations and prepare a revised budget which will then be used either alongside the original budget or in substitution for it.

In considering price changes, we envisaged cases where budget revision would be necessary. Under conditions of high inflation the need for budget revision may occur very frequently and to cope with this situation some companies have adopted a scheme of *rolling budgets*. Under such a system the annual budget is divided into two parts: (i) a relatively short period (say three or six months) for which detailed budgets are prepared for control purposes and (ii) the balance of the year for which budgets are in outline only. At the end of the control period the whole budget is reviewed, a new control budget is set for the next short period, and a new outline budget to cover a residual period to bring the total coverage up to a twelve-month total. For example:

At 1 January: Control budget for three months to 31 March
                       Outline budget for nine months April-December

At 31 March: Control budget of three months to 30 June
                       Outline budget for nine months July-March

You may find other methods of dealing with uncertainty in practice and in considering their merits you should bear in mind the two main purposes of preparing budgets:

♦   to define a commitment to profitability and funding arising from the board's longer-term plans; and

♦   to provide the basis for effective management control.

13 Zero-based budgeting

13.1 Introduction

Zero-based budgeting (ZBB) is a cost justification technique first developed by Texas Instruments, which is of particular use in controlling the costs of service departments and overheads. It does not simply look at last year's budget and add or subtract a bit (the traditional approach of **incremental budgeting**), but starts 'from scratch' each time a budget is prepared.

ZBB involves:

♦   developing *decision packages* for each company activity;
♦   *evaluating and ranking* these packages; and
♦   *allocating resources* to the various activities accordingly.

Decision packages include the following information:

♦   the function of the activity or department – this sets out the minimum goals that it must achieve;

♦   the goal of the department – this details the aim of the department (what it would like to achieve);

♦   the measure of the performance of the department;

♦   the costs and benefits associated with different ways of organising the department (at different levels of funding);

♦   the consequence of non-performance of the activity or department.

13.2 Advantages of ZBB

♦   It establishes minimum requirements for service departments, ranks departments and allocates resources.

♦   It produces a plan to work to when more resources are available.

♦   It makes managers think about what they are doing.

♦   It can be done annually, quarterly, or when crises are envisaged.

13.3   Disadvantages of ZBB

♦   It takes up a good deal of management time and so may not be used every year.

♦   It generates lots of paper, requires education and training, and results may be initially disappointing.

♦   It is costly.

Most budgets are prepared on an incremental basis, ie based on last time's figures plus/minus an incremental amount to cover inflation etc. However, this technique has the obvious disadvantage of perpetuating poor spending control. As an alternative zero-based or priority-based budgeting may be employed.

Practice questions 1 - 3 *(The answers are in the final chapter of this book)*

1   It is sometimes maintained that managers cannot be trusted to prepare their own budgets because they will tend to anticipate problems by understating income and overstating the staff and facilities they require. Budgets should therefore be prepared by the accounts department who, on the basis of past management reports, can decide more accurately what should happen in the future. Do you agree?

2   A capital expenditure budget is said to be merely a segment of a long-term on-going plan.

     Is this not equally true of all types of budget?

3   Describe the practical organisation and operation of a system of budgetary control.

---

14   Management by exception

The features of this method of reporting are:

♦   attention is drawn only to areas where operations are seen to be 'out of control';

♦   this may be achieved by identifying those variances from budget that are deemed to be 'exceptional';

♦   only these variances will be investigated and (where possible) corrected; and

♦   thus management time and expertise is utilised where it can be most effective in improving efficiency of future operations.

In order that this method is effective, it is important that:

♦   exceptional variances are correctly isolated;

♦   only such variances due to factors capable of correction should be considered for investigation; and

♦   costs and benefits of investigation are assessed.

15 Responsibility accounting

15.1 Introduction

The aim of a responsibility accounting system is to motivate management at all levels to work towards the company's objectives with the minimum of direction.

This involves:

♦ the use of budgets as 'targets' against which management performance can be measured; and

♦ the presentation of 'performance reports' relating to particular responsibility centres. These centres fall into three categories:

– **A cost centre**

Where a manager is held responsible for control of expenditure.

– **A profit centre**

Where a manager is held responsible for control of sales revenue and expenditure.

– **An investment centre**

Where a manager is held responsible for investment decisions as well as the control of sales revenue and expenditure.

♦ the requirement that the person deemed responsible for that area gives explanations of significant variances shown therein.

 Examination questions on this subject may concentrate on a practical application of the principles necessary for a system of responsibility accounting to work effectively, and require the preparation of a draft performance report, or the criticism of such a report. An in-depth theoretical knowledge of the work carried out in this field is not needed; a 'common sense' approach to a practical problem suffices.

After summarising the main points, the 'common sense' approach is used to answer a 'typical examination type question'. There is no need to learn the names of the academics who have contributed to the subject. What is more important is that you understand the relevance of what they said to the use of targets and performance reports in practice.

Three main areas need to be examined in relation to the use of budgets in responsibility accounting:

♦ participation in budget setting;
♦ budgets as motivational targets; and
♦ performance evaluation.

The conclusions under each of these headings are largely common sense – you should try to think up practical examples in relation to your own position in study or at work to help you remember them.

15.2 Participation

♦ Most academics agree that worker participation in the setting of budgets greatly improves commitment to and achievement of targets (**Bass & Leavitt, Coch & French, French, Kay and Meyer**).

♦ The extent to which participation enhances the quality of the budgets ultimately set, depends upon the market or technological conditions in which the business is working. The more uncertainty involved, the greater the benefit to be obtained from allowing information to flow vertically (from management to workers and vice versa) as well as horizontally (**Lawrence & Lorsch**).

15.3   *Budgets as motivational targets*

♦ In general it is accepted that corporate objectives are more likely to be met if they are expressed as quantified targets, often in the form of budgets.

♦ However, if a target is to have any influence on the performance the recipient must be aware of its existence and feel committed to achieving it.

♦ The target must be set at the right level of difficulty to act as a motivator. Both unrealistic and overgenerous targets will be demotivational. (**Hofstede**)

♦ In theory, there may be a need for two budgets to be prepared for the same area:

– a challenging (**aspirations**) budget to motivate the manager;

– a lower and more realistic **expectations** budget for planning and decision purposes. (**Hopwood**)

♦ Care should be taken to reward success as well as penalising failure, in order that a benefit is perceived in bettering rather than just achieving the target.

15.4   *Performance evaluation*

♦ A manager should only be held accountable for items over which they have control.

♦ Thus a manager of a profit centre may be judged by variances affecting *direct contribution* (before allocated fixed costs); the performance of the centre itself will be measured by *direct controllable contribution* (having accounted for costs that are directly attributable to that centre, but not necessarily all controlled by the manager).

♦ Measures of performance should be devised such that they promote decisions in line with corporate objectives.

♦ **Hopwood** has identified three main styles of management in the use of budget performance reports:

– the 'budget constrained' style, which lays particular emphasis on results being closely in accordance with the budget plan;

– the 'profit conscious' style, which is less concerned with current deviations from budget than with a manager's ability to achieve a trend of results which is acceptable in relation to changing conditions; and

– the 'non-accounting' style, which tends to disregard accounting reports as a means of measuring management performance and instead looks at factors such as:

– the number of customer complaints or substandard items produced;
– the staff turnover;
– morale in the department; and
– other qualitative measures.

Of the three styles, the middle one was felt to be most successful in achieving the company's long term goals. The first created good cost consciousness but also a lot of tension between a manager and his subordinates and manipulation of accounting information. The last promoted general good morale, but managers had a low involvement with costs.

15.5 Example

The following is a typical example of an examination question on this area.

A conference centre has a newly appointed (unqualified) management accountant who has sent the following report to the supervisor of the restaurant. Prior to the receipt of this report the restaurant supervisor has been congratulating herself on a good start to the year, with a substantial increase in the use of the restaurant.

To: Restaurant supervisor

From: Management accountant

Subject: Performance report   Date: 5 April

As part of the campaign to improve efficiency within the conference centre, quarterly budgets have been prepared for each department.

I attach a performance report for your department for the three months to the end of March, showing all discrepancies between budgeted and actual expenditure.

A indicates an adverse variance and F a favourable variance.

	Budget £	Actual £	Discrepancy £
Food and other consumables	97,500	111,540	14,040 A
Labour – hourly paid	15,000	16,500	1,500 A
– supervisor	3,750	3,700	50 F
Power	8,500	9,250	750 A
Breakages	1,000	800	200 F
Allocated overheads	21,000	24,000	3,000 A
	146,750	165,790	19,040 A
No. of meals served	32,500	39,000	6,500 F

You have apparently incurred costs which exceed the budget by £19,040.

Please explain this to me at the meeting of the management committee on 15 April.

Required

(a)   Discuss the various possible effects on the restaurant supervisor's behaviour caused by receipt of this report.

(b)   Redraft the performance report and supporting memorandum in a way which, in your opinion, would make them more effective management tools.

Before looking at the answer, have a go for yourself. Jot down the different aspects that need to be considered (headings) and the points that can be made under these headings, including relevant research findings.

15.6   Solution

♦   The possible effects have been considered under the various factors affecting motivation.

–   **The way in which the targets were communicated to and understood by the supervisor**

If a target is to have any influence on performance the recipient must be aware of its existence and feel committed to achieving it. From the wording of the memo, it would seem likely that until she received the performance report the restaurant supervisor was unaware of the budget.

Furthermore, the reaction of the supervisor to the memo comparing the department's performance to a previously unheard-of budget is likely to be defensive and rebellious. With no knowledge as to how the budget was calculated, the supervisor is very likely to devote time and energy to attacking the 'unfair budget'. How can management hope to obtain commitment by issuing budgets 'from on high', with no scope for consultation or explanation with those responsible for fulfilling the budget?

–   **Does the supervisor feel able to achieve the target?**

Is she being held responsible for costs which she is unable to control?

Has the budget been properly prepared?

If a target is to act as a motivator the recipients must feel that they are able to reach the target by their own efforts. Clearly the supervisor is not in a position to influence the level of allocated overheads, which is presumably determined by the amount paid for such things as rent, rates and administrative salaries, and the chosen method of allocation to the departments. Thus the inclusion of such costs in the performance report will demotivate the supervisor.

She can hardly be held responsible for the fact that her own salary differs from the budget. Indeed becoming aware that she has been paid less than anticipated is likely to alienate her from the senior management.

Finally, the variances have been calculated by comparing the original budget with actual costs. The original budget is based on an anticipated usage of the restaurant of 32,500 meals; in fact, 39,000 meals have been served. If the explanation of variances is to be meaningful it should have been based on a comparison of actual costs with flexed budget. (This has been done in the suggested redraft of the performance report.)

–   **Is the supervisor being offered rewards for achieving the target?**

The memo with the report is very brief, concentrating on the fact that costs have been above budget, with no mention of the fact that the restaurant has served more meals than was anticipated. There is no indication that the supervisor is to be rewarded in any way for her efforts to increase the use of the restaurant, and the summons to explain the 'excessive' costs at a formal meeting seems almost threatening. This is likely to demotivate the supervisor. She will feel that the successful aspects of the restaurant's operation are being ignored while the less successful are being unfairly highlighted.

– **Is the target of the right degree of difficulty?**

As discussed above, the target costs communicated to the supervisor in the performance report are unrealistic because they have been left at the level of the original budget and have not been flexed to take account of the greater use made of the restaurant. Unrealistic budgets are bound to demotivate. Indeed, rather than working to reach the target, management is likely to expend time and effort criticising the target as unfair.

– **Is the supervisor the sort of person who reacts well to targets?**

As a final consideration it is important to remember that even the most perfect responsibility accounting system will fail if the managers of the responsibility centres are the sort of people who find any target frightening and thus demotivating. Although there are such people, evidence supports the view that most managers are motivated by well designed, clearly understood targets.

♦ With all these considerations in mind we can now redraft the performance report and memo in a form which is more likely to have a positive effect on the performance of the restaurant supervisor.

To: Restaurant supervisor

From: Management accountant

Subject: Performance report   Date: 5 April

I enclose a performance report for your department for the three months to the end of March. The aim of this report is to aid in the efficient use of resources by providing information as to which costs differ from their expected level (the original budget figures) and why.

The original budget figures were based on last year's costs; I would like to meet you next Tuesday to discuss whether these figures are sensible targets for this year. I have tried to make the budget more realistic by adjusting the costs upward to reflect the increased use of the restaurant (the flexed budget figures). I would welcome any ideas you have as to:

– other adjustments that are necessary to the figures in this report; and
– how the budgets should be established for future periods.

	Original budget	Flexed budget	Actual	Variance flexed budget to actual
No of meals served	32,500	39,000	39,000	
	£	£	£	£
Controllable costs				
Food and other consumables	97,500	117,000	111,540	5,460 F
Labour – hourly paid	15,000	18,000	16,500	1,500 F
Power	8,500	10,200	9,250	950 F
Breakages	1,000	1,200	800	400 F
	122,000	146,400	138,090	8,310 F

Allocated costs

Overheads	21,000	21,000	24,000	3,000	A
	143,000	167,400	162,090	5,310	F

F = favourable variance
A = adverse variance

The restaurant is evidently being well managed, with many more meals served than in the same period last year, whilst costs have risen by a small proportion. Following our discussion on Tuesday, the performance report, with any agreed amendments, will be reviewed at the meeting of the management committee on 15 April; please ensure you attend to participate in the discussion and explain the reasons for the variances.

15.7   Learning outcomes

At this stage of the chapter we have now covered the following Learning Outcomes.

Explain why it is necessary to identify controllable and uncontrollable costs
Discuss alternative approaches to budgeting
Discuss the behavioural implications of planning and budgeting

16   Summary

This chapter has considered budgets as part of the planning and control process. You should have learned how budgets are used as the basis of comparison with actual performance and the importance of managers taking responsibility for targets.

Multiple choice questions (The answers are in the final chapter of this book)

1   A company's budget includes the following figures.

Monthly sales (60% of which are on credit)	£80,000
Gross profit margin on sales	30%
Stock turnover	10 times per annum
Debtors collection period	1.2 months
Creditors payment period (all purchases are on credit)	1 month

All non-trading expenses are paid in cash and there is no cash balance at the end of a month.

What bank overdraft will produce a current (working capital) ratio of 2 at the end of the month?

A   £25,600
B   £20,800
C   £6,400
D   £1,600

2   A company has developed a computerised financial model of its operations. By entering the sales forecast and values for parameters, the model will produce a profit and loss account and balance sheet.

Parameter values

Net profit margin	25%
Return on capital employed	10%
Ratio of fixed assets to working capital	1 : 1
Current ratio	2 : 1

The first trial run of the model will use a sales forecast of £96,000.

What value will the first trial run produce for current liabilities?

A   £160,000
B   £120,000
C   £80,000
D   £60,000

3   Jason is preparing a cash budget for July. His credit sales are as follows.

	£
April (actual)	40,000
May (actual)	30,000
June (actual)	20,000
July (estimated)	25,000

His recent debt collection experience has been as follows.

Current month's sales	20%
Prior month's sales	60%
Sales two months prior	10%
Cash discounts taken	5%
Bad debts	5%

How much may Jason expect to collect from debtors during July?

A   £18,000
B   £20,000
C   £21,000
D   £24,000

CHAPTER 5

Regression analysis and time series

EXAM FOCUS

This chapter considers the mathematical techniques which may be used to forecast future sales and cost values. Forecasting is an important part of the planning process.

LEARNING OUTCOMES

This chapter covers the following Learning Outcome of the CIMA Syllabus.

Calculate future sales and costs using forecasting techniques and evaluate the results

In order to cover this Learning Outcome the following topics are included.

The High/Low method
Regression Analysis
Time Series Analysis

1   Introduction

Before considering these techniques in detail a brief overview of the methods is helpful.

The techniques rely on the analysis of past data. The objective is to obtain a mathematical expression of the relationship between two variables, say for example, costs given levels of production output.

The high-low method is a quick approach which only utilises restricted quantities of data. While this method saves time it can lead to inaccurate estimates of variable values being obtained for budgeting purposes.

Linear regression is a much more involved procedure which usually utilises all the available past data which in turn should lead to more reliable variable relationships being derived. As a consequence the information obtained for budgeting purposes should be of a better quality. The strength of the relationships derived from linear regression are supported by correlation calculations.

If the relationship between the variables is not a straight line, then the alternative method of time series analysis can be used to forecast future values based on the trends observed in the past.

2   The high-low method

2.1   Introduction

 This is a simple method of estimating future costs from past results. It takes the costs for the highest and lowest activity levels, and assumes that a linear relationship covers the range in between.

2.2 Example

Widgets are produced by a process that incurs both fixed and variable costs.

Total costs have been recorded for the process for each of the last six months as follows:

Month	Output (units)	Total cost £
1	4,500	33,750
2	3,500	30,500
3	5,100	34,130
4	6,200	38,600
5	5,700	38,000
6	4,100	31,900

Required

(a)   Formulate an equation that relates cost to output.
(b)   Plot output against total cost on a graph.
(c)   Predict total cost at the budgeted activity level for month 7 of 6,000 units.

2.3 Solution

We select the months with the highest and lowest output levels as follows:

	Output	Total cost £
Lowest	3,500	30,500
Highest	6,200	38,600
Increase	2,700	8,100

For an increase of 2,700 units, cost has increased by £8,100. This cost element must therefore represent a change in variable costs only.

Assuming a straight-line relationship, then the variable cost per unit = $\dfrac{£8,100}{2,700}$ = £3 per unit

 Note carefully that the factor determining which values to choose is the total cost at the highest output level and the total cost at the lowest **output** level. These are not necessarily the highest and lowest costs. The high/low observations are always based on the independent variable.

We can now substitute back into either of the two output levels to obtain the fixed cost.

At the 3,500 units level:

	£
Total cost	30,500
Variable cost = (3,500 × £3)	(10,500)
Fixed costs	20,000

As a check on the accuracy of our calculations, at the 6,200 unit level.

		£
Total costs		38,600
Variable costs = (6,200 × £3)		18,600
Fixed costs		20,000

We can now answer the questions set

(a)   If we let   x   =   the production level in units
                          y   =   total cost in £

        Then   y   =   20,000 + 3x

(b)   We can now plot the data on a graph of cost against output.

Total cost
£000

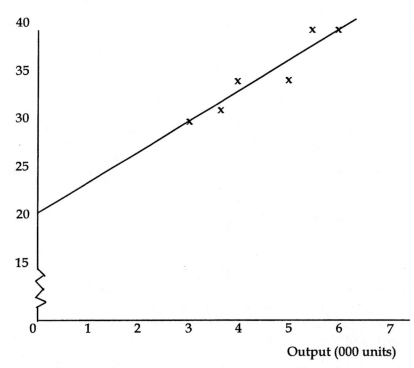

(c)   At an output level of 6,000 units, our equation would predict costs of:

        y   =   20,000 + (3 × 6,000) = £38,000

2.4   Advantages of the high – low method

♦   Simple to operate.
♦   Easy to understand.

2.5   Disadvantages of the high – low method

The problem with the high-low method is that it could give a completely inaccurate result. This is because we are only considering two sets of data, and ignoring all of the others. It is possible that the points we have chosen are completely unrepresentative of the rest of the data. This is a distinct possibility since we have chosen the two points at the extreme ends of our activity range. At these levels it is more likely that operating conditions will be atypical compared with more normal output. One way around this problem is to choose the 'next to highest' and 'next to lowest' figures, but this destroys some of the simplicity of the model.

3 Linear regression

3.1 Introduction

Repeated below are the data from the initial widgets example above, which we will use to illustrate the technique of linear regression.

Output (Units)	Total cost (£)
4,500	33,750
3,500	30,500
5,100	34,130
6,200	38,600
5,700	38,000
4,100	31,900

The technique of regression requires a particular choice of variables for the x and y axes.

The rule is:

  x axis – the independent variable
  y axis – the dependent variable

Thus we must designate output as x and total cost as y, since cost depends on output and not vice versa, ie. it is cost which is 'dependent' upon output.

The previous graph of cost against output shows that the points lie more or less on a straight line. Such a graph is called a 'scatter diagram', for obvious reasons.

One could draw a straight line through the points by eye, but there is an equation for the line which statistically fits the points most closely – the regression line.

3.2 The regression line

The regression line ('the line of best fit' or 'least squares line') is the line which minimises the sum of the squares of the **vertical** distances of the scatter points from the line. In other words, if you take each scatter point, measure how far above or below the line it lies, square each of the distances and then add them up, the regression line is designed to give you the smallest possible total.

This somewhat peculiar procedure for getting to the line is not important, as you are given formulae for working out what the line looks like. However, it is important to note that the **vertical** distances are used in the definition. This is why you must get the correct variable on each axis.

The equation of the regression line is:

  y   =   a + bx

and the constants 'a' and 'b' are given by:

$$b = \frac{n\Sigma xy - \Sigma x\Sigma y}{n\Sigma x^2 - (\Sigma x)^2} \quad \text{and} \quad a = \bar{y} - b\bar{x}$$

where

'a'   represents the point where the regression line crosses the y (vertical) axis, and

'b'   represents the slope (gradient) of the regression line

$\bar{x}$ and $\bar{y}$ are the average values of the x and y variables respectively and can be calculated from the general expression:

$$\bar{x} = \frac{\Sigma x}{n} \text{ and } \qquad \bar{y} = \frac{\Sigma y}{n}$$

Σ is the Greek letter sigma and stands for 'the sum of ....'. So in the context of $\bar{x}$ the expression $\frac{\Sigma x}{n}$ means 'sum together all the x values and divide this result by n (the number of x values)'.

Applying this to the figures in the example we get:

x	y	xy (millions)	x^2 (millions)
4,500	33,750	151.875	20.25
3,500	30,500	106.75	12.25
5,100	34,130	174.063	26.01
6,200	38,600	239.32	38.44
5,700	38,000	216.6	32.49
4,100	31,900	130.79	16.81

$\Sigma x = 29,100 \qquad \Sigma y = 206,880 \qquad \Sigma xy = 1,019.398m \qquad \Sigma x^2 = 146.25m$

$$\bar{x} = \frac{29,100}{6} \qquad\qquad \bar{y} = \frac{206,880}{6}$$

$$= 4,850 \qquad\qquad = 34,480$$

Thus   b $= \dfrac{(6 \times 1,019.398m) - (29,100 \times 206,880)}{(6 \times 146.25m) - (29,100 \times 29,100)}$

$\qquad\qquad = \dfrac{96.18m}{30.69m}$

$\qquad\qquad =$ £3.13 (this represents the variable cost per unit)

a $=$ 34,480 – (3.13 × 4,850)
$\quad =$ £19,300 (the fixed cost for a month)

The equation of the line is therefore:

y $=$ 19,300 + 3.13x

3.3   Interpolation and extrapolation

We can now use our regression line to estimate costs for different output levels.

For example:

♦   What is the expected cost for output of 4,900 units?

y $=$ 19,300 + (3.13 × 4,900) = £34,637

♦ What is the expected cost for output of 8,200 units?

$$y = 19,300 + (3.13 \times 8,200) = £44,966$$

At first glance there may seem to be little difference between the two computations we have just performed. Look more carefully at the value of x (output).

 For the first example we are considering an activity level that is within the range covered by our data. This is known as **interpolation**.

 For the second example we are looking at an output level above our range of data. What happens if the production capacity is limited to, say, 7,500 units? In order to produce 8,200 units we would have to purchase additional machinery and engage extra workers, which would make the cost far higher. It is for this sort of reason that extending beyond our data (**extrapolation**) can be very misleading.

Just because we have established a linear relationship within the range of data examined, it does not follow that the same relationship will persist beyond that range.

4 Reservations about linear regression

4.1 Measurement problems

In determining the values for use in regression or for plotting on a scatter diagram we would generally use historic cost analysis obtained from the accounting records of the firm. This gives rise to a number of potential problems such as:

♦ Timing differences

The relationship between output levels and costs could be obscured if costs are recorded after the output levels. For example, we would expect maintenance costs to increase as machinery is used more, but the increased costs may not be recorded in the same period as the output, if the maintenance work is deferred until after the peak period is past.

♦ The accounting treatment of some costs may obscure true cost behaviour. A common example here would be the allocation of fixed overhead costs to production departments. If the objective is to determine the cost behaviour pattern in a single department, then only those costs incurred within the department should be included.

♦ It is too simplistic to assume that it is only output level that affects costs.

Other factors that will affect costs will be:

– technological changes;

– the impact of learning effects;

– inflationary effects (we can compensate for this by discounting all costs to a common time period); and

– extraordinary circumstances in any given period(s).

4.2 The assumptions of regression analysis

The regression analysis is based on sample data and if we selected a different sample it is probable that a different regression line would be constructed. For this reason, regression analysis is most suited to conditions where there is a relatively stable relationship between cost and activity level.

If we are to make valid conclusions about the relationship between the two variables, then the following assumptions must be satisfied:

♦   linearity;
♦   constant variance;
♦   independence;
♦   representativeness of observations;
♦   the dependent variable is only influenced by one independent variable.

We briefly consider each of these assumptions in turn.

4.3   Linearity

In the majority of cases management will rely on linear models to relate costs to output levels. This in itself makes assumptions such as:

♦   each unit of output uses the same physical quantity of inputs; and

♦   unit prices of inputs remain constant regardless of the quantity used or purchased.

Management must carefully assess a range of output levels over which such assumptions are likely to hold good. Preliminary assessments as to linearity can be made by considering a scatter diagram.

However, we must be wary about defining the relevant range over which such linearity applies. For example, the following data is initially collected and plotted on a scatter diagram.

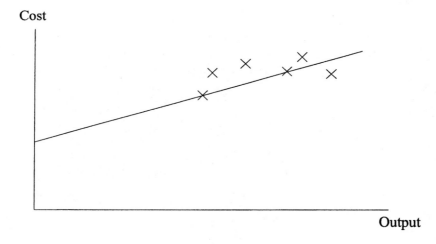

A straight line has been drawn by inspection.

When more data has been collected, the diagram may now look as follows:

Cost

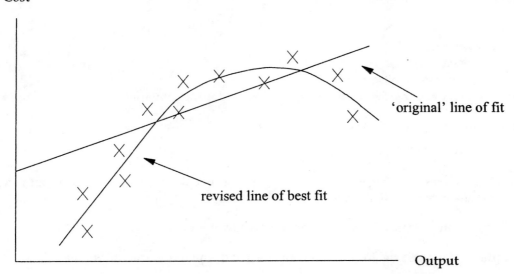

'original' line of fit

revised line of best fit

Output

4.4 Constant variance

This means that the spread of all individual observations from the regression line is uniform throughout the entire range of data.

Consider the two diagrams below:

Cost

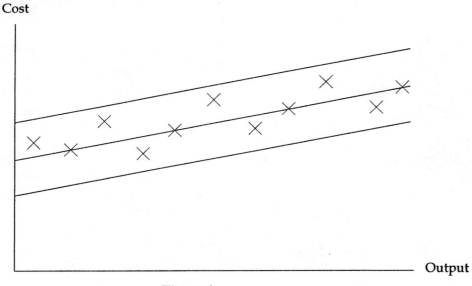

Output

Figure 1

Cost

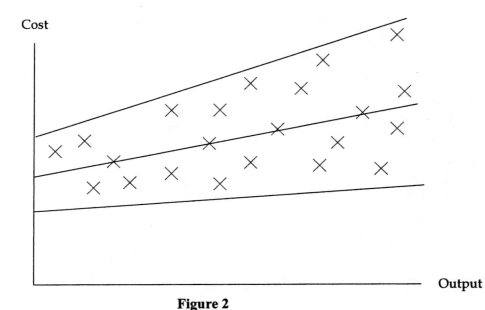

Figure 2

Output

In Figure 1 the constant variance assumption is correct. In Figure 2 the observations spread out further as volume increases. Thus, for Figure 2 the regression line would be a less reliable predictor of costs as activity increased.

In practice it may well be reasonable to expect a higher degree of variability of costs at high levels of output than at low levels of output.

4.5 Independence

The assumption here is that the deviations from the regression line are independent of each other. In other words the sequence of output levels makes no difference to the level of costs. This may not be the case in practice due to the 'stickiness' of costs. As production levels increase, costs increase because more workers are hired. As production levels fall, costs do not decrease at the same rate because workers are not laid off as rapidly. Consequently costs may well not fall as rapidly as they increase.

4.6 Representativeness of observations

Where the data includes one unusual observation, then the least-squares criterion gives a great deal of weight to that individual observation. For example results for a single period could have been distorted by a strike or material shortage, keeping costs artificially high compared with output level. In such circumstances we may be justified in eliminating such an outlying observation from our analysis, since it is wholly unrepresentative of our normal operating conditions.

Consider the diagram below:

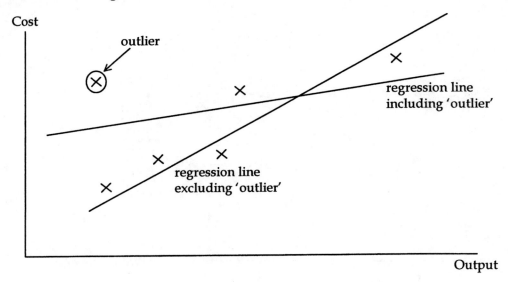

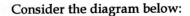 = *outlying observation that could be validly excluded from regression analysis*

It should be noted that we must not simply exclude observations just to get a line of good fit! There must be a valid reason for exclusion of any given data.

4.7 Dependence on more than one factor

We have assumed throughout the above that costs are only influenced by changes in volume. In reality many factors may influence costs, such that it may not be possible to predict costs purely on the basis of volume of output. Non-volume factors may include:

♦ Changes in production techniques.

♦ Human factors – such as efficiency of labour, new personnel or learning effects.

♦ Seasonal costs; costs such as heat and light are more closely related to the weather and time of year than output levels.

♦ Changes in price levels. Remember we have said already that historical data should be adjusted to reflect price changes.

Practice questions 1 and 2 *(The answers are in the final chapter of this book)*

1   (a)   Give three examples of pairs of variables which are linearly correlated over a certain range but where the linear relationship breaks down outside the range.

    (b)   Calculate the regression line of total cost on output from the figures given below and hence estimate the fixed and variable costs of production.

Output (thousands of units)	Cost of production (£000)
5	11.8
7	14.7
9	18.5
11	24.0
13	26.2
15	30.1

2   A machine is set up to produce components to a nominal dimension of 0.3750 cms. Six components are taken from the output at regular intervals and measured. The results are given in the table below.

Production sequence Number of piece	Difference of dimension from nominal (.0001 cms)
1	- 6
21	- 4
41	+ 2
61	+ 3
81	+ 7
101	+ 11

Use regression analysis to interpret these results for the quality control inspector.

4.8   Summary

We have examined techniques for estimating costs from sample data. Most important amongst them is the technique of linear regression. Be certain that you can, for a given set of data:

♦   compute the coefficients in the equation:

    y = a + bx from the least-squares regression criterion; and

♦   comment upon the methods used, the terms of uses and limitations.

5   Time series analysis

5.1   Introduction

So far we have looked at the technique of fitting a straight line to a set of data. This was useful for prediction purposes provided that the data varied reasonably linearly.

Now we shall be considering how we can go about forecasting future values of a time series, where although the underlying general direction of movement may well be linear, other factors cause fluctuations.

5.2   What is time series analysis?

A time series is a set of values for some variable (eg monthly production) which varies with time. The set of observations will be taken at specific times, usually at regular intervals. Examples of figures which can be plotted as a time series are:

♦   monthly rainfall in London;
♦   daily closing price of a share on the London Stock Exchange;
♦   weekly sales in a department store.

The following graph shows the volume of sales by month for a department store.

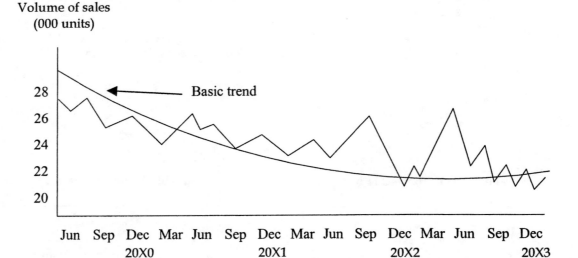

Volume of sales
(000 units)

In such a graph each point is joined by a straight line hence the typically 'jagged' appearance. Don't try to draw a smooth curve which will pass through all the points on a time series graph. You will find it practically impossible and, in any case, it is incorrect to do so. The only reason for joining the points at all is to give a clearer picture of the pattern, which would be more difficult to interpret from a series of dots.

5.3 Characteristic movements

Analysis of time series has revealed certain characteristic movements or variations. These movements are the components of the time series. Analysis of these components is essential for forecasting purposes.

The four main types of components are:

♦ long term movements or basic trends;
♦ cyclical movements;
♦ seasonal movements;
♦ irregular or random movements.

To illustrate these features, the figures below show the graphs of the components of a time series as they are built up into the graph of the complete time series.

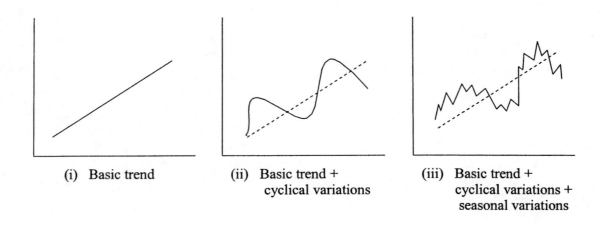

(i) Basic trend

(ii) Basic trend +
cyclical variations

(iii) Basic trend +
cyclical variations +
seasonal variations

5.4   *Basic trend*

The basic trend refers to the general direction in which the graph of a time series goes over a long interval of time. This movement can be represented on the graph by a trend curve or line. Three of the most common basic trends are:

♦   parabolic trend;
♦   arithmetic trend;
♦   compound interest trend.

Trend curves for these are illustrated below.

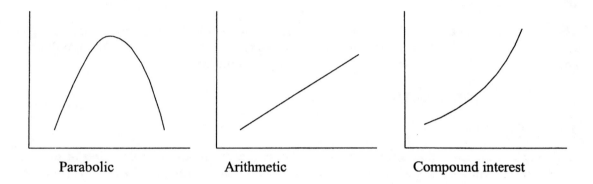

| Parabolic | Arithmetic | Compound interest |

5.5   *Cyclical variations*

Cyclical variations refer to long term oscillations or swings about the trend line or curve. These cycles may or may not be periodic; ie. they do not necessarily follow exactly similar patterns after equal intervals of time. In business and economic situations movements are said to be cyclical if they recur after time intervals of more than one year. A good example is the trade cycle, representing intervals of prosperity, recession, depression and recovery.

For cyclical variations to be apparent, data must be available over long periods of time since the periods of oscillation are so long. This is impractical for examination questions and for that reason the calculation of cyclical variations is ignored in this chapter although you must, of course, realise that they exist.

5.6   *Seasonal variations*

Seasonal fluctuations are the identical, or almost identical, patterns which a time series follows during corresponding intervals of successive periods. Such movements are due to recurring events such as the sudden increase in department store sales before Christmas. Although, in general, seasonal movements refer to a period of one year, this is not always the case and periods of hours, days, weeks, months etc. may also be considered depending on the type of data available.

5.7   *Random variations*

Random variations are the sporadic motions of time series due to chance events such as floods, strikes, elections etc.

By their very nature they are unpredictable and therefore cannot play a large part in any forecasting but it is possible to isolate the random variations by calculating all other types of variation and removing them from the time series data. It is important to extract any significant random variations from the data before using them for forecasting.

5.8   Analysis

The analysis of a time series consists of:

♦   breaking the series down into trend and seasonal variations;
♦   projecting each characteristic into the future;
♦   adding together all the individual projections to arrive at one forecast figure.

The analysis which follows concentrates on isolating only the basic trend and seasonal variations. As already stated, random movements are not usually included in analysis and, although cyclical movements may be treated in the same way as seasonal variations, they repeat over such long intervals of time that masses of historical data are required before the pattern becomes evident.

There are many methods of analysing time series, some sophisticated, others simple. The method considered here is known as the additive model. It is the best known and most commonly used although admittedly, it is not the most sophisticated.

6   Isolating the trend

6.1   Introduction

You may have noticed that a trend curve was drawn in on the time series graph in the first graph earlier. Indeed one way, admittedly not very scientific, of isolating the trend is simply to draw it in freehand on the graph. This is not usually good enough for examination purposes and the two common methods are:

♦   using moving averages; and
♦   calculating the line of best fit using regression analysis.

6.2   Moving averages

By using moving averages of appropriate order, the variations in a time series can be eliminated leaving a 'smoothed' set of figures which is taken as the trend. It is important that the correct cycle is chosen for the moving average otherwise the result will not be as good as it should be. For instance, if there are seasonal variations present in a time series and the pattern is repeated every fourth period then moving averages with a cycle of 4 should be used for the best results.

This may become clearer as you follow through the simple example in the next section.

6.3   Example

The following series is made up of two components, a simple seasonal variation of period 4 and an arithmetic trend. The moving average of order n is computed by moving down the time series, one value at a time, and averaging the next n values. Notice how different results are obtained from the different order moving averages.

	Trend		Variation		Time series	Moving averages Order 2	Order 3	Order 4
	1	+	2	=	3			
						4		
	2	+	3	=	5		4⅓	
						5		4½
	3	+	2	=	5		5	
						5		5½
	4	+	1	=	5		5⅔	
						6		6½
	5	+	2	=	7		7	
						8		7½
	6	+	3	=	9		8⅓	
						9		8½
	7	+	2	=	9		9	
						9		9½
	8	+	1	=	9		9⅔	
						10		10½
	9	+	2	=	11		11	
						12		11½
	10	+	3	=	13		12⅓	
						13		12½
	11	+	2	=	13		13	
						13		
	12	+	1	=	13			

The moving average of order 4 is the only one which captures the steadily increasing property of the original trend. It is therefore important to **examine** the figures before choosing which order moving average to use. (It will be fairly obvious which is the appropriate order in an examination question due to the way in which the data are presented, eg in 'quarters' (order 4) or days of working week (order 5).)

6.4 Centred averages

You may have been wondering about the peculiar positioning of the moving averages in the last paragraph. In fact each average has been written exactly opposite the middle of the figures from which it has been calculated. This results in the moving averages of **even** order being suspended half way between two of the original figures. In the next stage of the analysis it is essential that the moving averages are exactly aligned with the original figures. We need a centring process as demonstrated in the following illustration.

6.5 Illustration

Time series	Moving average	Moving total of previous column		Centred moving average
	Order 4	Order 2		Order 4
3				
5				
	4½			
5		10	÷ 2	5
	5½			
5		12	÷ 2	6
	6½			
7		14		7
	7½			
9		16		8
	8½			
9		18		9
	9½			
9				

As you can see by the centring process we have now arrived back at the original trend (although with some data missing). In this case it was rather a circular computation but since one of the main purposes of time series analysis questions is to identify the trend, it would not normally be known to start with! This illustration is to show that the technique does in fact give us the right answer.

6.6 Example – T S Ltd

The following data will be used to demonstrate the various techniques in the subsequent paragraphs. The data represents the quarterly sales of T S Ltd over the past five years.

	Quarter			
Year	1	2	3	4
1	73	99	93	126
2	81	114	108	148
3	91	121	117	154
4	106	131	135	175
5	134	149		

First, the trend could be isolated by moving averages.

Note: An alternative method of finding the centred moving average is shown here. Instead of averaging the 4 quarter moving totals then taking the average of each adjacent pair as in the previous illustration the averaging is left to the end. The **totals** of each adjacent pair are shown in column (d) and this is then averaged by dividing by eight. Either method gives the same answer.

6.7 Solution

Year + qtr (a)		Value (b)	4 quarter moving total (c)	8 quarter moving total (d)	Trend (T) (d)/8 (e)
1	1	73			
	2	99			
			391		
	3	93		790	98.75
			399		
	4	126		814	101.625
			414		
2	1	81		843	105.375
			429		
	2	114		880	110
			451		
	3	108		912	114
			461		
	4	148		929	116.125
			468		
3	1	91		945	118.125
			477		
	2	121		960	120
			483		
	3	117		981	122.625
			498		
	4	154		1,006	125.75
			508		
4	1	106		1,034	129.25
			526		
	2	131		1,073	134.125
			547		
	3	135		1,122	140.25
			575		
	4	175		1,168	146
			593		
5	1	134			
	2	149			
	3				
	4				

6.8 Disadvantages of moving averages

♦ Values at the beginning and end of the series are lost – therefore the moving averages do not cover the complete period.

♦ The moving averages may generate cycles or other movements that were not present in the original data.

♦ The averages are strongly affected by extreme values. To overcome this a 'weighted' moving average is sometimes used giving the largest weights to central items and small weights to extreme values.

6.9 Trend by linear regression

If, after plotting a time series on a graph, the trend appears to be approximately linear, it can alternatively be estimated by using the least squares line of best fit or regression line.

Provided a linear model is reasonable, this method has advantages over the moving average method including:

♦ values are not 'lost' – trend values will cover the whole period; and
♦ forecasting of future trend values is easier.

To apply the method, time periods should be numbered consecutively from 1 and used as the independent variable. This can be demonstrated using the same data for the example TS Ltd.

6.10 Illustration

Time period x	Value y	xy	x^2
1	73	73	1
2	99	198	4
3	93	279	9
4	126	504	16
5	81	405	25
6	114	684	36
7	108	756	49
8	148	1,184	64
9	91	819	81
10	121	1,210	100
11	117	1,287	121
12	154	1,848	144
13	106	1,378	169
14	131	1,834	196
15	135	2,025	225
16	175	2,800	256
17	134	2,278	289
18	149	2,682	324
171	2,155	22,244	2,109

$$\bar{x} = \frac{171}{18} = 9.5 \qquad \bar{y} = \frac{2,155}{18} = 119.7$$

$$b = \frac{n\Sigma xy - \Sigma x\Sigma y}{n\Sigma x^2 - (\Sigma x)^2}$$

$$= \frac{(18 \times 22,244) - (171 \times 2,155)}{(18 \times 2,109) - (171 \times 171)}$$

$$= \frac{31,887}{8,721}$$

$$= 3.66$$

$$a \quad = \quad \overline{y} - b\overline{x}$$

$$= \quad 119.7 - 3.66 \times 9.5$$

$$= \quad 85$$

Regression line is:

$$y \quad = \quad 3.66x + 85$$

To produce trend figures using this technique, simply substitute x values from 1 to 18 in the equation and the resulting value for y is then the trend. This is demonstrated for the first four quarters.

Quarter (x)	Value of y		Trend
1	3.66 + 85	=	88.7
2	3.66 × 2 + 85	=	92.3
3	3.66 × 3 + 85	=	96.0
4	3.66 × 4 + 85	=	99.6

7 Seasonal variations – the additive model

7.1 Introduction

Having isolated the trend we can consider how to deal with the seasonal variations. The additive model we will use expresses variations in absolute terms with above and below average figures designated by plus and minus signs.

7.2 The additive model

 The four components of a time series (T = trend; S = seasonal variation; C = cyclical variation; R = random variation) are expressed as absolute values which are simply added together to produce the actual figures, ie

Actual data (Time series) = T + S + C + R

For unsophisticated analysis over a relatively short period of time C and R are ignored. Random variations are ignored because they are unpredictable and would not normally exhibit any repetitive pattern, whereas cyclical variations (long term oscillations) are ignored because their effect is negligible over short periods of time. The model therefore simplifies to

Actual data = T + S

The seasonal variation is thus obtained for each time period by subtracting the computed trend figure from the original time series.

7.3 Example

Using the same data for T S Ltd from the list table produced in the answer earlier, the seasonal variations can be extracted by subtracting each trend value (using the moving averages method) from its corresponding time series value:

7.4 Solution

Year	Quarter	Seasonal variation (S) (b) – (e)
1	3	–5.75
	4	+24.375
2	1	–24.375
	2	+4
	3	–6
	4	+31.875
3	1	–27.125
	2	+1
	3	–5.625
	4	+28.25
4	1	–23.25
	2	–3.125
	3	–5.25
	4	+29

7.5 Average seasonal variations

One of the purposes of extracting the seasonal variations is to enable forecasts to be made for future time periods. Looking at the result obtained above, we have a problem – which variation to use?

Obviously, if we're making a prediction for a quarter 2 of a year in the future, we'll use a quarter 2 variation, but we have three of these in the above data, all different

One way to get a representative seasonal variation, if no obvious pattern exists, is to average out corresponding variations for each quarter:

Year	Quarter 1	2	3	4
1	–	–	–5.75	+24.375
2	–24.375	+4.00	–6.00	+31.875
3	–27.125	+1.00	–5.625	+28.25
4	–23.25	–3.125	–5.25	+29.00
5	–	–	–	–
Sum	–74.75	+1.875	–22.625	+113.5
Average	–24.917	+0.625	–5.656	+28.375

7.6 Deseasonalisation of data

Having isolated the seasonal variations we could now 'deseasonalise' the original data by removing these variations.

Note that, for example, quarter 1 has a generally **below** trend value (negative average seasonal variation) while quarter 4 is generally **above** trend. Thus in adjusting the original data to eliminate effects of seasonal variations, ('deseasonalising'), the quarter 1 data is **increased** by 24.917 whereas quarter 4 data is **reduced** by 28.375.

After data have been deseasonalised they still include trend, cyclical and random movements. The trend has already been found and can now be removed from the deseasonalised data to leave only cyclical and random movements (residual variations).

Year + qtr		Original data	Average seasonal variations	Deseasonal-ised data	Trend	Residual variations (cyclical and random)
1	3	93	−5.656	98.656	98.75	−0.094
	4	126	+28.375	97.625	101.625	−4.0
2	1	81	−24.917	105.917	105.375	+0.542
	2	114	+0.625	113.375	110.0	+3.375
	3	108	−5.656	113.656	114.0	−0.344
	4	148	+28.375	119.625	116.125	+3.5
3	1	91	−24.917	115.917	118.125	−2.208
	2	121	+0.625	120.375	120.0	+0.375
	3	117	−5.656	122.656	122.625	+0.031
	4	154	+28.375	125.625	125.75	−0.125
4	1	106	−24.917	130.917	129.25	+1.667
	2	131	+0.625	130.375	134.125	−3.75
	3	135	−5.656	140.656	140.25	+0.406
	4	175	+28.375	146.625	146.0	+0.625

8 Seasonal variations – the multiplicative model

8.1 Introduction

While the additive model calculates the seasonal variations by looking at the absolute differences between the trend and the observed values, the multiplicative model expresses the seasonal variations as proportions of the trend.

8.2 The multiplicative model

In the multiplicative model, the four components of a time series are multiplied together to produce the actual figure, ie:

Actual data (time series) $= T \times S \times C \times R$

where T = trend, S = seasonal variation, C = cyclical variation and R = random variation. For analysis over a short period of time, C and R can be ignored so that the model simplifier to:

Actual data $= T \times S$

8.3 Example

In a shop, the trend in sales of umbrellas each quarter has been calculated as :

$y = 8x + 1,000$

where y is the number of umbrellas sold and x is the number of the quarterly period (Q1 2000 in period 1, Q2 2000 in period 2 etc).

The quarterly seasonal variations are believed to be:

Q1	Q2	Q3	Q4
+ 20%	- 30%	- 15%	+ 25%

What are the expected sales in:

(a)   Q3 of 2001
(b)   Q4 of 2002?

8.4 Solution

(a)   In Q3 of 2001, the x value (the number of the quarterly period) is 7, so the trend value is:

$$y = 8x + 1,000 = 56 + 1,000 = 1,056$$

The quarterly variation for Q3 is –15%, so the forecast actual sales in Q3 of 2001 are:

$$0.85 \times 1,056 = 898 \text{ umbrellas}$$

(b)   In Q4 of 2002, the x value is 12, so the trend value is:

$$y = 8x + 1,000 = 96 + 1,000 = 1,096$$

The quarterly variation for Q4 is +25%, so the forecast actual value in Q4 of 2002 is:

$$1.25 \times 1,096 = 1,370 \text{ umbrellas}$$

8.5 Discussion of the multiplicative model

In the multiplicative model, the seasonal variations can either be expressed as percentages (as in the example above) or as factors. The variations in the example above would be expressed as factors as below:

Q1	Q2	Q3	Q4
1.2	0.7	0.85	1.25

The sum of all the percentages of the variations should be zero (check: 20% - 30% - 15% + 25% = 0). Similarly, the sum of variations expressed as factors should be the number of individual variations (check: 1.2 + 0.7 + 0.85 + 1.25 = 4).

The multiplicative model is preferred to the additive model when the trend in values is sharply rising or falling, since the seasonal variations will then typically increase in absolute terms as the trend value increases. In diagrammatic terms:

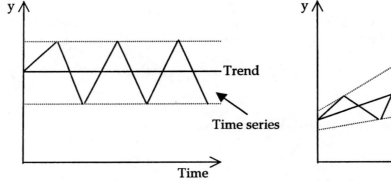

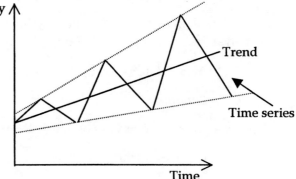

Flat trend with constant fluctuations about trend ∴ additive model is suitable.

Rising trend with increasing absolute fluctuations about trend ∴ multiplicative model is suitable.

8.6 Learning outcome

At this stage of the chapter we have now covered the following Learning Outcome:

Calculate future sales and costs using forecasting techniques and evaluate the results.

Practice questions 3 - 8 *(The answers are in the final chapter of this book)*

3   In what order should the following be placed to show movements that can be described as a trend, seasonal variation, cyclical variation and random variation respectively?

    (1)   The pattern of the number of cars going over Battersea Bridge in London each hour during a working day.

    (2)   The decline in the infant mortality rate due to improvements in intensive care treatment.

    (3)   Changes in house prices in the North relative to the Retail Price Index.

    (4)   The increase in buildings insurance claims due to the worst storms to hit England in history.

    A   2, 3, 1, 4
    B   2, 1, 3, 4
    C   3, 4, 1, 2
    D   3, 1, 2, 4

4   Which of the following statements concerning the trend of a time series is incorrect?

    A   The more exact method of linear regression for isolation of the trend is always preferable to the moving average method

    B   The trend may be linear or a curve

    C   The method of moving averages can always be used whatever the shape of the underlying trend

    D   Extraction of the trend can be by the same method whether the additive or proportional model is to be used

5   The following represents quarterly output for a product

	March	June	September	December
Year 1	100	104	110	109
Year 2	102	108	112	108

    The trend figures that would be obtained by centred moving averages of order 4 would be

    A   105.75, 106.25, 107.25, 107.75, 107.5
    B   106, 106.75, 107.5, 107.625
    C   212, 213.5, 215, 215.25
    D   423, 425, 429, 431, 430

6   Give an example of a time series and explain how the four characteristic movements would be caused in the example that you have chosen.

7   The following table shows capital expenditure by the distributive trades in £million.

	Quarter			
	1	2	3	4
Year 1	173	206	198	218
Year 2	216	223	219	221
Year 3	213	212	225	199

(a)   Calculate the trend by the method of moving averages and chart both the original figures and the trend.

(b)   Consider the case for using the method of least squares for deriving the trend for the above data.

8   The following data give the tonnage of shipping entered with cargoes at UK ports (in 100,000 tons).

	1st quarter	2nd quarter	3rd quarter	4th quarter
20X7	134	153	163	151
20X8	135	154	159	155
20X9	132	159	177	159

Compute the seasonal variations and apply these as seasonal corrections to the 20X8 figures to deseasonalise them.

9   Summary

In this chapter we have explained the high/low method, regression analysis and time series analysis as forecasting techniques. You should be able to make computations using these techniques and also explain the uses, advantages and disadvantages of each method.

CHAPTER 6

Modern business environment

EXAM FOCUS

This chapter explains the new methods of working found in the modern business environment and the accounting systems which have been developed to provide useful information to managers.

LEARNING OUTCOMES

This chapter covers the following Learning Outcomes of the CIMA Syllabus.

> Compare and contrast value analysis and functional analysis
> Apply and evaluate the use of activity-based, absorption, marginal and process costing and throughput accounting in the context of planning and decision making
> Explain total quality management
> Prepare and discuss cost of quality reports
> Apply and evaluate the use of throughput accounting

In order to cover these Learning Outcomes the following topics are included.

> Strategic management accounting
> Activity based approaches
> Modern developments in management accounting
> Throughput accounting

1 Strategic management accounting

1.1 The role of the accountant in business

The role of the accountant in business is in transition. Accountants need to adapt to changes in their environment and change the image that has been created over many years. Robert Townsend once said:

'Accountants can be smarter than anybody else or more ambitious or both, but essentially they are bean counters — their job is to serve operations. They can't run the ship'.

Robert Kaplan suggests that accountants should:

♦ become part of their organisation's value-added team

♦ participate in the formulation and implementation of strategy

♦ translate strategic intent and capabilities into operational and managerial measures

♦ move away from being scorekeepers of the past to become the designers of the organisation's critical management information systems.

These ideas have given rise to the concept of *strategic management accounting* (SMA), which is defined as 'a form of management accounting in which emphasis is placed on information which relates to factors external to the firm, as well as non-financial information and internally generated information'. (*Management Accounting Official Terminology*, CIMA, 1996).

1.2   *The work of Professor Michael Porter: cost leadership and differentiation*

Porter investigated the strategies that allow the organisation to grow through obtaining competitive advantage. Porter claims that there are four such generic strategies, as shown in Table 1. (Note that the two strategies based on focus are often amalgamated, so you may see references to three generic strategies rather than four.)

		Competitive advantage	
		Looking at cost	*Distinction from competitors*
Target market	*Across industry*	Cost leadership	Differentiation
	Specific industry niche	Focus based on cost	Focus based on differentiation

Table 1 Porter's generic strategies

 Two basic approaches are embodied in this analysis.

(a)   Producing goods of acceptable quality at a lower cost than competitors. This will allow lower prices to be charged, leading to increased market share.

(b)   Differentiating the product from its competitors in some way. This will lead to customers paying a premium for the product.

1.3   *Value analysis and functional analysis*

Cost reduction programmes can be implemented with the organisation to ensure that products are being offered to the market at the lowest possible unit cost. Two techniques that can be applied in cost reduction programmes are value analysis and functional analysis.

 Value analysis is defined as "a systematic interdisciplinary examination of factors affecting the cost of a product or service, in order to devise means of achieving the specified purpose most economically at the required standard of quality and reliability."

The specified purpose can best be identified from discussions with customers. What are the characteristics of the product that the customers really want and are prepared to pay for? If the customer uses the product as an internal component, perhaps they would be equally happy with the product unpainted, so that the cost of painting the end unit could be eliminated. Similarly, perhaps they would be happy with the case being cheap plastic rather than expensive metal.

Whereas traditional cost reduction tries to identify the cheapest method of producing a product to a specific fixed design, value analysis tries to identify the cheapest method of producing a product that still achieves its desired purpose.

Functional analysis is a similar process. It is defined as "an analysis of the relationships between product functions, their perceived value to the customer and their cost of provision." Functional analysis asserts that it is the functions of a product that customers are prepared to pay for, so attention should be concentrated on the functions already offered by a product and any possible additional functions that could be incorporated.

For example, the convergence of consumer electronics means that it is possible to add new functions to a piece of equipment at very low cost, simply by redesigning the chips on-board. We therefore see digital cameras that can also act as MP3 music players, or handheld computers that can also act as mobile phones. Profits can be improved by stripping out functions of no value, and adding new functions which customers are prepared to pay for.

1.4   *Management accounting in the modern business environment*

The modern business environment is characterised by:

♦   increased competition (eg former state monopolies being broken up and privatised)

♦   globalisation of sources and markets (eg the Internet allows the smallest of businesses to offer their products to the whole world)

♦   continuous improvements in quality are necessary

♦   reductions in product lifecycles

The old principles of batch manufacturing for stock have been swept away by cheaper methods of Just-in-Time procurement, eliminating the need for stocks but necessitating defect-free deliveries.

Various production management strategies have been introduced:

(i)   Material Requirements Planning (MRP I)

        MRP I is a system that converts a production schedule into a listing of the materials and components required to meet that schedule, so that adequate stock levels are maintained and items are available when needed.

(ii)   Manufacturing Resource Planning (MRP II)

        MRP I applies only to the manufacturing operation. MRP II expands on MRP I to give a broader approach to the planning and scheduling of resources, embracing areas such as finance, logistics, engineering and marketing.

(iii)   Enterprise Resource Planning (ERP)

        With increased computer power now available, MRP II has evolved into ERP. ERP refers to integrated business software systems that use database technology to control the corporate information resource, helping businesses to control all aspects of their operations (stock, purchasing, personnel, finance etc). Common data can be accessed across the whole enterprise in a real-time environment.

2   The pursuit of quality

2.1   *Introduction*

The last twenty years has seen a switch in emphasis in manufacturing from quantity to quality. Previously the objective was to produce as much as possible, carrying out quality tests on the output, and scrapping or reworking the output units that were of insufficient quality. It has now been recognised that it is cheaper in the long run to get things right first time, so that a defect-free philosophy should be designed into the system. The name for this philosophy is Total Quality Management (TQM).

2.2   *Total Quality Management*

TQM has been defined as "the continuous improvement in quality, productivity and effectiveness obtained by establishing management responsibility for processes as well as outputs. In this every process has an identified process owner and every person in an entity operates within a process and contributes to its improvement".

In a traditional system, operators in the production department are responsible for producing a batch of units, which are then checked for quality by a separate quality control department. In a TQM system, quality is designed into the system, so that operators are responsible for producing defect-free output.

Features of TQM are:

♦ It aims towards an environment of zero defects at a minimum cost.

♦ It requires an awareness by all personnel of the quality requirements of supplying the customer with products of the agreed design specification.

♦ It aims towards the elimination of waste where waste is defined as anything other than the minimum essential amount of equipment, materials, space and workers' time.

♦ It must embrace all aspects of operation from pre-production to post-production stages in the business cycle.

♦ It recognises the need to maximise the ratio of added value time to total cycle time. Non-added value activities incur costs which should be eliminated. For example stockholding cost, inspection costs, costs incurred in the unnecessary movement of goods.

Total quality management will, therefore, seek methods changes which will help in achieving such objectives. Examples include the use of **Just-in-time** (JIT) production procedures and the use of a **dedicated cell production layout** where a bank of machinery and personnel is dedicated to the performance of a specific sequence of operations.

The widespread introduction of TQM principles has led to a structured analysis of the costs involved in ensuring quality.

2.3 Quality related costs

Quality-related costs are the expenditure incurred in defect prevention and appraisal activities and the losses due to internal and external failure of a product or service through failure to meet agreed specifications.

 Quality-related costs may be classified as failure costs (both internal and external), appraisal costs and prevention costs.

Failure costs are the costs required to evaluate, dispose of, and either correct or replace a defective or deficient product.

2.4 Internal failure costs

Internal failure costs are costs discovered before the product is delivered to the customer. Examples include the following.

♦ Rework costs
♦ Net cost of scrap
♦ Disposal of defective products
♦ Downtime due to quality problems

2.5 External failure costs

External failure costs are costs discovered after the product is delivered to customers. Examples include the following.

♦ Complaint investigation and processing
♦ Warranty claims
♦ Cost of lost sales
♦ Product recalls

2.6   Appraisal costs

Appraisal costs are costs of monitoring and inspecting products in terms of specified standards before the products are released to the customer. Examples include the following.

- Measurement equipment
- Inspection and tests
- Product quality audits
- Process control monitoring
- Test equipment expense

2.7   Prevention costs

Prevention costs include investments in machinery, technology, and education programmes designed to reduce the number of defective products during production. Examples include the following.

- Customer surveys
- Research of customer needs
- Field trials
- Quality education and training programmes
- Supplier reviews
- Investment in improved production equipment
- Quality engineering
- Quality circles

Practice questions 1-3 *(The answers are in the final chapter of this book)*

1   Planning

Lack of co-ordination between strategic planning and operational planning may result in unrealistic plans, inconsistent goals, poor communication and inadequate performance measurement.

(a)   State key features or characteristics which should be incorporated in each of strategic planning and operational planning.

(b)   Name and comment on examples of the cost implications of each of the factors shown in italics in the above statement which may occur from lack of relevant and appropriate operational planning. Your answer should be in the context of a strategic planning goal of sustaining competitive advantage at minimum cost through speedy delivery of quality products to customers.

2   Total quality

(a)   'It may be argued that in a total quality environment, variance analysis from a standard costing system is redundant'.

Discuss the validity of this statement.

(b)   Using labour cost as the focus, discuss the differences in the measurement of labour efficiency/effectiveness where (i) total quality management techniques and (ii) standard cost variance analysis are implemented.

3   Calton

Calton Ltd make and sell a single product.   The existing product unit specifications are as follows.

Direct material X:	8 sq metres at £4 per sq metre
Machine time:	0.6 running hours
Machine cost per gross hour:	£40
Selling price	£100

Calton Ltd require to fulfil orders for 5,000 product units per period.   There are no stocks of product units at the beginning or end of the period under review.   The stock level of material X remains unchanged throughout the period.

The following additional information affects the costs and revenues.

1   5% of incoming material from suppliers is scrapped owing to poor receipt and storage organisation.

2   4% of material X input to the machine process is wasted owing to processing problems.

3   Inspection and storage of material X costs 10 pence per sq metre purchased.

4   Inspection during the production cycle, calibration checks on inspection equipment, vendor rating and other checks cost £25,000 per period.

5   Production quantity is increased to allow for the downgrading of 12.5% of product units at the final inspection stage.   Downgraded units are sold as 'second quality' units at a discount of 30% on the standard selling price.

6   Production quantity is increased to allow for returns from customers which are replaced free of charge.   Returns are due to specification failure and account for 5% of units initially delivered to customers.   Replacement units incur a delivery cost of £8 per unit.   80% of the returns from customers are rectified using 0.2 hours of machine running time per unit and are re-sold as 'third quality' products at a discount of 50% on the standard selling price.   The remaining returned units are sold as scrap for £5 per unit.

7   Product liability and other claims by customers are estimated at 3% of sales revenue from standard product sales.

8   Machine idle time is 20% of gross machine hours used (ie running hours = 80% of gross hours).

9   Sundry costs of administration, selling and distribution total £60,000 per period.

10   Calton Ltd is aware of the problem of excess costs and currently spends £20,000 per period in efforts to prevent a number of such problems from occurring.

Calton Ltd is planning a quality management programme which will increase its excess cost prevention expenditure from £20,000 to £60,000 per period.   It is estimated that this will have the following impact.

1   A reduction in stores losses of material X to 3% of incoming material.

2   A reduction in the downgrading of product units at inspection to 7.5% of units inspected.

3   A reduction in material X losses in process to 2.5% of input to the machine process.

4   A reduction in returns of products from customers to 2.5% of units delivered.

5   A reduction in machine idle time to 12.5% of gross hours used.

6   A reduction in product liability and other claims to 1% of sales revenue from standard product sales.

7   A reduction in inspection, calibration, vendor rating and other checks by 40% of the existing figure.

8   A reduction in sundry administration, selling and distribution costs by 10% of the existing figure.

9   A reduction in machine running time required per product unit to 0.5 hours.

Required

(a)   Prepare summaries showing the calculation of (i) total production units (pre-inspection), (ii) purchases of material X (sq metres), (iii) gross machine hours. In each case the figures are required for the situation both before and after the implementation of the additional quality management programme, in order that the orders for 5,000 product units may be fulfilled.

(b)   Prepare profit and loss accounts for Calton Ltd for the period showing the profit earned both before and after the implementation of the additional quality management programme.

(c)   Comment on the relevance of a quality management programme and explain the meaning of the terms internal failure costs, external failure costs, appraisal costs and prevention costs giving examples for each, taken where possible from the information in the question.

3   Activity-based budgeting and activity based costing

3.1   Activity-based budgeting (ABB)

ABB is a strategically based resource allocation system designed to ensure that resources are allocated primarily around value added activities.

Advocates of ABB argue that traditional budgeting over-emphasises the importance of financial forecasting, and that planning too often takes a remote, rather detached view. Budgeting (of the ABB variety) should be closely integrated with planning and have a focus of continuous innovation, leading in the long term to strategic advantage.

Budgeting is important because:

♦   it is the single most important vehicle for making decisions

♦   the budgetary process provides a method for the systematic, continuous, and intensive review of operations (otherwise it is feared that innovation might occur only in a sporadic manner).

ABB has been described as a management process, focusing on controlling costs at the activity level. There is a slant on process, as ABB should result in the continuous and systematic improvement in cost (considering performance, or value added).

ABB thus involves defining the activities underlying the financial figures and, for each function, the level of activity is used to determine appropriate budget targets. In other words, costs are 'flexed', or 'modelled' to the activity levels. The variances obtained in the actual to budget comparison process are arguably more meaningful than those obtained under orthodox costing methods.

ABB has developed from a number of related management techniques.

(a) *ZBB (zero-based budgeting)* — in which budget expenditure is prioritised amongst activities according to the value added by each.

(b) *TQM (total quality management)* — the essence of which is continuous innovation in all aspects of production; the goal being quality (which is often the most vital aspect of the product's positioning in the market).

(c) *VA (value analysis)* — which checks that the level of quality (or value) required in the product's positioning is delivered to the consumer at the lowest possible cost.

(d) *ABC (activity-based costing)* — which assumes that management cannot control costs directly, but instead, must control the activities which drive the costs. Precisely which activities are required is decided strategically; whilst the operational control of the chosen activities is effected by the actual versus budget variance analysis.

To be effective ABB requires:

♦ activity analysis techniques (including the activity cost matrix which is considered below)
♦ the identification of cost improvement opportunities
♦ careful analysis of discretionary expenditure
♦ the establishment of performance targets
♦ a participative organisational culture to encourage ideas.

In short, organisational flexibility is required: organisations should be 'organic' rather than 'mechanistic'.

3.2 Activity cost matrix (ACM)

An activity cost matrix is a simple way of analysing activities — an essential prerequisite for ABB. Below we illustrate the use of the ACM for a sales order department.

Activity cost matrix for a sales order department (figures in £000)

	No of customers	No of orders	No of export orders	No of despatches	Price list sales literature sustaining cost	Dept sustaining cost	Total
Management salary	-	-	-	-	10	30	40
Clerical salaries	30	80	70	40	20	-	240
Overtime	-	-	10	15	-	-	25
Stationery and consumables	-	8	3	4	30	-	45
IT costs	8	12	4	8	-	-	32
Other costs	3	4	2	6	7	10	32
Total (£000)	41	104	89	73	67	40	414
Volume of activity	650	2,300	500	6,000	-	-	
Cost per unit of activity	£63	£45	£178	£12	£67,000	£40,000	

The orthodox line-by-line budget splits the total departmental costs by resource type (management salary; clerical salaries; overtime and so on). This resource analysis is seen on the far left-hand column of the matrix.

In addition, the total departmental costs are split by function, ie between:

♦   activity-related functions (number of customers, orders, export orders and despatches);
♦   sustaining functions (sustaining price lists, sales literature, and the department itself).

The significance of a sustaining function is that its cost is unrelated to the volume of any activity; the cost of sustaining functions is fixed.

The functional analysis of cost can be seen in the bottom horizontal row.

The total activity related costs are divided by budgeted activity levels to arrive at costs per unit of activity; these form the vital yardstick of control.

3.3   Problems with short-term fluctuations

The 'costs per unit of activity' derived above should be seen as a long-term performance target. For instance, let us suppose that the number of orders increases by 10%. In the short term, the number of clerks may remain as before; but increased overtime, at premium rates, may be worked. In this way, one might expect the actual 'variable' cost per order to exceed the budgeted standard, but this would only be so in the short term. In the long term the firm would hire more clerks, no overtime would be worked, thus pushing down the long-term cost per order.

3.4   Controllability

Users of ABB should carefully consider whether managers are in a position to control activities, or whether they can only control the costs of each activity.

For example, quality control procedures may require (say) 5% of production batches to be tested: the number of testings (ie the volume of the activity) is fixed. However, the manager of the testing department is in a position to control:

♦   the technicians' productivity (by changing the remuneration, degree of motivation, etc);
♦   the speed and flexibility of the equipment; and
♦   the operating procedures and processes.

All three are described in the terminology as cost-level drivers.

3.5   Benefits of ABB

♦   Costs of activities are highlighted; this may lead to improved decision making. For instance, if salesmen are aware that processing each order costs £45, they may be dissuaded from selling items (value say £50).

♦   Resources are allocated on the basis of levels of activity, rather than on an ad hoc basis (eg 'let's spend 5% more than last year').

♦   Costs have nowhere to hide; all costs must be justified by their functional benefit.

♦   Creativity is encouraged; ABB can be seen as a vehicle to encourage an innovative culture.

3.6 Activity-based costing (ABC)

ABC is the attribution of costs to cost units on the basis of benefit received from indirect activities (eg ordering, setting-up, assuring quality). ABC is studied further in a later chapter of this book.

The key features of ABC are listed below

♦ ABC emphasises the need to obtain a better understanding of the behaviour of costs.

♦ In the long run most manufacturing costs are not fixed.

♦ Activities cause costs and customers create the demands for activities.

♦ Cost drivers are the factors which cause costs to occur at a given level of activity.

♦ ABC improves product costing by linking costs to the activities and the cost drivers which cause the relative use of each activity.

3.7 Example

The following data relates to Publications Ltd in the month of April 20X8.

| | *Products* | |
	A	B
Quantity produced	5,000	7,000
Direct labour hours per unit	1	2
Machine hours per unit	3	1
Set-ups in the period	10	40
Orders handled in the period	15	60
Overhead costs		
	£000	
Relating to machine activity	220	
Relating to production run set-ups	20	
Relating to handling of orders	45	
	———	
	285	
	———	

Required

Calculate the production overhead to be absorbed by one unit of A and B using a traditional costing approach absorbing on the basis of direct labour hours and an ABC approach.

3.8 Solution

Traditional absorption approach

Direct labour hours (DLH)

Product A	$1 \times 5,000$	=	5,000
Product B	$2 \times 7,000$	=	14,000
			———
Total DLH			19,000
			———

$$\text{Overhead absorption rate} \quad = \quad \frac{£285,000}{19,000}$$

$$= \quad £15 \text{ per hour}$$

Absorbed overheads would be

Product A 1 hr × £15   =   £15 per unit

Product B 2 hrs × £15   =   £30 per unit

ABC - overheads absorbed according to cost drivers

Machine overheads

	A		B	
Total machine hours	(5,000 × 3)	+	(7,000 × 1)	= 22,000
Machine-hour driver costs	£220,000/22,000	=	£10 per machine hour	
Set-up driver costs	£20,000/50 set-ups	=	£400 per set-up	
Order-driver costs	£45,000/75 orders	=	£600 per order	

		A		B
		A		*B*
Machine-driver costs	(15,000 × £10)	150,000	(7,000 × £10)	70,000
Set-up costs	(10 × £400)	4,000	(40 × £400)	16,000
Order-driver costs	(15 × £600)	9,000	(60 × £600)	36,000
		———		———
		163,000		122,000
		———		———

$$\text{Overhead cost per unit} \quad = \quad \frac{£163,000}{5,000} \qquad = \quad \frac{£122,000}{7,000}$$

$$= \quad £32.60 \qquad\qquad £17.43$$

Comparison of traditional and ABC overhead absorbed per unit

	A	B
Traditional	£15	£30
ABC	£32.60	£17.43
Percentage change	117% ↑	41.9% ↓

Practice questions 4 and 5 *(The answers are in the final chapter of this book)*

4   Snecas

Snecas Ltd manufacture a range of products using a series of machine operations. One product type is made from steel bar. At present the factory layout is somewhat haphazard and machines are used for a particular job as they become available. Company management have decided to create a 'dedicated cell' of machines which will specialise in the manufacture of steel bar products with specialist machine minders. The machines in the 'cell' will be grouped by machine type to facilitate a smooth flow of steel bar products. There are three steel bar products which are manufactured.

Product A   saw the steel bar to size; turn the bar on a turning machine; harden in a hardening process; grind the bar on a grinding machine.

Product B   saw the steel bar to size; turn on a turning machine, grind on a grinding machine.

Product C   saw the steel bar to size; turn on a turning machine; drill on a drilling machine; harden in a hardening process; grind on a grinding machine.

Snecas Ltd currently operate a system whereby labour and overhead costs for all products are absorbed into product units at 225% of direct material costs. The direct material cost per metre of each steel bar product is £70.

This system results in the net profit or loss per metre of steel bar product being reported as £12.50 profit, £27.50 loss and £12.50 profit for products A, B and C respectively.

A study by the management accountant has resulted in the following budget data for the coming year for the steel bar product 'cell'.

(i)   *Machine operation*

	Fixed labour and overhead (total) £000	*Variable labour and overhead per metre* £
Saw	88	36
Turn	110	14
Drill	108	40
Harden	320	26
Grind	154	25

(ii)   Production/sales quantity

Product A	8,000 metres
Product B	2,000 metres
Product C	12,000 metres

(iii)   Direct material prices will rise by 6% from the current year level.

(iv)   Selling prices will be increased by 5% from the current year level.

(v)   Variable labour and overhead costs will be absorbed at the budgeted rate per metre for each machine type listed in (i) above.

(vi)   Fixed costs for each machine type will be absorbed at a rate per metre based on the aggregate quantity of products A, B and C budgeted to pass through each machine type.

Required

(a)   Prepare a diagram which illustrates the layout and steel bar 'flow' of the new steel bar product machine group and shows the aggregate quantity (metres) of products passing through each machine type.

(b)   Prepare a budget summary for the coming year which details for each product:

  (i)   fixed and variable costs by machine operation (per metre and in total)
  (ii)   contribution earned per metre and in total for each product
  (iii) net profit or loss per metre and in total for each product.

(c)   Suggest ways in which the cost and revenue analysis for the amended machine layout indicates possible change in the product pricing and mix strategy.

(d)   Itemise and briefly comment on five distinct ways in which the steel bar product dedicated cell layout may result in reductions in cost.

5   Repak

Repak Ltd is a warehousing and distribution company which receives products from customers, stores the products and then re-packs them for distribution as required. There are three customers for whom the service is provided — John Ltd, George Ltd and Paul Ltd. The products from all three customers are similar in nature but of varying degrees of fragility. Basic budget information has been gathered for the year to 30 June 20X3 and is shown in the following table.

	Products handled *(cubic metres)*
John Ltd	30,000
George Ltd	45,000
Paul Ltd	25,000

	Costs *£000*
Packaging material (see note)	1,950
Labour – basic	350
– overtime	30
Occupancy	500
Administration and management	60

Note. Packaging materials are used in re-packing each cubic metre of product for John Ltd, George Ltd and Paul Ltd in the ratio 1:2:3 respectively. This ratio is linked to the relative fragility of the goods for each customer.

Additional information has been obtained in order to enable unit costs to be prepared for each of the three customers using an activity based costing approach. The additional information for the year to 30 June 20X3 has been estimated as follows.

(i)   Labour and overhead costs have been identified as attributable to each of three work centres – receipt and inspection, storage and packing as follows:

	Cost allocation proportions		
	Receipt and inspection %	*Storage* %	*Packing* %
Labour – basic	15	10	75
– overtime	50	15	35
Occupancy	20	60	20
Administration and management	40	10	50

(ii)   Studies have revealed that the fragility of different goods affects the receipt and inspection time needed for the products for each customer. Storage required is related to the average size of the basic incoming product units from each customer. The re-packing of goods for distribution is related to the complexity of packaging required by each customer. The relevant requirements per cubic metre of product for each customer have been evaluated as follows.

	John Ltd	*George Ltd*	*Paul Ltd*
Receipt and inspection (minutes)	5	9	15
Storage (square metres)	0.3	0.3	0.2
Packing (minutes)	36	45	60

Required

(a) Calculate the budgeted average cost per cubic metre of packaged products for each customer for each of the following circumstances:

   (i) where only the basic budget information is to be used

   (ii) where the additional information enables an activity-based costing approach to be applied.

(b) Comment on the activities and cost drivers which have been identified as relevant for the implementation of activity based costing by Repak Ltd and discuss ways in which activity-based costing might improve product costing and cost control in Repak Ltd. Make reference to your answer to part (a) of the question, as appropriate.

4 Target costing and target pricing

4.1 Introduction

The use of activity-based methods has been discussed in the previous section of this chapter. The aim of the present section is to show how such methods can be extended to develop a system of target costing and target pricing.

A target cost is defined as 'a product cost estimate derived by subtracting a desired profit margin from a competitive market price [the target price]. This may be less than the planned initial product cost, but will be expected to be achieved by the time the product reaches the mature production stage'. (*Management Accounting Official Terminology*, CIMA, 1996).

In other words, managers set a target selling price by reference to their assessment of the market. They then work backwards to calculate what production cost must be achieved in order to earn a desired level of profit. This is the opposite of traditional cost-plus pricing, in which production costs are regarded as a 'given' and managers add a mark-up to arrive at a price that may or may not be acceptable to customers.

We show how this works by means of the following extended illustration, which also exemplifies the activity-based principles explained in the previous section.

4.2 Scenario

GB Ltd assembles and tests electronic instrument products including printed-circuit boards (PCBs). Two types of PCBs are produced: PCBA and PCBB. The following budgeted data is available on the assembly and testing of each product.

	PCBA	PCBB
Machine fitted parts per board	70	90
Manually fitted parts per board	10	30
Test hours per board	1.5 hrs	2.5 hrs
Direct labour hours per board	2.5 hrs	4.5 hrs
Budgeted production (boards)	750	2,000

Total budgeted production overhead is estimated to be £565,000 for the period. The existing management accounting information system absorbs production overhead on the basis of budgeted direct labour hours (DLH).

The predetermined overhead recovery rate is established as follows.

	PCBA	PCBB
DLH per unit	2.5 hrs	4.5 hrs
Budgeted production	750 boards	2,000 boards
Total DLH	1,875 hrs	9,000 hrs

Overhead recovery rate	=	Total overhead / Total DLH
	=	£565,000 / 10,875
	=	£51.95 per DLH

Using this system gives the following budgeted production overhead per board:

PCBA	=	2.5 × £51.95 = £130 (rounded)
PCBB	=	4.5 × £51.95 = £234 (rounded)

Miss Harrison, a newly qualified accountant employed by GB Ltd, suggests that an 'ABA system would produce a more accurate product cost per unit and this information is essential in today's competitive environment'. The Managing Director, Mr Chenng, requests Miss Harrison to detail the steps required in setting up an ABA system. The following memo was sent to Mr Chenng for his consideration.

MEMO

To : Mr Chenng

From : Miss Harrison

Date : 7 December 20XX

Establishing an activity-based accounting system

Step 1 — Prepare an inventory of activities

An activity analysis is undertaken with the objective of eliminating non-value activities. Costs are managed in the long term by controlling the activities which drive them. The aim is to control the causes of cost (cost drivers).

Step 2 — Determine the cost drivers

The factors which influence the cost of a particular activity are identified. The term cost driver is used to describe the factors that are the determinants of the cost of activities.

Step 3 — Establish a cost pool for each activity

A cost pool is a grouping of individual costs for each activity.

Step 4 — Trace the cost of activities to products

The costs of activities are traced to products on the basis of the product's demand for these activities.

Signed :

Date:

4.3 Implementing an activity-based system

It was decided that an ABA system should be implemented within GB Ltd. The following steps were undertaken:

Step 1 — Prepare an inventory of activities

The following value added activities were identified in the production of PCBA and PCBB.

1   *Material handling* All the parts necessary for constructing the PCBs are combined into a kit.

2   *Machine fitted parts* Automated machines fit components onto the board.

3   *Manually fitted parts* Operatives fit components onto the board.

4   *Soldering* Automated machines solder all fitted parts onto the board.

5   *Product testing* All boards are tested to ensure that products conform to quality standards.

6   *CAM* The computer aided manufacturing system controls the automated machines once programmed by the computer operatives.

Step 2 — Determine the cost drivers

	Activity	Cost driver
1	Material handling	Number of parts
2	Machine fitted parts	Number of machine parts
3	Manually fitted parts	Number of manually fitted parts
4	Soldering	Number of PCBs
5	Product testing	Number of hours on test
6	CAM	Number of PCBs

Step 3 — Establish a cost pool for each activity

	Activity	Cost driver	Cost pool
1	Material handling	Number of parts	£150,000
2	Machine fitted parts	Number of machine parts	£58,125
3	Manually fitted parts	Number of manually fitted parts	£135,000
4	Soldering	Number of PCBs	£41,250
5	Product testing	Number of hours on test	£153,125
6	CAM	Number of PCBs	£27,500

Step 4 — Trace the cost of activities to products

Costs are traced to each product using the following drivers.

Material handling	=	Budgeted overhead / Total number of parts
	=	£150,000 / 300,000 = £0.50 per part

Machine fitted parts	=	Budgeted overhead / Total number of machine parts
	=	£58,125 / 232,500 = £0.25 per part

Manually fitted parts	=	Budgeted overhead / Total number of manually fitted parts
	=	£135,000 / 67,500 = £2 per part

Soldering	=	Budgeted overhead / Total number of PCBs
	=	£41,250 / 2,750 = £15 per board
Product testing	=	Total overhead / Total number of hours on test
	=	£153,125 / 6,125 = £25 per hour
CAM	=	Total overhead / Total number of PCBs
	=	£27,500 / 2,750 = £10 per board

Overheads are traced to each product using the cost drivers as follows.

	PCBA £	PCBB £
Material handling 0.5 × 80 / 120	40	60
Machine fitted parts 0.25 × 70 / 90	17.5	22.5
Manually fitted parts 2 × 10 / 30	20	60
Soldering 15 × 1 / 1	15	15
Product testing 25 × 1.5 / 2.5	37.5	62.5
CAM 10 × 1 / 1	10	10
Total production overhead per board	140	230

A comparison of the overhead cost per board shows the following:

	PCBA	PCBB
Overhead per board:		
Traditional approach	£130	£234
ABA approach	£140	£230

The ABA approach should result in a more accurate production overhead product cost. In today's competitive environment, information for control and decision making needs to be as accurate as possible.

4.4   Target costing and pricing

The ABA system could be used to gain a competitive advantage by developing the system further into a target costing and pricing system for new products.

The key characteristics of a target costing and pricing system are as follows.

♦   Product costs are determined by market price requirements.

♦   A target price is determined by marketing management — set to achieve a desired level of market share.

♦   The organisation can examine the design specification for each product and the production methods in order to look for ways in which costs may be reduced without impairing the acceptability of the products to customers.

The development of the ABA system within GB Ltd is now considered.

4.5 Illustration

GB Ltd is considering the launch of a new car alarm system (CAS). Market research indicates that customers would be prepared to pay £700 per system. Product designers produced a prototype specification for CAS-MOD1 and the cost drivers previously established resulted in the following costings.

		CAS-MOD1 £
1	Material handling 209 parts × £0.5	104.50
2	Machine fitted parts 142 parts × £0.25	35.50
3	Manually fitted parts 67 parts × £2	134.00
4	Soldering 1 PCB × £15	15.00
5	Product testing 5.8 hrs × £25	145.00
6	CAM 1 PCB × £10	10.00
Production overhead per system		£444.00

Direct material and labour costs are estimated to be £200 per system resulting in a total cost of £644. Given a market price of £700 per system, management are not happy with the expected profit margin of £56 per system. The product designers within GB Ltd have been asked to re-design CAS-MOD1 with the objective of increasing the profit margin per system.

The product design team produced the following specification for CAS-MOD2 and believe that the quality will be superior to the CAS-MOD1.

		CAS-MOD2 £
1	Material handling 169 parts × £0.5	84.50
2	Machine fitted parts 138 parts × £0.25	34.50
3	Manually fitted parts 31 parts × £2	62.00
4	Soldering 1 PCB × £15	15.00
5	Product testing 3.6 hrs × £25	90.00
6	CAM 1 PCB × £10	10.00
Production overhead per system		£296.00

Direct material and labour costs are also estimated to be £200 per system resulting in a total cost of £496 per system. The management of GB Ltd are happy with a profit margin of £204 per system and agree to launch the new product within the next six months.

The conclusion is that organisations need to develop accounting information systems to help them gain a competitive advantage. Cost plus pricing systems are not deemed to be 'strategic' in the sense that no account is taken of the external environment facing the enterprise.

Practice question 6 (The answer is in the final chapter of this book)

Sapu

Sapu plc make and sell a number of products. Products A and B are products for which market prices are available at which Sapu plc can obtain a share of the market as detailed below. Estimated data for the forthcoming period is as follows.

(i)   Product data

	Product A	Product B	Other products
Production/sales (units)	5,000	10,000	40,000
Total direct material cost (£000)	80	300	2,020
Total direct labour cost (£000)	40	100	660

(ii)   Variable overhead cost is £1,500,000 of which 40% is related to the acquisition, storage and use of direct materials and 60% is related to the control and use of direct labour.

(iii)   It is current practice in Sapu plc to absorb variable overhead cost into product units using overall company wide percentages on direct material cost and direct labour cost as the absorption bases.

(iv)   Market prices for Products A and B are £75 and £95 per unit respectively.

(v)   Sapu plc require a minimum estimated contribution: sales ratio of 40% before proceeding with the production/sale of any product.

Required

(a)   Prepare estimated unit product costs for Product A and Product B where variable overhead is charged to product units as follows:

   (i)   using the existing absorption basis as detailed above.

   (ii)   using an activity based costing approach where cost drivers have been estimated for material and labour related overhead costs as follows:

	Product A	Product B	Other products
Direct material related overheads — cost driver is material bulk. The bulk proportions per unit are:	4	1	1.5
Direct labour related overheads — cost driver is number of labour operations (not directly time related). Labour operations per product unit are:	6	1	2

(b)   Prepare an analysis of the decision strategy which Sapu plc may implement with regard to the production and sale of Products A and B. Use unit costs as calculated in (a) (i) and (a)(ii) together with other information given in the question in your analysis. Your answers should include relevant calculations and discussion and be prepared in a form suitable for presentation to management.

(c)   Explain how Sapu plc could make use of target costing in conjunction with activity-based costing with respect to Products A and B.

(d)   If spare production capacity exists in Sapu plc, comment on the relevance of the present decision criterion of a minimum contribution: sales ratio of 40%.

5 Zero-based budgeting

Zero-based budgeting (ZBB) is a cost justification technique first developed by Texas Instruments, which is of particular use in controlling the costs of service departments and overheads. It does not simply look at last year's budget and add or subtract a little, but starts 'from scratch' each time a budget is prepared. It is particularly applicable for service cost centres, for non-product costs.

ZBB involves:

♦ developing decision packages for each company activity;
♦ evaluating and ranking these packages; and
♦ allocating resources to the various activities accordingly.

Decision packages include the following information.

♦ The function of the activity or department. This sets out the minimum goals that it must achieve.

♦ The goal of the department. This details the aim of the department — what it would like to achieve.

♦ The measure of the performance of the department.

♦ The costs and benefits associated with different ways of organising the department (at different levels of funding).

♦ The consequence of non-performance of the activity or department.

Advantages of ZBB are as follows.

♦ It establishes minimum requirements for service departments, ranks departments, and allocates resources.

♦ It produces a plan to work to when more resources are available.

♦ It makes managers think about what they are doing.

♦ It can be done annually, quarterly, or when crises are envisaged.

Disadvantages of ZBB are as follows.

♦ It takes up a good deal of management time and so may not be used every year.

♦ It generates a great deal of paper, requires education and training, and results may be initially disappointing.

♦ It is costly.

Most budgets are prepared on an incremental basis. In other words, they are based on last time's figures plus/minus an incremental amount to cover inflation, etc. However, this technique has the obvious disadvantage of perpetuating poor spending control. As an alternative, zero-based or priority-based budgeting may be employed.

Practice question 7 *(The answer is in the final chapter of this book)*

Energy costs

Energy costs may include the following items in a company which manufactures and sells products.

♦ Maintaining a statutory temperature range in the workplace
♦ The operation of a specially humidified materials store
♦ Power costs per unit of output
♦ Power costs in the movement of raw materials and work in progress
♦ Losses from steam pipelines and steam valves
♦ Heat losses through windows

Explain how management may be assisted in the implementation of an energy cost reduction strategy through the application of (a) zero-based budgeting and (b) total quality management. Your answers to (a) and (b) should refer to any THREE of the energy cost examples given in the question.

6   Just in time (JIT)

6.1   The concept of JIT

Just in time stock systems are in common use in many businesses now. They are an attempt to improve the efficiency of stock control systems, thus reducing cost. However, they are nothing revolutionary and can be viewed as an attempt to re-engineer the EOQ and re-order level systems already studied in this chapter.

We first revisit EOQ. JIT attempts to reduce stockholding costs. To do this, it is important to reduce stock levels as the main holding cost (the finance cost) is outside the control of the company. Reduced stock levels require smaller orders to be placed.

The problem with smaller orders is that they must be placed more frequently to satisfy demand. Any attempt to reduce holding costs will simply incur much higher ordering costs as we move away from the EOQ.

Realising this, advocates of JIT attempt to change the business practices so that the cost of placing orders is much reduced. This effectively reduces the EOQ size, with the result that both holding costs and ordering costs are cut considerably from the existing case.

The reduction in the cost of placing orders is achieved by the following steps.

♦ Office practices are streamlined so that the expense of raising order documents is reduced. Ideally ordering is carried out by phone or computer link only so paperwork is largely avoided.

♦ A part of ordering cost is delivery as this follows on from orders. By using local suppliers delivery charges are much reduced.

♦ After delivery, quality control inspections are carried out. Therefore quality control costs are still part of the ordering cost function. By using reliable suppliers with sound internal quality control procedures themselves, much of this inspection work can be avoided without risk to the company.

We now look again at re-order levels in the light of JIT. By using a low re-order level and therefore carrying few safety stocks, further holding costs can be avoided. However, as we know from previous studies, this would normally be unsatisfactory as stockout costs would rise alarmingly.

JIT considers why safety stocks are needed. We need safety stocks to deal firstly with uncertainty as to customer demand, and secondly with uncertainty as to supplier lead times.

JIT therefore takes steps to improve the situation in these areas, making low re-order levels optimal.

This is attempted as follows.

♦ Work closely with customers, so that customer demand is more accurately known. This reduces the need for safety stocks.

♦ Use suppliers who are nearby. This should reduce lead times considerably, reducing uncertainty, and hence the need for safety stocks.

♦ Use suppliers who are reliable. This means that lead times will be adhered to and further uncertainty removed, reducing the need for safety stocks further.

6.2 The results of JIT

The results of JIT are as follows:

♦ The cost of placing orders is vastly reduced.
♦ Lead times are shorter and less variable.
♦ Customer demand is more predictable.

This means, within the frameworks of our existing models, that small EOQs and low re-order levels are justified, thus leading to huge savings in stock-related costs.

There are problems with JIT however. JIT systems are heavily dependent on supplier reliability in terms of quality control and adherence to lead times. If this reliability fails, then disruption and stockouts occur at considerable expense.

JIT systems work best when a tied supplier relationship is formed. The company has the exclusive attention of its suppliers at all times as it is their only customer, and the tight working relationship between parties ensures the aims of JIT are achieved.

6.3 Learning outcomes

At this stage of the chapter we have now covered the following Learning Outcomes.

> Describe the modern business environment
> Compare and contrast alternative production and management strategies
> Compare and contrast value analysis and functional analysis
> Explain total quality management
> Prepare and discuss cost of quality reports

7 Throughput accounting

Throughput accounting, which can also be referred to as the 'Theory of Constraints (TOC)', focuses on organisational constraints or bottlenecks which restrict production.

The objective is to maximise output (or throughput) by converting raw materials to finished items as quickly as possible. These finished items are then despatched to customers as soon as possible (as in a JIT system).

7.1   Bottlenecks

The most important aspect of the theory of Throughput Accounting (TA) is that the speed of output of the factory is restricted to the speed of the bottleneck which is, in effect, the limiting factor or constraining resource. The objectives, therefore, are:

♦   Identify the bottleneck(s)

♦   Remove them, or reduce the extent to which they constrain activity.

7.2   Terminology

Throughput accounting uses three key terms:

Throughput contribution

Sales revenue – completely variable costs.

(Completely variable costs usually comprise direct materials **only** because labour costs usually include a fixed element).

Conversion costs

= all operating costs excluding completely variable costs incurred to produce the product.

Investment

= all types of stock, equipment costs, buildings costs etc.

The purpose of throughput accounting is to maximise throughput contribution whilst minimising conversion costs and investment.

7.3   Throughput per hour

One of the key measures of throughput is the ratio:

$$\frac{\text{Throughput contribution}}{\text{Time}}$$

which provides us with a value of throughput contribution per hour. By emphasising time as a key factor, managers' attention is drawn to areas of the business which reduce the speed of operations, ie bottlenecks.

This can be used in decision making by ranking products according to the time they spend using bottleneck resources.

To do this, the formula is modified thus:

$$\text{Product return per minute} \quad = \quad \frac{\text{Throughput contribution}}{\text{Minutes on bottleneck resource}}$$

7.4 Example

A company produces two products X and Y which have unit selling price and cost values as follows:

Product	X	Y
	£	£
Selling price	130	104
Direct materials	20	20
Direct labour	10	18
Variable overhead	10	18
Fixed overhead	10	18
	50	74
Profit	80	30

Fixed overhead costs are absorbed on the basis of direct labour costs. The direct labour cost is incurred at the rate of £20 per hour in respect of the time spent in the two processes.

Process	Product	
	X	Y
A	8 min	30 min
B	22 min	14 min
	30 min	44 min

The maximum process times available per week are as follows:

Process A	2000 minutes
Process B	800 minutes

Calculate the production plan to maximise profits.

7.5 Solution

The first step is to recognise that this is a limiting factor problem with two possible constraints: process A time and/or process B time.

Firstly consider the maximum numbers of product X and Y that can be produced:

	Product X	Product Y
Process A	$\dfrac{2000}{8} = 250$	$\dfrac{2000}{30} = 67$
Process B	$\dfrac{800}{22} = 36$	$\dfrac{800}{14} = 57$

As the maximum number of units of both products is limited by the time available in process B, we can see that process A is not an effective constraint.

The **traditional** approach to this type of problem is to use the contribution per process B minute to rank the products.

This gives:

$$\text{Product X} \quad = \quad \frac{£(130-20-10-10)}{22}$$

$$= \quad \frac{£90}{22} \quad = \quad £4.09 \text{ per minute}$$

$$\text{Product Y} \quad = \quad \frac{£(104-20-18-18)}{14}$$

$$= \quad \frac{£48}{14} \quad = \quad £3.43 \text{ per minute}$$

On this basis product X would be preferred.

If the same problem is considered using throughput contribution as the basis of ranking:

$$\text{Product X} \qquad \frac{£(130-20)}{22} \quad = \quad £5.00 \text{ per minute}$$

$$\text{Product Y} \qquad \frac{£(104-20)}{14} \quad = \quad £6.00 \text{ per minute}$$

On this basis product Y is preferred.

Clearly since the ranking basis changes the decision, they cannot both provide an optimum solution.

Which is correct? The answer depends on the variability of the labour and variable overhead cost. In the short term it is now more likely that the labour cost is fixed, so under these circumstances the throughput accounting approach probably provides the better solution.

7.6   Controlling costs

Whilst the measurement of throughput per hour is important, we must recognise the need to consider any costs associated with increasing the throughput.

To do this we use the throughput accounting ratio:

$$\frac{\text{Value added per time period}}{\text{Conversion cost per time period}}$$

where 'value added' equals 'sales less material costs' equals throughout contribution.

Traditional efficiency measures are no longer valid as they encourage production for stock. Instead efficiency is measured by:

$$\frac{\text{Standard minutes of throughput achieved}}{\text{Minutes available}}$$

7.7   Summary of throughput accounting

In principle there is little difference between throughput accounting and marginal costing, both relying on the contribution concept. However, they differ in their classification of labour and other costs.

8   Summary

In this chapter we have explained the effect of the modern business environment on accounting systems. It is now recognised that production of goods is not the purpose of businesses; the purpose is to satisfy customer wants by delivering quality products at an acceptable price. The past twenty years has seen the emphasis shift to quality and target pricing, away from producing the maximum quantity of goods which would be offered to the market at cost plus.

Multiple choice questions *(The answers are in the final chapter of this book)*

1   A travel company provides 7-day and 14-day package holidays. The expected cost data for the forthcoming period are as follows:

	7-day	14-day	Total £
Number of customers	350	120	
Variable cost	£76,000	£66,000	142,000
Fixed cost			58,000
Total expenses			200,000

What is the price per customer (to the nearest £) for 14-day holidays if the mark-up percentage over variable cost is twice that for 7-day holidays and the company wishes to achieve a target profit of £50,000?

A   £772
B   £828
C   £1,121
D   £1,872

2   A travel company provides 7-day and 14-day package holidays, details of which are as follows:

	7-day	14-day
Total direct cost	£50,000	£40,000
Sales	200 units	150 units

Indirect expenses amount to 40% of total costs (ie including indirect expenses) and the mark-up over direct costs for 14-day holidays is 50% more than the mark-up for 7-day holidays.

What is the unit price to the nearest £ for 7-day holidays, assuming that the company wishes to achieve a target profit of £40,000?

A   £341
B   £423
C   £432
D   £477

3   A company estimates indirect costs to be 40% of direct costs and its price to recover the full cost plus 50%.

What mark-up on direct costs would give rise to the same price strategy?

A   90%
B   110%
C   190%
D   210%

CHAPTER 7

Modern performance measures

EXAM FOCUS

This chapter builds upon your knowledge of the modern business environment, and considers the performance measures which are used.

LEARNING OUTCOMES

This chapter covers the following Learning Outcomes of the CIMA Syllabus.

> Prepare reports using a range of internal and external benchmarks and interpret the results
>
> Evaluate the balanced scorecard

In order to cover these Learning Outcomes the following topics are included.

> Non-financial performance indicators
> The balanced scorecard

---

1 Non-financial performance indicators

1.1 Measuring success and ensuring success

The academics H.T. Johnson and R.S. Kaplan (particularly in their book *Relevance Lost: The Rise and Fall of Management Accounting,* 1987) have developed a wide-ranging critique of traditional methods of management accounting. In particular, they believe that traditional methods are failing to give managers the information they need for effective decision making.

The declining relevance of traditional management accounting systems is attributed by Johnson and Kaplan to three failure types.

♦ *Use-type failure:* a failure to adopt flexible budgets, to evaluate discretionary expenditures or to adopt appropriate measures to control fixed costs.

♦ *Relevance-type failure:* a failure to develop quality control and factor productivity measures or to highlight opportunity costs.

♦ *Control-type failure:* a failure to consider non-financial factors, through undue emphasis devoted to short-term financial performance indicators and financial accounting considerations in most calculations.

In each case, there is a need for non-financial indicators (NFIs) as measures which improve the decision usefulness of management accounting information and facilitate evaluation and control. The following table gives a range of NFIs encompassing production, marketing and customer-oriented aspects.

	Focus of measurement	Non-financial indicators (NFI)	
Input	Quality of purchased components	1	Proportion of defects
	Quantity of raw material inputs	2	Actual v target units
Work	Equipment productivity	3	Actual v standard units
	Equipment failure	4	Downtime/total time
		5	Time between failures
	Maintenance effort	6	Time between overhauls
		7	Time spent on repeat work
		8	Mean time to effect repairs
		9	Total time in backlog jobs
		10	Number of production units lost through maintenance
		11	Number of repeat jobs
		12	Number of backlog jobs
		13	Number of failures in planned jobs prior to schedule
		14	% failures: planned/unplanned jobs
		15	Preventive maintenance/total maintenance
		16	Corrective maintenance/total maintenance
		17	Breakdown maintenance/total maintenance
	Overtime	18	Overtime hours/total hours
	Waste	19	% faulty items
		20	% scrap
		21	% rework
	Throughput	22	Production rate achieved
	Production flexibility	23	Set-up time
	Product complexity	24	Number of component parts
Product	Quantity of output	25	Actual units
		26	% completion: actual v target
	Quality of output	27	% yield
		28	Index of key product characteristics
	Safety	29	Serious industrial injury rate (SIIR)
	Reliability	30	Warranty claims/costs
	Availability	31	% stockouts
	Obsolescence	32	% shrinkage
	Commitment to quality	33	% dependence on post-inspection
		34	% conformance to quality standards
Market	Market share	35	Local/domestic/world volume
	Market leadership	36	% R & D expenditure
		37	% new production innovation
	Growth	38	% increase in market share
		39	New clients/total clients
	Strengths	40	Index of competitive value
	Competition	41	Index of vulnerability
Employees	Employee skills	42	Index of educational attainment
		43	% training costs
		44	% staff turnover lost to competitors
		45	Age/experience profiles
	Employee morale	46	% absenteeism
		47	Cost of employee downtime
		48	% Leadership impact (eg cancelled meetings)
		49	New staff/total staff
		50	New support staff/total staff

	Focus of measurement	Non-financial indicators (NFI)	
	Employee productivity	51	Direct labour hours per unit
		52	Managed labour hours per unit
		53	Labour effectiveness $= \dfrac{\text{Standard hours achieved}}{\text{Total labour hours worked}}$
		54	Output efficiency $= \dfrac{\text{Output}}{\text{Payroll Cost}}$
Customers	Customer awareness	55	% approval rating
		56	% service calls/claims
		57	Number of complaints
		58	% repeat orders
	Timeliness	59	Number of overdue deliveries
		60	Mean delivery delay

It has been argued that financial performance measures such as ROI etc simply *measure success*. It is essential for businesses to set up non-financial performance measures since it is factors such as quality which *ensure success*.

In other words, in order for an organisation to achieve its objectives, critical success factors (CSFs) need to be identified and key activities need to be performed at a high level in these 'key factors'. The financial resource of an organisation should, therefore, be allocated behind the critical success factors.

This is illustrated in Figure 1.

Figure 1   Critical success factors

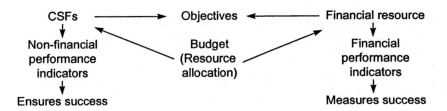

Figure 1 shows the need to establish both financial and non-financial performance evaluation systems. The 'circular flow' of resource through the budgetary control system should enable the organisation to achieve its objectives.

The circular sequence of events therefore becomes as follows.

♦   Set objectives and identify critical success factors to ensure that objectives are achieved. Set up NFIs around the CSFs.

♦   Allocate the financial resource around the key activities which are critical to the achievement of objectives. Set up financial performance indicators which measure the achievement of (success) financial objectives.

1.2 Operational performance control

A well-known saying in this context is that 'what you measure is what you get'. There is little doubt that if you measure, or reward, managers on budget achievement, profit performance or return on investment (ROI) ratios, that is what they will manage, or manipulate, their operations to achieve. Similarly, many standard cost variances can motivate sub-optimal behaviour: purchasing inferior materials, performing unwanted operations to improve volume or efficiency variances, and so on.

The conclusion from this analysis is to recommend a performance measurement system with two essential characteristics: firstly, it should derive in a direct causal line from strategic objectives, as in Figure 2.

Figure 2   From strategic objectives to performance indicators

In this schema the CSFs should be the three or four factors which are fundamental to the achievement of each particular strategic objective. KPIs translate the appraisal of CSF achievement into quantifiable measures.

Secondly, CSFs and KPIs should be multi-dimensional so as to reflect the full spectrum of strategic goals and to prevent managers from focusing on a single dimension to the neglect of others. In practice, this will mean that the strategies have to satisfy multiple criteria, eg EPS growth for shareholders, survival and security for employees and quality and service for customers.

1.3 The balanced scorecard

 Robert Kaplan and David Norton have suggested a balanced scorecard approach which combines financial measures with operational, organisational innovation and customer service measures: see Figure 3.

The balanced scorecard becomes the manager's instrument panel for managing the complexity of the organisation within a dynamic external environment.

The table included in Figure 3 is an example of a balanced scorecard performance management system which demonstrates the role of CSFs and KPIs in this process.

Figure 3   The balanced scorecard

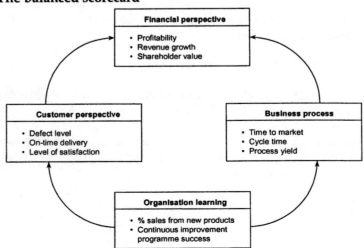

	Financial aspect	Customer aspect	Business process aspect	Organisational learning aspect
Strategic objective	Shareholder satisfaction	Customer satisfaction	Manufacturing excellence	New product innovation
Critical success factor	Grow shareholder wealth	Achieve preferred supplier status	State-of-the-art process plant	Successful new product development
Key performance indicators	Shareholder value annual growth %	Number of customer partnerships	Cycle times Unit cost % yield	% of sales represented by new products

A balanced scorecard performance management system

1.4 Example

The following illustration demonstrates the approach to calculating non-financial performance indicators for management control and decision making.

EVCO plc produces and sells a single product by passing a single raw material through three consecutive production processes; making, converting and finishing. A system of standard process costing is in operation for which the following information is available for the period ended 30 April 20X6.

♦ Stocks are held at constant levels at the beginning and end of the period as follows: raw material (4,000 kg at £0.75 per kg); WIP-converting (500 units); WIP-finishing (500 units); finished goods (500 units).

♦ Process accounts are debited with the actual costs incurred for the period.

♦ All losses and transfers between processes or into finished goods are valued at standard cost at their stage of completion. Such unit standard costs may be determined from the information in Table A below.

♦ WIP in converting and finishing is held at the beginning of each process.

♦ The units transferred into finished goods will eventually comprise free replacements to customers, finished goods stock losses and the balance as net sales to customers.

Table B shows the summary profit and loss account for the period ended 30 April 20X6 showing budget and actual analysis of gross profit/(loss).

Information relevant to the profit and loss account is as follows.

♦ Free replacements to customers and finished goods stock losses are valued at standard cost per unit.

♦ The price reduction penalty is allowable on goods delivered late to customers at 5% of the normal selling price of £30 per unit.

EVCO plc presently relies on the variances (£) reported in its standard process system as its main source of control information.

Table A
EVCO plc: Standard process accounts for the period ended 30 April 20X6

	Making process Product units	£	Converting process Product units	£	Finishing process Product units	£
Debit						
WIP brought forward			500	7,909	500	10,054
Transfers from previous process			6,800	107,563	6,025	121,156
Raw material cost	8,000	96,000				
Conversion costs		18,800		30,100		14,390
	8,000	114,800	7,300	145,572	6,525	145,600
Credit						
Normal losses	800		504		298	
Transfers to next process	6,800	107,563	6,025	121,156	5,365	124,655
WIP damage (written off)			75	1,186	60	1,207
Abnormal process losses	400	6,327	196	3,934	302	6,822
Residual variance		910		11,387		2,862
WIP, carried forward			500	7,909	500	10,054
	8,000	114,800	7,300	145,572	6,525	145,600

Table B
EVCO plc: Summary profit and loss account for the period ended 30 April 20X6

	Actual £	Actual £	Budget £	Budget £
Sales revenue		145,050		150,000
Less standard cost of sales		112,341		116,175
Standard contribution		32,709		33,825
WIP damage losses	2,393		1,437	
Finished goods losses	697		232	
Abnormal losses	17,083			
Residual process variances	15,159			
Free replacements to customers	11,617		4,832	
Price reduction penalty	1,160		750	
Raw material stock damage losses	240		120	
		48,349		7,371
Gross profit/(loss)		(15,640)		26,454

Prepare a report for the period ended 30 April 20X6 to the management team of EVCO plc which:

(a)   details the factors which have contributed to the poor performance of EVCO plc

(b)   expresses budget and actual levels (units and percentage) for each of the following as examples of non-financial indicators of performance:

♦   free replacements to customers (compared to units delivered)
♦   late deliveries to customers (against net sales units)
♦   finished goods stock losses (compared to stock level).

(Show all relevant workings)

1.5   Solution

(Note that the answer is produced in report format. Note also that there is a lot of data in the illustration which is irrelevant for the calculations. You will be expected to 'sift' through this type of data and use what you think is appropriate.)

EVCO plc   **Report to management team**

Subject: Performance measurement

(a)   The accounting information for the period ended 30 April 20X6 highlights a number of major problems as follows.

♦   Deteriorating profit levels with an actual loss of £15,640 instead of a budget profit of £26,454

♦   Reduction in sales volume of approximately 3.5%

♦   High levels of process losses as indicated by high abnormal losses written off

♦   High levels of losses to raw materials, WIP and finished goods

♦   High levels of residual process variances which probably indicate poor levels of productivity and high idle time

♦   Likely customer dissatisfaction through high replacement of faulty units and late deliveries.

(b)   Customer dissatisfaction may be due to high level of faulty goods and late deliveries which may be worsened by losses of finished goods before delivery. The following budget and actual figures apply.

	Budget	*Actual*
Free replacement (as percentage of sales delivered)	208/5,208 = 4%	500/5,335 = 9.4%
Late deliveries (as percentage of net sales)	500/5,000 = 10%	773/4,835 = 16%
Finished goods stock losses (as percentage of stock)	10/500 = 2%	30/500 = 6%

(*Note.* The units in the above calculations are obtained from Table B values (£) using £23.235 as unit valuation and a price penalty reduction value of £1.50 per unit as appropriate.

Eg   Actual finished goods losses = £697/23.235 = 30 units
          Budget late deliveries = £750/1.50 = 500 units).

Practice question 1 *(The answer is in the final chapter of this book)*

Critical success factors

(a) Explain the meaning and relevance of the term 'critical success factors' in a business, giving examples of such factors.

(b) If productivity is seen as a critical success factor in a manufacturing environment, suggest ways in which the management accountant should check that adequate control is being exercised over productivity measurement and over its use as a control mechanism.

2 Service businesses

2.1 Introduction

The problems of measuring performance are particularly acute in service businesses, mainly because the 'output' is intangible.

2.2 Six-factor scorecard

Fitzgerald et al argue for a six factor scorecard which separates the *results* of action (measures of success) from the *determination* of those results (ensure success). Thus, quality of service, flexibility, resource utilisation and innovation represent the means whereby competitive success is achieved.

The following table illustrates the type of performance measure which could be used to control the level of performance in each area.

	Dimensions of performance	Types of measures
Results	Competitiveness	Relative market share and position Sales growth Measures of the customer base
	Financial performance	Cashflows Shareholder value Gearing Market ratios
Determinants	Quality of service	Reliability Responsiveness Aesthetics/appearance Cleanliness/tidiness Comfort Friendliness Communication Courtesy Competence Access Availability Security
	Flexibility	Volume flexibility Delivery speed flexibility Specification flexibility
	Resource utilisation	Productivity Efficiency
	Innovation	Performance of the innovation process Performance of individual innovations

Practice question 2 *(The answer is in the final chapter of this book)*

BS

BS Ltd provides consultancy services to small and medium sized businesses. Three types of consultants are employed offering administrative, data processing and marketing advice respectively. The consultants work partly on the client's premises and partly in BS Ltd premises, where chargeable development work in relation to each client contract will be undertaken. Consultants spend some time negotiating with potential clients attempting to secure contracts from them. BS Ltd has recently implemented a policy change which allows for a number of follow-up (remedial) hours at the client's premises after completion of the contract in order to eliminate any problems which have arisen in the initial stages of operation of the system. Contract negotiation and remedial work hours are not charged directly to each client. BS Ltd carries out consultancy for new systems and also offers advice on existing systems which a client may have introduced before BS Ltd became involved. BS Ltd has a policy of retaining its consultancy staff at a level of 60 consultants on an ongoing basis.

Additional information for the year ended 30 April 20X5 is as follows.

♦   BS Ltd invoices clients at £75 per chargeable consultant hour.

♦   Consultant salaries are budgeted at an average per consultant of £30,000 per annum. Actual salaries include a bonus for hours in excess of budget paid for at the budgeted average rate per hour.

♦   Sundry operating costs (other than consultant salaries) were budgeted at £3,500,000. Actual was £4,100,000.

♦   BS Ltd capital employed (start year) was £6,500,000.

♦   Table 1 shows an analysis of sundry budgeted and actual quantitative data.

Required

(a)   (i)   Prepare an analysis of actual consultancy hours for the year ended 30 April 20X5 which shows the increase or decrease from the standard/allowed non chargeable hours. This increase or decrease should be analysed to show the extent to which it may be shown to be attributable to a change from standard in:

        (1)   standard chargeable hours
        (2)   remedial advice hours
        (3)   contract negotiation hours
        (4)   other non–chargeable hours.

      (ii)   Calculate the total value of each of (1) to (4) in (a) (i) above in terms of chargeable client income per hour.

(b)   BS Ltd measure business performance in a number of ways. For each of the undernoted measures, comment on the performance of BS Ltd using quantitative data from the question and your answer to (a) to assist in illustrating your answer:

      (i)   Financial performance
      (ii)   Competitive performance
     (iii)   Quality of service
     (iv)   Flexibility
      (v)   Resource utilisation
     (vi)   Innovation.

Table 1
BS Ltd
Sundry statistics for year ended 30 April 20X5

	Budget	Actual
Number of consultants		
Administration	30	23
Data processing	12	20
Marketing	18	17
Consultants hours analysis		
Contract negotiation hours	4,800	9,240
Remedial advice hours	2,400	7,920
Other non-chargeable hours	12,000	22,440
General development work hours (chargeable)	12,000	6,600
Customer premises contract hours	88,800	85,800
Gross hours	120,000	132,000
Chargeable hours analysis		
New systems	70%	60%
Existing systems advice	30%	40%
Number of clients enquiries received		
New systems	450	600
Existing systems advice	400	360
Number of client contracts worked on		
New systems	180	210
Existing systems advice	300	288
Number of client complaints	5	20
Contracts requiring remedial advice	48	75

2.3 Learning outcomes

At this stage of the chapter we have now covered the following Learning Outcomes.

Prepare reports using a range of internal and external benchmarks and interpret the results

Evaluate the balanced scorecard.

3 Summary

Performance measurement is an important aspect of management control. Whatever measurement system is adopted, one of the objectives should be to achieve goal congruence. This means motivating managers to take decisions that benefit the organisation in the long term as well as benefiting themselves.

In service businesses the problems of performance measurement are particularly acute. The use of non-financial performance indicators has been an important feature in this sector in recent years, and the concept of a 'balanced scorecard' has won wide acceptance in both service and manufacturing contexts.

Multiple choice questions *(The answers are in the final chapter of this book)*

1   Which of the following is not a non-financial indicator?

    A   Actual number of units produced
    B   Time spent repairing machines
    C   Cost of overtime per month
    D   Number of new clients achieved

2   Which of the following is not a perspective examined in Kaplan's balanced scorecard approach?

    A   Employee perspective
    B   Financial perspective
    C   Internal business process perspective
    D   Customer perspective

3   Why is performance measurement particularly difficult in service businesses?

    A   Low profitability
    B   Intangibility of output
    C   Accounting standards are not applicable
    D   Lack of objectives

CHAPTER 8

Accounting for overheads

EXAM FOCUS

Basic overhead costing is covered in Management Accounting Fundamentals but is expanded upon here, and contrasted with ABC.

We have already covered activity-based costing (ABC) in an earlier chapter, but study it now specifically in relation to the treatment of overheads.

LEARNING OUTCOMES

This chapter covers the following Learning Outcomes of the CIMA Syllabus.

> Prepare and discuss a report which reconciles budget and actual profit using absorption and/or marginal costing principles

In order to cover these Learning Outcomes the following topics are included.

> Traditional overhead costing
> Service departments in traditional overhead costing
> Activity-based costing
> Marginal v Absorption costing

1 Traditional overhead costing

1.1 Introduction

Many of the costs incurred by an organisation are easily related to the outputs produced by the organisation. For example, a manufacturer of Product X may use two kilos of Material Q for every unit of X produced. The cost of Material Q is a direct cost of Product X.

However, the manufacturer will also incur many *indirect* (overhead) costs that are not so easily related to units of output. For example, suppose that the cost of factory rental is £50,000 per year.

How is this cost to be attributed to the many units of Product X (and Product Y and Product Z...) produced in the year?

The technique that has been in use since the introduction of cost accounting in industry is described below.

The aim of the technique is ultimately to calculate the overhead cost of products.

First the factory organisation is split into logical departments or *cost centres* to structure the approach.

Typical cost centres could be machining, assembly, finishing, painting, lathing, turning.

 In exam questions the production or factory cost centres will already have been selected in the question for you.

1.2   The traditional approach

 The traditional approach is sometimes referred to as the 3 As system.

- Allocation
- Apportionment
- Absorption

From a list of factory overheads it is often possible to *allocate* many to production cost centres directly. The salaries of supervisors can often be allocated as the cost accountant will know which supervisors work in which departments. The examiner will already have indicated which overheads are to be allocated to which departments for you.

Once any allocated overheads are dealt with any remaining overheads are those that relate to more than one department. These must be *apportioned* to the departments on some sensible basis.

 In exam questions the question will give hints as to the basis of apportionment. Sometimes percentages will be given or in more complicated questions a sensible basis of apportionment must be selected from the statistics given in the question.

The following table shows some typical bases of apportionment that have appeared in costing questions down the years.

Overhead	Apportionment basis
Factory rent	Floor area
Machine insurance	Number of machines
	Value of machines
Canteen costs	Number of employees
Light and heat	Floor area
Materials handling	Quantity of material handled
	Number of times material handled

Once a basis of apportionment has been selected a simple ratio is then calculated.

Illustration

Factory rent	£50,000

Production departments	Floor area (m^2)
Machining	20,000
Assembly	30,000
Finishing	50,000

The factory rent overhead will be apportioned in the ratio 20 : 30 : 50 or, simplifying, 2 : 3 : 5.

Thus the overhead cost sheet would bear the following.

	Machining	Assembly	Finishing	Total
Factory rent (2 : 3 : 5) (Floor area)	£10,000	£15,000	£25,000	£50,000

After the overheads have been allocated and apportioned to the production cost centres the overhead must then be related to a level of the activity of each department. We can then calculate an overhead *absorption* rate for each department.

In exam questions an activity measure may be given or you may have to select one from the statistics available.

The most common absorption rates are direct labour hours and machine hours.

1.3   Example

	Production departments	
	Machining	Assembly
Budgeted overheads allocated and apportioned	£100,000	£75,000
Budgeted hours:		
Labour hours	10,000	37,500
Machine hours	200,000	25,000

1.4   Solution

For the machining department the dominant activity measure is machine hours so a machine hour rate will be calculated as follows.

Overhead absorption rate (machining department) $=$ $\dfrac{£100,000}{200,000}$

$=$ 50p per machine hour

This means that if a product requires one hour of work in the machining department we attribute 50p of overhead cost to that product.

For the assembly department the dominant activity measure is labour hours so a labour hour rate will be calculated.

Overhead absorption rate (assembly department) $=$ $\dfrac{£75,000}{37,500}$

$=$ £2 per direct labour hour

As an example, a product that requires 30 minutes of work in the assembly department would absorb £1 of overhead cost. This of course is in addition to the direct cost of the product and any overhead absorbed by the product in other departments.

Note that in traditional overhead costing there is only one absorption rate per department.

Throughout this process, we normally work with budgeted overhead figures to provide feedback control information to management. However, it can alternatively be done after the event using *actual* data.

An exam question could stop with calculation of absorption rates. However, the end result is calculation of an overhead cost for a product.

Thus to finish off we follow a product through its production process, absorbing overhead as it goes using the overhead absorption rates already calculated.

1.5 Example

Product X is produced in two departments: A and B.

Overhead absorption rates are:

Department A : £3 per direct labour hour
Department B : £1.40 per machine hour

One unit of Product X is expected to take the following times in the production departments.

Time in Department A

Labour hours	1 hour
Machine hours	½ hour

Time in Department B

Labour hours	1 hour
Machine hours	2½ hours

Required

Calculate the total overhead absorbed per unit of Product X.

1.6 Solution

			£
Department		A	
1 direct labour hour @ £3 per hour			3.00
Department		B	
2½ machine hours @ £1.40 per hour			3.50
Total overhead absorbed by one unit of Product X			6.50

If the above calculations were based on budgeted figures (as is normal) then the overhead figure of £6.50 per unit would be added to the materials and direct labour cost per unit to form the fully absorbed standard cost of a unit of Product X.

Practice question 1 (The answer is in the final chapter of this book)

Luda

Luda Ltd manufactures three products known as P, Q and R. Each product is started in the machining area and completed in the finishing shop. The direct costs associated with each product forecast for the next trading period are as follows.

	P	Q	R
	£	£	£
Materials	18.50	15.00	22.50
Wages			
Machining area at £5 per hour	10.00	5.00	10.00
Finishing shop at £4 per hour	6.00	4.00	8.00
	34.50	24.00	40.50

There are machines in both departments. Machine hours required to complete one of each product, budgeted output and fixed overheads are as follows.

	P	Q	R
Machine area (hours per unit)	4	1.5	3
Finishing shop (hours per unit)	0.5	0.5	1
Budget output in units	6,000	8,000	2,000
Fixed overheads			
Machine area			£100,800
Finishing shop			£94,500

Required

(a)   Calculate the overhead absorption rate for fixed overheads using:

   (i)   a labour hour rate for each department,
   (ii)   a machine hour rate for each department.

(b)   Calculate the total cost of each product using:

   (i)   the labour hour rate,
   (ii)   the machine hour rate, as calculated in (a) above.

(c)   Set out your comments to the factory manager who has suggested that one overhead rate for both departments would simplify matters.

2   Service departments in traditional overhead costing

2.1   The problem of accounting for service department overheads

A service department in these questions is a part of the factory organisation that provides services to the production departments. Product units pass through production cost centres but not through service departments.

Typical service departments in exam questions are the factory canteen, machine maintenance department and materials handling departments.

In exam questions the required service centres will be indicated in the question.

As with production cost centres the budgeted overheads must be allocated and apportioned to the service cost centres as relevant using a suitable basis of apportionment.

Before absorption rates are calculated for the production cost centres the service department overhead must be re-apportioned between the production departments. The aim is to remove overhead costs from the service departments and re-locate them in production departments. That way, we ensure that all overheads are picked up as the products make their way through the production process.

The re-apportionment of service department overheads between production departments is carried out using the most sensible statistic available in the question.

When there is a single service department the re-apportionment is relatively straightforward.

2.2 Example

| | Production departments | | Service department |
	Machining	Assembly	Canteen
Overheads allocated and apportioned	£50,000	£70,000	£10,000
Number of employees	15	40	2

2.3 Solution

The most sensible basis of apportionment is the number of employees using the canteen. The two employees in the canteen itself are ignored as the aim is to remove the overhead from the service departments.

Therefore the canteen overhead will be re-apportioned in the ratio 15:40 (or, simplifying, 3 : 8) between the production departments.

The end result will be as follows.

| | Production department | | Service department |
	Machining £	Assembly £	Canteen £
Overheads allocated and apportioned	50,000	70,000	10,000
Re-apportion canteen costs (3 : 8) based on number of employees	2,727	7,273	(10,000)
Total overhead allocated and apportioned to production departments	52,727	77,273	–

Departmental absorption rates will now be calculated as described earlier.

2.4 Additional complications

When there is more than one service department additional complications can arise. The first is the possibility of a single cross-service. This means that one service department does work for another service department, but not *vice versa*.

The approach here is to re-apportion the service department overheads of the department providing the cross–service first so no great difficulties arise.

2.5 Example

| | Production departments | | Service departments | |
	Machining	Assembly	Canteen	Maintenance
Overheads allocated and apportioned	£50,000	£70,000	£10,000	£20,000
Number of employees	15	40	2	5
Number of maintenance call outs	150	50	-	-

2.6 Solution

In this case the maintenance people use the canteen but the maintenance department does not work for the canteen. It is therefore appropriate to re-apportion the canteen costs first, once again ignoring the employees in the canteen itself.

	Production departments		Service departments	
	Machining £	Assembly £	Canteen £	Maintenance £
Overheads	50,000	70,000	10,000	20,000
Re-apportion canteen (number of employees 15:40:0:5 or 3:8:0:1)	2,500	6,667	(10,000)	833
Subtotal	52,500	76,667	-	20,833
Re-apportion maintenance (number of call outs 150:50 or 3:1)	15,625	5,208	-	(20,833)
Total overhead allocated and apportioned to production departments	68,125	81,875	-	-

2.7   The repeated distribution method

A greater complication arises when the service departments do work for each other. This is known as *reciprocal services*. The most common approach for dealing with this is the *repeated distribution method*. The service department overheads are re-apportioned until the numbers become small so the cross–service is finally disregarded as immaterial to finish the computation off.

2.8   Example

	Production departments		Service departments	
	Machining	Assembly	Canteen	Maintenance
Overheads allocated and apportioned	£50,000	£70,000	£10,000	£20,000
Number of employees	15	40	2	5
Number of maintenance call outs	150	50	25	-

2.9   Solution

Here the maintenance department employees use the canteen and also do work for the canteen so a reciprocal services situation is present.

	Production departments		Service departments	
	Machining £	Assembly £	Canteen £	Maintenance £
Overheads	50,000	70,000	10,000	20,000
Re-apportion canteen 3:8:0:1	2,500	6,667	(10,000)	833
Subtotal	52,500	76,667	-	20,833
Re-apportion maintenance (150:50:25:0 or 6:2:1:0)	13,889	4,630	2,314	(20,833)
Subtotal	66,389	81,297	2,314	-
Re-apportion canteen (3:8:0:1)	578	1,543	(2,314)	193
Subtotal	66,967	82,840	-	193

Re-apportion maintenance 15:50:0:0 or 3:1	145	48	-	(193)
Total overheads in production departments	67,112	82,888	-	-

When the overhead remaining in the maintenance department falls to £193 it is sensible to stop the process of repeated distribution and simply charge the whole £193 to the two production departments.

Practice questions 2 and 3 *(The answers are in the final chapter of this book)*

2   Cross-services

A company is preparing its production overhead budgets and determining the apportionment of these overheads to products.

Cost centre expenses and related information have been budgeted as follows:

	Total	Machine shop A	Machine shop B	Assembly	Canteen	Maintenance
Indirect wages (£)	78,560	8,586	9,190	15,674	29,650	15,460
Consumable materials (inc. maintenance) (£)	16,900	6,400	8,700	1,200	600	-
Rent and rates (£)	16,700					
Buildings insurance (£)	2,400					
Power (£)	8,600					
Heat and light (£)	3,400					
Depreciation of machinery (£)	40,200					
Area (sq ft)	45,000	10,000	12,000	15,000	6,000	2,000
Value of machinery (£)	402,000	201,000	179,000	22,000	-	-
Power usage – technical estimates (%)	100	55	40	3	-	2
Direct labour (hours)	35,000	8,000	6,200	20,800	-	-
Machine usage (hours)	25,200	7,200	18,000	-	-	-

Required

Determine budgeted overhead absorption rates for each of the production departments, using bases of apportionment and absorption which you consider most appropriate from the information provided.

3   Reciprocal services

Company P makes several products which pass through the two production departments in its factory. These two departments are concerned with filling and sealing operations. There are two service departments in the factory: maintenance and canteen.

Predetermined overhead absorption rates, based on direct labour hours, are established for the two production departments. The budgeted expenditure for these departments for the period just ended, including the apportionment of service department overheads, was £110,040 for filling, and £53,300 for sealing. Budgeted direct labour hours were 13,100 for filling and 10,250 for sealing.

Service department overheads are apportioned as follows.

Maintenance

Filling	70%
Sealing	27%
Canteen	3%

Canteen

Filling	60%
Sealing	32%
Maintenance	8%

During the period just ended, actual overhead costs and activity were as follows.

	£	*Direct labour hours*
Filling	74,260	12,820
Sealing	38,115	10,075
Maintenance	25,050	
Canteen	24,375	

Required

(a)   Calculate the overheads absorbed in the period.

(b)   State, and critically assess, the objectives of overhead apportionment and absorption.

3   Activity-based costing

3.1   Problems with the traditional method

We have already studied activity-based costing techniques in the context of budgeting. We now revisit these techniques in the related area of overhead absorption.

Activity-based costing of overheads is an attempt to produce more accurate product overhead costs than the traditional approach.

 In the modern industrial environment it is thought that more accurate product overhead costing is required for two reasons.

Firstly, owing to international competition in the modern environment profitability is under threat and the high margins that could be earned under a protectionist umbrella are no longer available. Thus accurate product cost information is vital to assessing the true profitability of individual products as an aid in decision making and resource allocation.

Secondly a move in the cost base in many modern industries means that a higher proportion of product cost than ever is in the form of overhead. True direct labour has disappeared from many factories because of increased use of robotics and technology, with any remaining labour falling into the indirect and hence overhead category. In addition extra emphasis on quality has led to new categories of production overhead arising. The result is that a far higher proportion of costs nowadays fall into the category of overheads; this means that accurate attribution of overhead costs for products is more important than ever.

3.2   Principles of ABC

Activity-based costing starts by claiming that traditional views of cost behaviour are not always applicable. Overheads are traditionally viewed as either variable directly with production or fixed in relation to time periods. This analysis may be simplistic.

ABC claims that many overheads are incurred in relation to some other measure of activity. These activities are termed *cost drivers* – activities that cause costs to be incurred. If appropriate cost drivers can be isolated, these can be used to calculate more appropriate absorption rates for overheads, leading to more accurate product costing.

In overview we can now see that ABC is not a wholly new technique but a refinement of the traditional approach. Whereas the traditional approach calculates a single absorption rate per production department, the ABC approach calculates multiple absorption rates for a department based on the different categories of overhead present and the cost drivers that are relevant.

In most exam questions you will often find a simplifying assumption, namely that the firm has only one production department. Therefore many of the complications of allocation and apportionment are avoided in ABC questions.

An additional simplification in questions is that similar overheads in the department relating to a common cost driver will already have been grouped in a *cost pool*. In reality, the cost accountant would normally have to do this as a preliminary step. In some questions the appropriate cost driver will be specifically identified, whereas in others you may be required to isolate these from the data available.

There now follow some illustrations showing the principles of ABC.

3.3 Example

The following products are budgeted for production over the forthcoming period.

Product	X	Y	Z
Production	100	500	800
Number of set-ups required	10	20	40
Budgeted overhead in the set-up cost pool			£70,000

Set-ups are required at the end of a production run to make the machines serviceable for the next run. The appropriate cost driver would appear to be the number of set-ups required, because it is this that will determine how much overhead is incurred.

3.4 Solution

We therefore calculate an absorption rate based on the number of set-ups.

Total set-up overhead	£70,000
Total number of set-ups	70
Set-up overhead per set-up	$\dfrac{£70,000}{70}$
	= £1,000

Product	X	Y	Z
Production (units)	100	500	800
Set-ups in total	10	20	40
Set-ups per unit	0.1	0.04	0.05

Set-up overhead absorbed

	X	Y	Z
X 0.1 × £1,000	£100		
Y 0.04 × £1,000		£40	
Z 0.05 × £1,000			£50

This approach should reflect the product set-up cost more accurately than using labour or machine hours as is traditionally used.

3.5   Example

For the same firm another cost pool has been established for minor machine drill parts.

Product	X	Y	Z
Production (units)	100	500	800
Drill holes per unit	3	2	5
Cost pool for drill parts			£10,600

3.6   Solution

Here the number of holes drilled will be the appropriate cost driver, as the drills will wear out more, the more they are used. Thus an absorption rate based on drill operations will be used.

Budgeted number of drill holes

X	100 × 3	=	300
Y	500 × 2	=	1,000
Z	800 × 5	=	4,000
Total			5,300

Drill parts overhead per operation

$$= \frac{£10,600}{5,300} = £2 \text{ per operation}$$

	X	Y	Z
Drill holes per unit	3	2	5
Absorption rate per operation	£2	£2	£2
Drill part overhead absorbed per unit	£6	£4	£10

Again, this should give a more accurate picture of the drill part overhead cost per product than using labour hours or machine hours as in the traditional approach.

The above illustrations demonstrate the principles of ABC. We would continue through the cost pools calculating each product's cost per unit for that particular style of overhead and cost driver. Once this is complete we would simply add up the individual figures computed to give a total overhead cost for each product.

As we can now see, the ABC method is similar to the traditional approach, except that within a production department multiple absorption rates are calculated to improve accuracy. Alternatively, we could also say that the traditional approach is a simplified version of ABC. In other words, we might argue that, with hindsight, cost drivers were used in the traditional method, but it was assumed that only one would apply to all the overheads in a department (normally either labour hours or machine hours).

Practice questions 4 and 5 *(The answers are in the final chapter of this book)*

4 Hensau

Hensau Ltd has a single production process for which the following costs have been estimated for the period ending 31 December 20X1.

	£
Material receipt and inspection cost	15,600
Power cost	19,500
Material handling cost	13,650

Three products (X, Y and Z) are produced by workers who perform a number of operations on material blanks using hand–held electrically powered drills. The workers have a wage rate of £4 per hour.

The following budgeted information has been obtained for the period ending 31 December 20X1.

	Product X	Product Y	Product Z
Production quantity (units)	2,000	1,500	800
Batches of material	10	5	16
Data per product unit			
Direct material (sq metres)	4	6	3
Direct material (£)	5	3	6
Direct labour (minutes)	24	40	60
Number of power drill operations	6	3	2

Overhead costs for material receipt and inspection, process power and material handling are presently each absorbed by product units using rates per direct labour hour.

An activity based costing investigation has revealed that the cost drivers for the overhead costs are as follows.

♦ Material receipt and inspection: number of batches of material.
♦ Process power: number of power drill operations.
♦ Material handling: quantity of material (sq metres) handled.

Required

Prepare a summary which shows the budgeted product cost per unit for each of the products X, Y and Z for the period ending 31 December 20X1 detailing the unit costs for each cost element:

(a) using the existing method for the absorption of overhead costs

(b) using an approach which recognises the cost drivers revealed in the activity-based costing investigation.

5   Experiment

Having attended a course on activity-based costing (ABC) you decide to experiment by applying the principles of ABC to the four products currently made and sold by your company. Details of the four products and relevant information are given below for one period.

Product	A	B	C	D
Output in units	120	100	80	120
Costs per unit	£	£	£	£
Direct material	40	50	30	60
Direct labour	28	21	14	21
Machine hours (per unit)	4	3	2	3

The four products are similar and are usually produced in production runs of 20 units and sold in batches of 10 units.

The production overhead is currently absorbed by using a machine hour rate, and the total of the production overhead for the period has been analysed as follows.

	£
Machine department costs (rent, business rates, depreciation and supervision)	10,430
Set-up costs	5,250
Stores receiving	3,600
Inspection/quality control	2,100
Materials handling and despatch	4,620

You have ascertained that the 'cost drivers' to be used are as listed below for the overhead costs shown:

Cost	Cost driver
Set-up costs	Number of production runs
Stores receiving	Requisitions raised
Inspection/quality control	Number of production runs
Materials handling and despatch	Orders executed

The number of requisitions raised on the stores was 20 for each product and the number of orders executed was 42, each order being for a batch of 10 of a product.

Required

(a)   Calculate the total costs for each product if all overhead costs are absorbed on a machine hour basis.

(b)   Calculate the total costs for each product, using activity-based costing.

(c)   Calculate and list the unit product costs from your figures in (a) and (b) above, show the differences and comment briefly on any conclusions which may be drawn which could have pricing and profit implications.

3.7 Activity-based costing in practice

Activity-based costing principles have been in use for a number of years now and the following comments can be made.

 Many firms found initially that the additional complexity of ABC systems compared to the traditional approach meant that higher costs of obtaining the improved information outweighed the resulting benefits. This was mainly due to the use of too many cost pools and cost drivers. By streamlining the systems so as to use fewer pools and drivers the balance can be redressed. An attempt at too much precision can be costly.

Some firms found that when they moved to an ABC approach their low-volume products appeared far more costly than was previously thought to be the case. It appears with hindsight that the traditional method tended to undercost the 'hassle factor' associated with low-volume products. For example, short production runs require many set-ups with their associated cost, but this was ignored in the traditional approach based on labour or machine hours which effectively provided a blanket rate for the department.

ABC was originally envisaged for use in a manufacturing environment, the traditional home of cost accounting techniques. Over recent decades in many western countries, the UK included, there has been an economic shift away from a manufacturing environment towards an economy based on services. In many service businesses there is little in the way of direct unit cost, the main cost being overhead. Thus the adoption of ABC within service businesses has provided many with the first accurate cost information ever achieved. It is not uncommon to see banks, building societies and even the health service use ABC.

In conclusion, it appears that ABC is here to stay and sensible use of the technique can bring substantial information benefits to a firm.

3.8 Learning outcome

At this stage of the chapter we have now covered the following Learning Outcome:

> Explain activity-based costing

Practice question 6 *(The answer is in the final chapter of this book)*

Brunti

The following budgeted information relates to Brunti plc for the forthcoming period.

	XYI	Products YZT	ABW
	(000)	(000)	(000)
Sales and production (units)	50	40	30
	£	£	£
Selling price (per unit)	45	95	73
Prime cost (per unit)	32	84	65
	Hours	Hours	Hours
Machine department (machine hours per unit)	2	5	4
Assembly department (direct labour hours per unit)	7	3	2

Overheads allocated and apportioned to production departments (including service cost centre costs) were to be recovered in product costs as follows.

♦   Machine department at £1.20 per machine hour
♦   Assembly department at £0.825 per direct labour hour

You ascertain that the above overheads could be re-analysed into 'cost pools' as follows.

Cost pool	£000	Cost driver	Quantity for the period
Machining services	357	Machine hours	420,000
Assembly services	318	Direct labour hours	530,000
Set-up costs	26	Set-ups	520
Order processing	156	Customer orders	32,000
Purchasing	84	Suppliers' orders	11,200
	941		

You have also been provided with the following estimates for the period.

	Products		
	XYI	YZT	ABW
Number of set-ups	120	200	200
Customer orders	8,000	8,000	16,000
Suppliers' orders	3,000	4,000	4,200

Required

(a)   Prepare and present profit statements using:

    (i)   conventional absorption costing; and

    (ii)   activity-based costing.

(b)   Comment on why activity-based costing is considered to present a fairer valuation of the product cost per unit.

4   Total absorption costing and marginal costing

4.1   Introduction

To determine the total cost of a unit of product, we bring in a share of the overheads. The cost of a unit is then as follows:

	£
Materials	X
Labour	X
Variable overhead	X
Marginal cost	X
Fixed overhead	X
Total absorption cost	X

Here we have defined two types of cost.

Marginal cost is the sum of all the variable production costs.

Total absorption cost is the sum of all the variable production costs plus a share of the fixed production cost.

As we shall see, because we have two possible bases for costing our production, marginal and total absorption costing, we will therefore have differences in our possible stock valuation which may give rise to differences in profits.

These two types of cost give rise to two alternative methods of preparing our management accounts/budgets.

4.2 Total absorption costing

Stock is valued at total absorption cost.

Production cost is the total absorption cost per unit, times the number of units produced.

4.3 Marginal costing

Stock is valued at marginal cost.

Production cost is the marginal cost per unit, multiplied by the number of units produced.

Fixed costs, which are not included as a production cost, are charged as a period cost.

4.4 Example

Sally makes dudars. Each dudar has a variable cost of £3 and can be sold for £5.

Sally's fixed overheads are expected to amount to £50,000 for the coming year. During this year she expects to make and sell 100,000 dudars.

Required

(a)   Calculate the total absorption cost of a dudar.

(b)   Prepare Sally's budgeted profit and loss account under:

   (i)   marginal costing; and

   (ii)   total absorption costing.

4.5 Solution

		£
(a)	Variable cost per unit	3.00
	Fixed cost per unit (W)	0.50
	Total absorption cost per unit	3.50

WORKING

$$\frac{\text{Total budgeted fixed overhead}}{\text{Total expected production}} = \frac{£50,000}{100,000} = £0.50 \text{ per unit}$$

(b)   (i)   The budgeted profit and loss account of Sally for next year

Marginal costing

	Notes	£	£
Sales (100,000 × £5)			500,000
Opening stock	(1)	–	
Production (100,000 × £3)	(2)	300,000	
		300,000	
Closing stock	(1)	–	
			300,000
Contribution			200,000
Fixed cost	(3)		50,000
Profit			150,000

Notes

(1)   Normally these lines would be omitted as they have a value of nil.

(2)   Production is charged with the marginal cost of the goods produced.

(3)   Fixed costs are charged as a period cost.

Note that sales revenue less the marginal cost of sales is equal to *contribution* not profit. Profit is only obtained when the fixed costs are then taken off the contribution figure.

(ii)   The budgeted profit and loss account of Sally for next year.

Total absorption costing

	Notes	£	£
Sales			500,000
Opening stock	(1)	–	
Production (100,000 × £3.50)	(2)	350,000	
Closing stock	(1)	–	
			350,000
Profit			150,000

Notes

(1)   Normally these figures will be omitted as they have a value of nil.

(2)   Production is charged with total absorption cost of the goods produced.

Here you will notice that the fixed overhead is charged to production rather than as a period cost. This happens because the total absorption cost includes a proportion of the fixed overhead.

You will probably notice that the profit is the same using either method of costing. This is only because there was no change in stock levels. There was no opening stock and no closing stock, so therefore using a different method of valuing stock will not give rise to any difference in the profit figures.

4.6 The effect of changes in stock

Suppose that in the following year Sally plans to produce 100,000 units but to sell only 90,000 (all other items remaining as before).

Budgeted profit and loss account of Sally for year 2

			TAC		MC	
	Notes	£	£		£	£
Sales (90,000 × £5)			450,000			450,000
Opening stock		–			–	
Production (as before)		350,000			300,000	
		350,000			300,000	
Closing stock (10,000 × £3.50)	(1)	(35,000)				
(10,000 × £3.00)	(2)				(30,000)	
			315,000			270,000
			135,000			180,000
Fixed overheads (3)		–			50,000	
Profit			135,000			130,000

Notes

(1) Closing stock valued at total absorption cost.

(2) Closing stock valued at marginal cost.

(3) Remember that, in TAC, fixed overheads are included in production costs, whereas in MC they are taken off in total as a period cost.

As you can see there is a difference in profit.

The only difference between the two profit and loss accounts is the value of closing stock.

(Remember: Fixed cost + Cost of production under MC = Cost of production under TAC)

What has happened is that £35,000 of the production cost has been carried forward to the next period under TAC but only £30,000 under MC.

More precisely under total absorption costing £5,000 of fixed overheads (10,000 units × £0.50 per unit) have been carried forward while under marginal costing none have.

This leads us to some standard rules.

4.7 The relationship between TAC profit and MC profit

If closing stock is greater than opening stock	TAC profit will be greater than MC profit
If closing stock is less than opening stock	TAC profit will be less than MC profit
If closing stock is equal to opening stock	TAC profit will be equal to MC profit

Our two examples have illustrated the first and the third rule. You should be able to illustrate the second for yourself.

4.8   Over/under-absorption of fixed overhead

In our two examples so far we have seen that the fixed overhead is charged to the TAC profit and loss account as part of the cost of production.

Consider the following situation:

In year 3 Sally expects to produce and sell 90,000 units.

Prepare her budgeted profit and loss account using total absorption costing (all other items remaining as before). You might start by preparing the account as follows:

	£	£
Sales		450,000
Opening stock	35,000	
Production (90,000 × £3.50)	315,000	
	350,000	
Closing stock	(35,000)	
		315,000
Profit		135,000

This is not complete.

Consider the fixed overheads. They are £50,000.

How much has been included in our cost of production?

Answer: 90,000 × £0.50 = £45,000

We have not included enough fixed overheads, ie. we have *under-absorbed* our fixed overhead.

We need an adjustment to rectify this. It is useful to show this adjustment as a separate item in the profit and loss account so that management can see the effect of the different production level.

The profit and loss account becomes:

The budgeted profit and loss account of Sally for year 3

	£	£
Sales		450,000
Opening stock	35,000	
Production	315,000	
	350,000	
Closing stock	35,000	
		315,000
		135,000
Under-absorption of fixed overhead		5,000
		130,000

It is, of course, equally possible to have over-absorption.

This leads us to another set of standard rules.

4.9 Absorption rules

If the overheads absorbed (charged) in the production costs within the profit and loss account exceed the overheads actually incurred, they have been over-absorbed. If they are less than the actual overheads, they have been under-absorbed.

 As the overheads are absorbed via units produced, then, in particular, if actual *production* is greater than expected *production* over-absorption will occur.

If actual *production* is less than expected *production* under-absorption will occur.

Note that over/under-absorption occurs when production figures differ. It has nothing at all to do with sales figures and stock levels. Remember you absorb fixed overheads into production not into sales.

Also note that any over/under-absorption must be corrected in the profit and loss account, as in the previous example.

4.10 The effect of over/under-absorption on the comparison of total absorption cost profit and marginal cost profit

Over/under-absorption of fixed overhead does not cause a difference between TAC profit and MC profit. The fixed overhead charge in the TAC profit and loss account must always be corrected to make it equal to the actual fixed overhead.

It is a source of grief to tutors and the examiner alike that many students forget this fact as soon as they enter the examination room. You should not be one of them.

If you are not convinced, please review the following example.

4.11 Example

Prepare the budgeted profit and loss account of Sally for year 3 using marginal costing.

4.12 Solution

The budgeted profit and loss account of Sally for year 3

	£	£
Sales		450,000
Opening stock (@ MC)	30,000	
Production (90,000 × £3)	270,000	
	———	
	300,000	
Closing stock	(30,000)	
	———	
		270,000
		———
		180,000
Fixed overhead		50,000
		———
Profit – same as TAC		*130,000
		———

*Note that the TAC profit is only the same as the MC profit because there has been no change in stock levels. What is important is that now both the TAC and MC profit and loss accounts include £50,000 of fixed overheads.

4.13   Merits of the two costing approaches

 TAC and MC adopt fundamentally different attitudes towards the treatment of fixed overheads. Consequently the cost per unit derived under both methods will be quite different. However, each method has a use depending on the circumstances faced by the business and the purpose for which the cost per unit is to be used.

The advantages of one method are the disadvantages of the other and vice versa. These are considered below by focusing on TAC.

4.14   Advantages claimed for TAC

♦   Complies with SSAP 9

SSAP 9 does not permit marginal costing to be used in the preparation of published financial accounts.

For management accounts this is irrelevant. Management accounts are used for decision-making purposes and should contain information in the form that is most useful to management. If a TAC figure is required for the financial accounts, then it should be calculated separately.

In practice, the use of erroneous financial accounting information for management decisions is most likely in small companies whose staff have limited financial expertise and regard the accounts as something they have to get past the auditor.

♦   Reminds managers of the true cost of production

It is argued that the use of marginal costing will lead managers to believe that products cost less than they actually do. (Remember that stock is valued at marginal cost under a marginal cost system of accounting.)

Others argue that good managers should be aware that this is not so.

Here again, we may have a difference between the theoretical ideal and the practical reality that not every manager has financial expertise.

♦   Ensures that fixed costs are covered

This is an extension of the above point.

4.15   Example

The following details apply to a grodget.

	£
Variable cost	700
Fixed cost	3,000
Total cost	3,700

Discuss the impact that MC and TAC stock valuation might have on management.

4.16   Solution

It is argued that if stock is valued at £700 a manager might agree to sell it at £2,000 and believe he has struck a beneficial deal when in fact he has not.

In contrast, if stock is valued at £3,700 the manager will know that he has to achieve this price in order to cover the fixed costs.

This is a very simplistic view that can be challenged on two fronts. The first point will be considered in detail under decision-making.

We shall consider the second point here. Quite simply fixed costs will not be covered by a price of £3,700 unless the required volume is achieved.

Suppose that fixed costs are £30,000; we need to sell ten units at £3,700 to cover our costs. Selling one is not enough, but selling one at £2,000 at least gives a contribution of £1,300 to help cover fixed costs.

4.17 Disadvantage of TAC

♦ Unsuitable for one-off decision-making

Using the example set out above, suppose that a one-off order from an overseas customer was received. Suppose further that the order would have no effect on the price obtainable from existing customers.

Under these circumstances it would be worthwhile accepting the order if the price were above £700 because it would make a contribution to profits/fixed costs.

4.18 Conclusion

It can be seen that neither method is superior in all circumstances.

You have now seen the two main different costing systems adopted in practice. You must be able to prepare profit and loss accounts on either basis. In particular points to remember are:

♦ TAC profit can be different from MC profit. This is solely due to a change in stock levels over the period, ie. opening stock does not equal closing stock at the end of the period.

♦ In a TAC profit and loss account, adjustment might have to be made for any over/under-absorption of fixed overhead which arises when actual production does not equal budgeted production.

4.19 Learning outcome

At this stage of the chapter we have now covered the basis of the Learning Outcome.

Prepare and discuss a report which reconciles budget and actual profit using absorption and/or marginal costing principles

---

Practice questions 7 and 8 *(The answers are in the final chapter of this book)*

7 Sunshine

Sunshine Sales Ltd is drafting a budget on the basis of the following data.

Direct material	£10 per unit
Direct labour	£5 per unit
Variable production expenses	£8 per unit
Fixed production costs	£27,000 per month
Normal output 9,000 units per month	90% capacity
Sales price	£30 per unit

In order to build up stock in anticipation of an increase in demand which is expected later in the year, production is to exceed sales in the first three months of the year as follows.

	Month 1	Month 2	Month 3
Production	6,500	9,000	10,000
Sales	5,000	8,500	9,500

Required

(a)   Prepare two profit statements, each in comparative columnar form, covering each of the three months

(i)   on a marginal costing basis

(ii)   on a full absorption costing basis.

(b)   Reconcile the difference in profits for each month.

8   Ladenis

Ladenis has produced his budget for the coming year based on the manufacture and sale of 6,000 Nicos as shown below.

		£
Manufacturing costs		
	Variable	48,000
	Fixed	72,000
Selling and administrative costs		
	Variable	36,000
	Fixed	60,000
Profit		24,000
Sales revenue		240,000

Demand is seasonal and at the end of each year Ladenis runs down his stock levels to zero. Production and sales figures for the first three months of the year are estimated as follows.

	January	February	March
Production (units)	500	400	300
Sales (units)	300	400	400

Ladenis currently uses an absorption costing system but is considering changing to a marginal costing system.

Required

(a)   Produce budgeted profit statements (do not merely compute profit figures) for the first three months, both individually and in total, using an absorption costing format.

(b)   Produce a revised set of statements using a marginal costing format.

(c)   Reconcile the profit figures in (a) and (b).

(d)   Discuss the relative merits of the two systems.

5   Summary

The accounting treatment of overhead costs is a very important area as it underpins your study of cost control procedures.

The development of ABC and its application to the modern business environment is also a significant part of this syllabus.

Multiple choice questions *(The answers are in the final chapter of this book)*

1   Trimdon plc has just completed its first year of trading. The following information has been collected from the accounting records.

		£
Variable cost per unit		
	Manufacturing	6.00
	Selling and administration	0.20
Fixed costs		
	Manufacturing	90,000
	Selling and administration	22,500

Production was 75,000 units and sales were 70,000 units. The selling price was £8 per unit throughout the year.

The *difference* in annual net income using direct costing for inventory valuation, rather than absorption costing, is:

A   £2,500
B   £6,000
C   £7,500
D   £8,500

The following information relates to questions 2 and 3.

The budget for Bright's first month's trading, producing and selling showed the following:

	£000
Variable production costs of boats	45
Fixed production costs	30
Production costs of 750 boats	75
Closing stock of 250 boats	(25)
Production cost of 500 sold	50
Variable selling costs	5
Fixed selling costs	25
Profit	10
Sales revenue	90

The budget has been produced using an absorption costing system.

2   If a marginal costing system were used, the budgeted profit would be:

A   £22,500 lower
B   £10,000 lower
C   £10,000 higher
D   £22,500 higher

3   At the end of the first month unit variable costs and fixed costs and selling price for the month were in line with the budget, and any stock was valued at the same unit cost as in the above budget.

However, if production were actually 700 and sales 600, what would be the reported profit?

A   £9,000
B   £12,000
C   £14,000
D   £15,000

CHAPTER 9

Contribution analysis

EXAM FOCUS

This chapter explains the vital concept of contribution which is fundamental to resource planning in the context of budgets and performance management.

LEARNING OUTCOMES

This chapter covers the following Learning Outcomes of the CIMA Syllabus.

> Calculate and interpret the breakeven point, profit target, margin of safety and profit/volume ratio for multiple products
>
> Prepare breakeven charts and profit/volume charts for multiple products
>
> Discuss multiple product CVP analysis

In order to cover these Learning Outcomes the following topics are included.

> Contribution
> Breakeven

---

1 Cost classification

1.1 Introduction

There are many different types of cost. Classification involves forming logical, useful groups of costs. By doing this it makes it easier to understand, use and communicate to others.

The type of classification depends on the purpose to which the information will be put.

There are four main classification groups:

♦ By nature of the cost
♦ By direct/indirect cost
♦ By function
♦ By behaviour of the cost

1.2 Classification by nature

This involves grouping costs according to their type:

Material - Cost of materials directly or indirectly used in production

Labour - Cost of labour directly or indirectly used in production

Expenses - Costs which are neither materials or labour directly or indirectly used in production

1.3 Classification by direct/indirect cost

This involves grouping costs according to their relationship with production ie:

Direct cost

 Direct costs are those which can be related specifically to a cost unit. They are normally identified under three headings:

(a) *Direct materials* – the cost of materials entering into and becoming constituent elements of a product or service. The term "materials" covers raw materials (like the quantity of raw cotton used to produce a length of thread), components (like those used in assembling a television set) and finished products (like the quantity of paper used in printing a book).

(b) *Direct labour* – the cost of remuneration for working time applied directly to a product or service, such as the manual assembly time for the television set or the time spent in carrying out a property conveyancing by a solicitor.

(c) *Direct expenses* – other costs which are incurred for a specific product or service. Typical examples would be the hire of earth-moving equipment for a particular public works contract, or the cost of work sub-contracted to a third party.

 The total of all direct costs is sometimes referred to as the **prime cost** of the product or activity concerned.

Indirect costs

 All other costs, whether materials, wages or expenses, are termed indirect costs or "overheads".

They will normally be identified with cost centres, where they can be controlled by the managers responsible. The costs of management at all levels and of the provision of administrative services will fall into this category.

It may also include certain items which enter into a product but could not be identified with particular cost units without analytical effort disproportionate to any improvement in the accuracy of the product cost. A possible example is the relatively minor cost of screws, fixings and fastenings used in an assembly operation. The cost of such items, although classified as indirect, would be "variable" with the quantity of output achieved.

1.4 Classification by function

A manufacturing organisation is usually split into three broad functions:

♦ Production – cost of converting the raw materials into finished goods
♦ Administration – cost of managing the organisation
♦ Selling and distribution – cost of securing orders and despatching goods

Most costs will fall into these three categories.

 The distinction between production and other costs is essential for stock valuation purposes, as we shall see.

1.5 Classification by cost behaviour

 This involves grouping costs on the basis of their reaction to changes in activity.

Costs which change with activity are known as **variable costs.**

Costs which remain constant regardless of changes in activity are known as **fixed costs** (which may be **stepped**).

Costs which react to changes in activity but contain an element that doesn't are known **as semi-variable costs**.

We now consider these in more detail:

(a)   *Variable cost*

A cost which varies with a measure of activity eg direct materials.

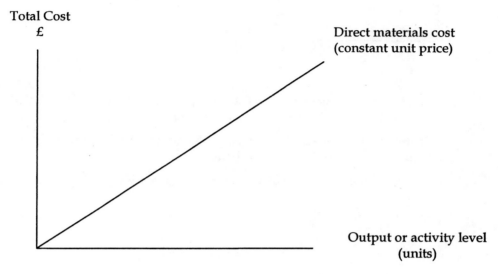

(b)   *Fixed cost*

This is a cost which is incurred for an accounting period, and which within certain output or turnover limits, tends to be unaffected by fluctuations in the levels of activity eg rent.

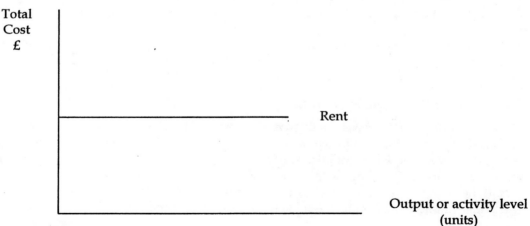

(c)   *Semi-variable cost*

This is a cost which contains both fixed and variable components and which is thus partly affected by a change in the level of activity. Two examples are shown below:

(i)   Salesmen's remuneration with added commission from a certain level of activity.

(ii)   Electricity charges comprising fixed standing charge and variable unit charge.

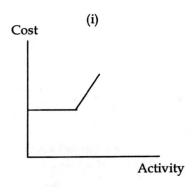

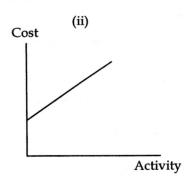

(d)   *Stepped fixed cost*

A stepped fixed cost is where the fixed cost increases to a different level when certain levels of activity are reached. Two examples are shown below:

(i)   Canteen cost where additional assistants are required as increases in activity result in larger numbers of factory personnel.

(ii)   Rent of premises, additional accommodation eventually being required.

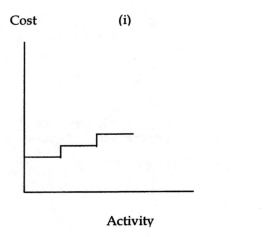

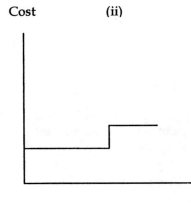

1.6   Splitting semi-variable costs

Where fixed and variable costs are known with reasonable accuracy total and unit costs may be predicted. Where semi-variable costs are present the situation is complicated and, in order to keep the model simple, the semi-variable costs are dealt with by splitting their fixed and variable portions and adding them to the other fixed and variable costs respectively. In order to split the semi-variable cost into fixed and variable components we use the high low method. This is an extremely important technique for your examination.

1.7   High Low Method - Example

Consider the following data:

Units produced per week	200	300	400	500	600	700	800
Total cost per week (£)	3,500	4,000	5,200	6,800	7,500	8,900	9,100

This method simply takes the highest and lowest numbers of units produced (activity levels) and bases the approximation on these.

Calculate the:

(a)   variable cost per unit

(b)   total fixed costs.

1.8   Solution

(a)   *Variable costs*

increase in output between highest and lowest values = 800 – 200	600 units
increase in total costs = £9,100 – 3,500	£5,600

Assuming this increase is purely due to the additional variable cost attributable (at a constant rate per unit) to the extra 600 units:

variable cost per unit = $\dfrac{£5,600}{600}$ £9.33

(b)   *Fixed costs*

These are calculated as a balancing figure, as follows:

                                                                                                          £

(i)   Variable cost of 200 units = 200 × £9.33   1,866

         Total cost of 200 units   3,500

         Therefore, fixed cost   1,634

(ii)   The answer would be the same if we considered 800 units

                                                                                                          £

         Variable cost of 800 units = 800 × £9.33   7,464

         Total cost of 800 units   9,100

         Therefore, fixed cost   1,636

(Note that there is a small rounding error because the variable cost per unit is £9.33 recurring.)

1.9   Linear assumption of cost behaviour

The accountant is normally quite happy to assume that the cost function of a firm is linear even when this is not quite true. He argues that, while it may well be true that the function is not represented by a straight line on a graph, the activity range being considered is narrow enough to ensure that any loss of mathematical accuracy is not material to his calculations.

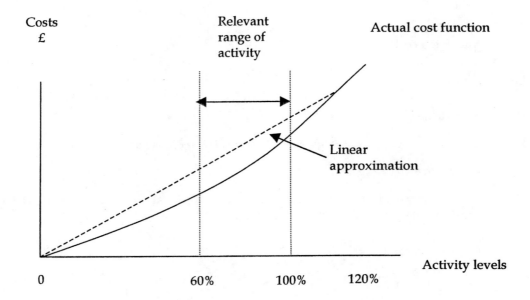

While the error taken between activity levels 0% and 120% may be quite large, a line drawn on the basis of the range of activity 60% to 100% shows a relatively close fit to the function curve. We can thus use our computed fixed and variable costs over this 'relevant range of activity'.

For examination purposes it may be assumed that costs are linear unless the contrary is made clear. Practically, the assumption of linearity is still prevalent and acceptable – so long as the assumption is recognised – but as computers become more widely used it is likely that curvilinear cost behaviour will be recognised and used for prediction purposes; the benefits no longer being outweighed by the cost of calculation.

2 Contribution and profit

2.1 Introduction

Under marginal costing we calculate the **contribution per item** by taking the sales price and deducting all variable production and selling costs. As we have seen, this procedure is a useful starting point for a wide variety of calculations used in management decision making.

2.2 Illustration

We illustrate the relevance of contribution with the example of a product selling at a unit price of £15, with variable materials cost of £4 per unit and other variable costs of £2 per unit. Contribution is therefore £9 per unit (£15 – £4 – £2). Suppose that fixed costs are £40,000 per period.

♦ If 5,000 units are produced and sold what is the total contribution and the net profit?

Contribution	=	5,000 × £9	=	£45,000
Profit	=	£45,000 – £40,000	=	£5,000

♦ What is the total contribution and profit if 7,000 units are produced and sold?

Contribution	=	7,000 × £9	=	£63,000
Profit	=	£63,000 – £40,000	=	£23,000

♦ What is total contribution and profit if 3,000 units are sold?

Contribution	=	3,000 × £9	=	£27,000
Profit	=	£27,000 – £40,000	=	£(13,000), ie a loss of £13,000

2.3   Contribution and profit graph

These results can be plotted on a graph as follows.

Cost, Revenue

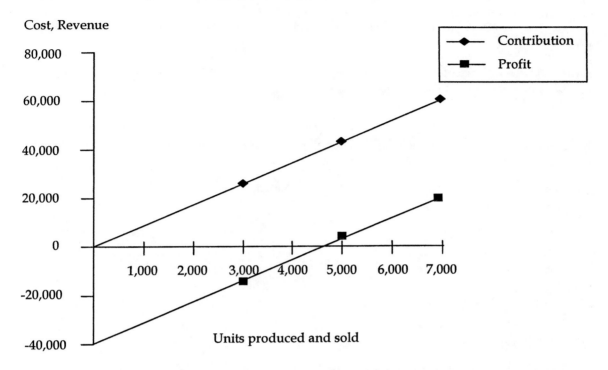

Notice that the two lines are parallel to one another. The **steepness** of the line represents the **contribution per item**; the **vertical distance** between the two lines represents the **fixed costs**. In other words if you know the total contribution, subtract £40,000 to arrive at the net profit. If zero units are made then no contribution is earned, but all the fixed costs must still be paid, resulting in a loss of £40,000.

If you look at the chart above, you will see that as the output doubles, so does the total contribution. Since this relationship is not true of profit, contribution is a more useful indicator. In this chapter we will look at some of the uses to which contribution can be put.

3   Contribution – vital concept

3.1   Introduction

Throughout much of your studies for this Paper you will be looking at techniques concerned with decision-making. This may be with regard to the relationship between output and profit, determining the strategy in the light of a restricted resource, or in general terms. What will become apparent is that the concept of contribution is vital in many areas.

Contribution is defined as the difference between selling price and the variable cost of producing and selling that item. This is in contrast to profit per unit, which is the difference between selling price and the total absorption cost of producing and selling that item, which includes an element of fixed cost.

When we are faced with a decision to make, we need to assess which course of action will be most beneficial. We therefore need to consider the revenues and costs under each alternative. Fixed costs, by definition, are unavoidable and do not change with the level of production. Therefore, in any decision which is connected with varying the level of production, fixed costs are not a relevant cost as they do not change regardless of which course of action is taken.

3.2 Example

Katie Ltd is currently producing baby rattles. Each rattle sells at £10 each, and has a variable cost of production of £8 per unit. Current production is 900 units per period. Fixed costs are expected to be £900 for the coming period, and therefore are charged at £1 per unit to production.

Katie has been approached to supply a new customer with 100 rattles, but at a discounted price of £8.25 per rattle. Should she accept the order?

3.3 Solution

If we look at profit per unit, then the decision would be to reject the order, as we would not sell for £8.25 per unit something which has cost us (£8 + £1) = £9 to produce.

However, if we look at total profits generated by the business before and after the acceptance of the project, we find:

		Reject £	Accept £
Revenue	(900 @ £10)	9,000	9,000
	(100 @ £8.25)		825
			9,825
Variable costs	(900/1,000 @ £8)	(7,200)	(8,000)
Fixed costs		(900)	(900)
Profit		900	925

Therefore we can see that profits are improved by accepting the contract. Whilst revenue is increasing by £825, costs only increase by £800 as **fixed costs do not change**.

We could have derived the same answer by looking at contribution generated by the contract.

 Remember contribution is calculated as Selling Price – Variable Cost. On a per unit basis for the contract, this is £8.25 – £8 = £0.25 contribution on each extra unit sold.

As we sell 100 units more, this generates a total increase in contribution of £25 (100 × £0.25).

We should accept the project – the use of contribution analysis enables us to determine this quickly.

4 Breakeven analysis

4.1 Introduction

How many units do we need to sell to make a profit?

By how much will profit fall if price is lowered by £1?

What will happen to our profits if we rent an extra factory but find that we can operate at only half capacity?

All of the above are realistic business questions. One solution would be to set up a model of the business on a computer and feed in the various pieces of information. The development of the microcomputer and associated software packages such as Lotus 123 and Excel mean that this may be a feasible option.

If there is no computer model readily available, breakeven analysis provides a quick and often surprisingly accurate alternative.

It is worth noting that another name for breakeven analysis is CVP analysis. This stands for cost, volume, profit analysis.

4.2   Approach

Costs are assumed to be either fixed or variable.

Economies or diseconomies of scale are ignored; this ensures that our cost functions are strictly linear.

The effect of changes in volume is determined by looking at the effect that change in volume has on **contribution** (not profit).

Remember, Selling price per unit – Total variable cost per unit = Contribution per unit.

5   Breakeven point

5.1   Introduction

The breakeven point is the volume of sales at which neither a profit nor a loss is made. It is also the volume of sales at which total contribution (contribution per unit multiplied by number of units sold) is equal to fixed costs. The fixed costs are total fixed costs, ie. fixed production and fixed selling costs.

The breakeven point can be found using the following formula.

$$\text{Breakeven point} = \frac{\text{Fixed costs}}{\text{Contribution per unit}}$$

This formula can be derived by considering the composition of profit; for sales of Q units:

	per unit £	*total* £
Sales	S	
Variable costs	(V)	
Contribution	C × Q =	CQ
Fixed costs		(F)
Profit		P

To breakeven, P = nil

so CQ = F

and $Q = \dfrac{F}{C} = \dfrac{\text{Fixed costs}}{\text{Contribution per unit}}$

5.2   Example

Rachel's product, the 'Steadyarm' sells for £50. It has a variable cost of £30 per unit. Rachel's fixed costs are £40,000 per annum. What is her breakeven point?

5.3 Solution

$$\text{Breakeven point} = \frac{\text{Fixed costs}}{\text{Contribution per unit}} = \frac{£40,000}{£20} = 2,000 \text{ units pa}$$

WORKING

	£
Selling price	50
Less variable cost	(30)
Contribution per unit	20

We can show that this is the case with a summarised profit and loss account.

	£
Sales (2,000 × £50)	100,000
Variable cost (2,000 × £30)	(60,000)
Fixed cost	(40,000)
Profit/loss	-

6 Sales volume to achieve a particular profit

6.1 Approach

 A similar approach to the above can be adopted.

$$\text{Sales volume to achieve a particular profit} = \frac{\text{Fixed costs} + \text{required profit}}{\text{Contribution per unit}}$$

6.2 Example

Information as above but we now want to know how many units must be sold to make a profit of £100,000.

6.3 Solution

To achieve a profit of £100,000, we require sufficient contribution to firstly cover the fixed costs (£40,000) and secondly, having covered fixed costs, we require sufficient contribution to give a profit of £100,000. Therefore our required contribution is £140,000.

Sales volume to achieve a profit of £100,000

$$= \frac{\text{Fixed costs} + \text{Required profit}}{\text{Contribution per unit}}$$

$$= \frac{£40,000 + £100,000}{£20} = 7,000 \text{ units}$$

We can show that this is the case with a summarised profit and loss account.

	£
Sales (7,000 × £50)	350,000
Variable cost (7,000 × £30)	(210,000)
Fixed cost	(40,000)
Profit	100,000

7   Breakeven charts

It is possible to show the approach diagrammatically.

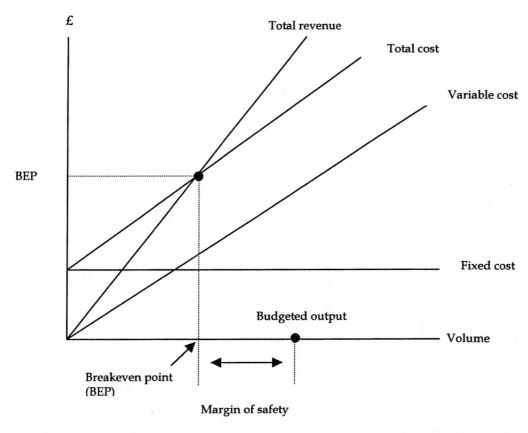

The variable cost and fixed cost line add little to the diagram which may be shown as:

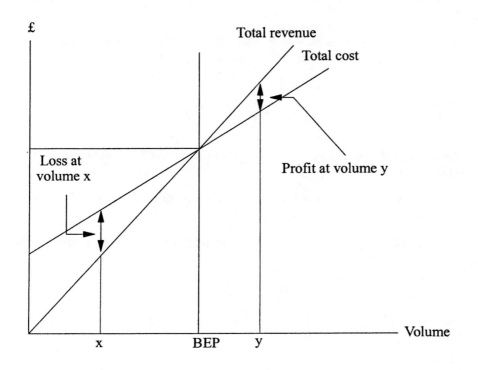

8   Profit-volume (P/V) chart

This is another way of presenting the information.

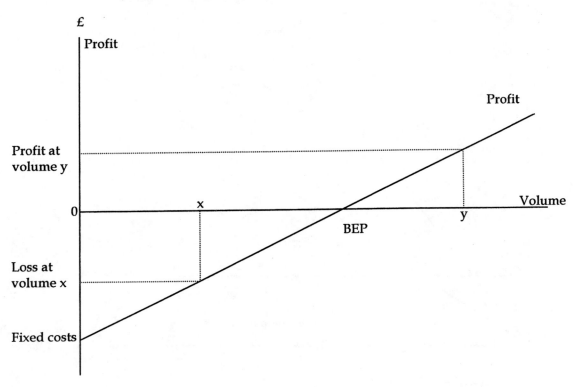

 Note that at a sales volume of nil, the total loss will be the same as the business's fixed costs.

9   P/V ratio

9.1   Introduction

The P/V ratio is a measure of the rate at which profit is generated with sales volume. An alternative name which provides a more accurate description is the contribution/sales (C/S) ratio.

 P/V ratio= $\dfrac{\text{Contribution}}{\text{Selling price}}$

It tells us what proportion of the selling price is contributing to our fixed overhead and profits. It is comparable to the gross profit margin.

If for example the C/S ratio was 40% this would mean that 40% of the selling price was contribution which means therefore that the remaining 60% is variable cost.

It can be used to find the breakeven point or the point at which profit is £x in terms of **sales value** (rather than volume).

 Sales value giving a profit £x = $\dfrac{\text{Fixed cost} + \text{Profit}}{\text{P/V ratio}}$

9.2   *Example*

As before.

What value of sales will give a profit of £100,000?

9.3   *Solution*

Sales value giving profit £100,000 = required contribution £140,000

$$= \quad \frac{\text{Fixed cost} + £100,000}{\text{P/V ratio}}$$

$$= \quad \frac{£40,000 + £100,000}{0.4(\text{W})}$$

$$= \quad £350,000$$

which is the same answer that we obtained before.

WORKING

$$\text{P/V ratio} = \frac{\text{Contribution}}{\text{Selling price}} = \frac{£20}{£50} = 0.4$$

10   Sensitivity analysis

10.1   *Introduction*

A very important aspect of decision-making is concerned with sensitivity analysis, ie how sensitive is our decision to a change in a particular component? Sensitivity analysis is thus concerned with when does our original decision change.

10.2   *Example*

Jonathan plans to manufacture 2,000 units of a product which he can sell for £150 each, the variable cost per unit being £70. Budgeted fixed costs are estimated to be £100,000.

Calculate – breakeven volume;
     – margin of safety; and
     – sensitivity of the decision to a change in the fixed costs.

10.3   *Solution*

♦ The breakeven point is as before:

$$\frac{\text{Fixed costs}}{\text{Unit contribution}} = \frac{£100,000}{£150 - £70 = £80} = 1,250 \text{ units}$$

Note: Our budgeted level of output of 2,000 units will therefore result in a budgeted profit of:

	£
Total contribution = 2,000 × £80	160,000
Less: Fixed costs	(100,000)
Budgeted profit	60,000

♦ **The margin of safety** is the amount by which anticipated sales can fall before the business makes a loss. It can be expressed in units or sales revenue or in relative terms.

Budgeted sales – Breakeven sales = Margin of safety

2,000 units – 1,250 units = 750 units

or $\dfrac{\text{Budgeted sales - Breakeven sales}}{\text{Budgeted sales}} \times 100\%$

$= \dfrac{2,000 - 1,250}{2,000} \times 100\% = 37\frac{1}{2}\%$

ie if budgeted sales fall by more than 37½%, then Jonathan will make a loss. For example consider a fall of 40% on the original budget:

	£
Revised contribution = 0.6 × 2,000 × 80	96,000
Less: Fixed costs	(100,000)
Budgeted loss	(4,000)

♦ **Sensitivity of the decision to a change in fixed costs** As we have seen earlier, currently Jonathan has a budgeted profit of £60,000. Thus the original decision will change if fixed costs increase by more than £60,000 and soak up all of the profits we are currently making, ie. an increase of $\dfrac{60,000}{100,000} \times 100\% = 60\%$: fixed costs can increase by up to 60% before Jonathan will make a loss, one could therefore argue fixed costs are fairly insensitive.

11 Assumptions of breakeven analysis

11.1 The assumptions

The approach makes a number of assumptions which are set out below:

♦ Fixed costs remain fixed throughout the range charted.
♦ Variable costs fluctuate proportionally with volume.
♦ Selling prices do not change.
♦ Efficiency and productivity do not change.
♦ The analysis is applied to a single product or static mix of products.
♦ Volume is the only factor affecting cost.
♦ Linearity is appropriate.

While some of the assumptions may seem unrealistic, over the range of activity considered this usually has little effect.

We will now consider each of the assumptions in more detail.

11.2 Fixed costs remain fixed

If fixed costs are actually stepped fixed costs, it would be possible to have more than one breakeven point.

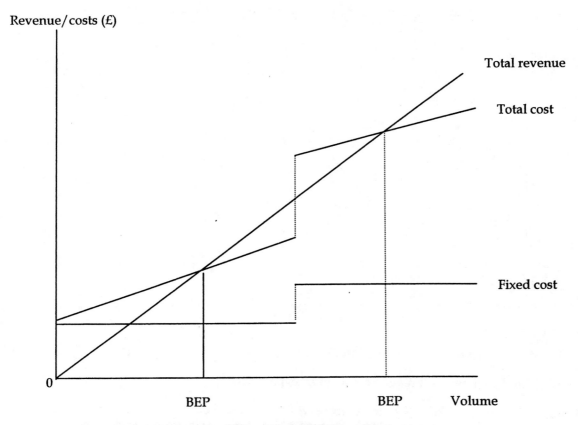

11.3 *Variable costs change in direct proportion to volume*

If this is not the case, then it is invalid to say that a further x units will increase contribution by x multiplied by the existing contribution per unit.

Direct labour is one variable cost that might not change in direct proportion to volume. There might be a learning situation in which case the relationship would be as shown in the following diagram.

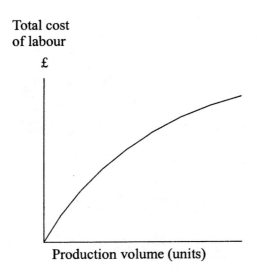

Alternatively there may be no learning effect but overtime is paid at a premium.

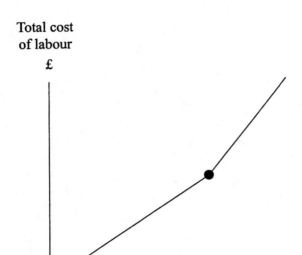

11.4 Selling prices and productivity do not change

A change in these items will require a new breakeven chart.

It might be thought likely that to increase volume a reduction in selling price would be necessary. Equally, discounts could be achieved if supplies were bought in bulk.

Productivity may fall as volume increases and overtime is worked because the workers become tired.

11.5 Product mix does not change

 If we are performing breakeven analysis for a mix of products, then we are working with **average** revenue and **average** variable cost.

11.6 Example

Bob sells X and Y in equal quantities.

	X £	Y £
Selling price	200	180
Variable cost	(100)	(130)
Contribution	100	50

Fixed costs £150,000

11.7 Solution

$$BEP = \frac{£150,000}{£75(W)} = 2,000 \text{ units}$$

ie. 1,000 X and 1,000 Y.

WORKING

Average of £100 and £50, in equal quantities = £75 average contribution per unit.

You may check that this does indeed give a breakeven situation.

Suppose now Bob is able to sell three X for every Y.

$$\text{BEP} = \frac{£150,000}{£87.50(W)} = 1{,}715 \text{ units}$$

ie approximately 429 Y and 1,286 X.

WORKING

$$\frac{[(3 \times £100) + (1 \times £50)]}{4} = £87.50$$

It can be seen then that the change in mix has changed the breakeven point from 2,000 units to 1,715 units.

11.8   Volume is the only factor affecting cost

It may be the case that government action will affect cost. For example, the government might raise taxes on our inputs and hence raise our total costs. This will of course raise our breakeven point.

A similar situation can be conceived as a result of overseas events or even unusual weather conditions.

11.9   Linearity is appropriate

In many ways this is a summary of the above assumptions. The economist would argue that the laws of diminishing returns would give us the following breakeven chart.

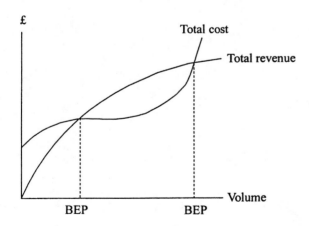

This diagram represents the view that:

♦   to sell more we have to reduce our price; and
♦   to buy more raw materials we have to pay more because they are in scarce supply.

12   Multi-product CVP revisited

12.1   Introduction

It has already been explained that, in order to carry out CVP analysis in a multi-product business, a constant sales mix has to be assumed. The purpose of this section is to illustrate multi-product CVP in a little more detail.

12.2   C/S ratio for multiple products

Consider again the example of Bob introduced earlier. His business faced the situation of selling products X and Y in equal quantities:

	X £	Y £
Selling price	200	180
Variable cost	(100)	(130)
Contribution	100	50

The fixed costs for the period are £150,000.

The contribution/sales ratio for multiple products is given by considering the mix of the products taken together. Each standard mix of one X and one Y generates contribution of £150 on sales of £380 ie:

$$\text{C/S ratio} = \frac{£150}{£380} = 39.474\%$$

The breakeven sales level is therefore given by

$$\frac{\text{Fixed costs}}{\text{C/S ratio}} = \frac{£150,000}{39.474\%} = £380,000$$

As before, this is achieved by selling 1,000 X and 1,000 Y.

12.3   CVP charts for multiple products

If Bob plans to sell 2,000 X and 2,000 Y next period, then we can draw a multi-product P/V chart for this situation.

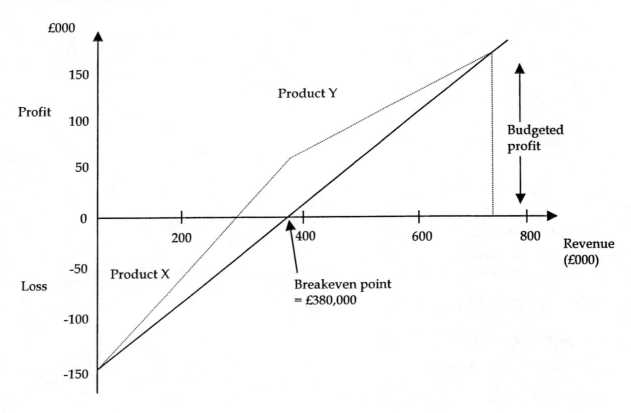

WORKINGS

Budgeted profit = (2,000 × £100) + (2,000 × £50) - £150,000 = £150,000

Budgeted revenue = 2,000 × (£200 + £180) = £760,000

Product X offers revenue of £400,000 and contribution of £200,000.

Product Y offers revenue of £360,000 and contribution of £100,000.

 Note that in multi-product P/V charts, the convention is to show the individual products on the chart from left to right, in order of their C/S ratios. We have Product X with the highest C/S ratio, so it is shown on the graph before Product Y.

12.4   Learning outcomes

At this stage of the chapter we have now covered the following Learning Outcomes.

Calculate and interpret the breakeven point, profit target, margin of safety and profit/volume ratio for multiple products.

Prepare breakeven charts and profit/volume charts for multiple products.

Discuss multiple product CVP analysis.

 Practice questions 1-7 *(The answers are in the final chapter of this book)*

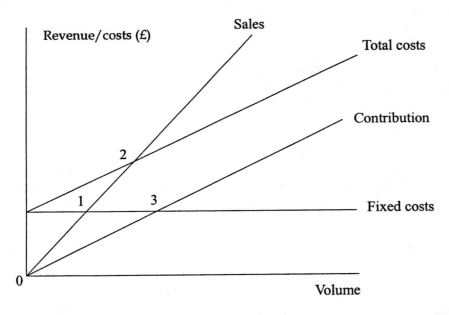

1   Which two points on the above graph could represent breakeven points?

        A   0, 1
        B   1, 2
        C   2, 3
        D   3, 1

2   Which of the following correctly defines the breakeven point? When

     A   total profit equals total costs
     B   total contribution equals total fixed costs
     C   total contribution equals total overheads
     D   total variable costs equals total revenue

3   Which of the following is not an assumption underlying the accountant's breakeven chart?

     A   Volume is the only factor affecting total cost
     B   Fixed costs remain fixed throughout the range charted
     C   Selling prices do not change
     D   Variable costs fluctuate inversely with volume

4   With regard to breakeven charts and breakeven analysis, which of the following is true?

     A   It is assumed that variable costs fluctuate in direct proportion to output
     B   The breakeven point is at the intersection of the sales line and the variable cost line
     C   A breakeven chart shows the maximum profit possible
     D   A breakeven chart is capable of dealing with any change of product mix

5   A company produced 500 units of a product and incurred the following costs:

	£
Direct materials	8,000
Direct wages	10,000
Overheads (20% fixed)	45,000

If the sales value of 500 units was £102,000, what is the P/V ratio?

     A   44%
     B   47%
     C   53%
     D   74%

6   Roger makes a single product, the Morton. During 20X4 he plans to make and sell 10,000 Mortons and accordingly has estimated the cost of each to be £50 (see below). Each Morton sells for £75.

	Cost of a Morton
	£
Material	12
Labour	24
Variable overhead	10
Fixed overhead	4
	50

(a)   Calculate Roger's total fixed overhead.

(b)   Calculate the contribution per unit earned by each Morton.

(c)   What is the total revenue earned if Roger sells 2,000 Mortons?

(d)   Using the information calculated in (a), (b) and (c) above, draw Roger's breakeven chart and estimate his breakeven point.

(e)   Confirm your estimate of the breakeven point by calculating it.

(f)   If Roger makes and sells 1,000 Mortons how much extra profit will he make?

7   The accountant of XYZ has produced the following statement of costs and profit for a company's product, the annual production/sales level of which is 50,000 units.

	£
Direct materials	25
Direct labour	3
Variable overhead	2
Fixed overhead	5
Profit	15
Selling price	50

(a)   (i)   Prepare a breakeven chart from which the contribution and profit at levels of activity up to 50,000 units per annum may be read.

(ii)   Show on your chart any adjustment(s) necessary to reflect an increase of 5% in direct materials cost.

(b)   Calculate the additional production/sales which would be necessary to maintain the company's annual profit, taking into account the additional cost referred to in (a)(ii) above, assuming there are no other changes in costs or in selling price.

(c)   State and comment upon the assumptions inherent in charts of the type required in (a) above.

---

13   Summary

This chapter defined contribution as the difference between selling price and total variable costs per unit. Since contribution per unit remains the same when sales volumes change, decision-making is best carried out in terms of contribution rather than profit.

The chapter explained how a number of contribution charts should be presented to illustrate the situation facing businesses in deciding on sales volumes.

CHAPTER 10

Scarce resource allocation

EXAM FOCUS

The problem of scarce resource allocation (limited factors) is fundamental to the budget setting process. Examination questions may test your understanding of this area either numerically or by a written question.

LEARNING OUTCOMES

This chapter covers the following Learning Outcomes of the CIMA Syllabus.

> Calculate and interpret the profit-maximising sales mix for a company with a single resource constraint and limited freedom of action
>
> Apply and evaluate relevant costs and revenues
>
> Solve a two-plus constraint/limitation problem for two products using the graphical method and explain the results

In order to cover these Learning Outcomes the following topics are included.

> Single scarce resources
> Linear programming

1   Introduction

Often production processes rely on the use of multiple inputs. Each of these inputs will be subject to short and long-term constraints.

When making a choice between alternative products or activities, or considering the most profitable mix, it will sometimes be found that there are factors limiting the achievable output. The limiting factor might be the number of operatives or machine hours available, or the availability of material, or the market demand. In such instances, the preferred product or activity will be that which yields the highest contribution per unit of the limiting factor. If several resources are in short supply another approach is needed: *linear programming*.

2   Single scarce resource

2.1   Ranking criterion

 Where resources are scarce, products competing for the scarce resources must be ranked so that the most efficient use is made of those resources (ie so that the maximum total contribution is earned). Where only one resource is scarce, a criterion which leads to maximum contribution is to rank products according to the contribution produced per unit of the scarce resource they require. Products producing higher contributions per unit of scarce resource are preferred.

2.2 Example

X Ltd is considering producing three products: A B and C. The information regarding these products is as follows.

	A		B		C	
	£	£	£	£	£	£
Selling price		60		80		100
Labour (£2 per hour)	30		20		60	
Material (£1 per kg)	15		30		20	
	—		—		—	
		45		50		80
		—		—		—
Contribution per unit		15		30		20
		—		—		—
Labour hours per unit		15		10		30
Maximum demand per annum	1,000 units		800 units		600 units	

What production plan will maximise the annual contribution, assuming that labour is restricted to 20,000 hours per annum?

2.3 Solution

(a) Calculate whether the limit on the availability of the factor will prevent annual demand being satisfied.

	A	B	C
Annual demand	1,000	800	600
Hours per unit	15	10	30
Hours required to satisfy annual demand	15,000	8,000	18,000

Total hours required = 41,000. Therefore labour is a limiting factor.

(b) Calculate the contribution per unit of the limiting factor:

	A	B	C
Contribution per unit	£15	£30	£20
Labour hours per unit	15	10	30
Contribution per hour	£1.00	£3.00	£0.67
Ranking	2	1	3

(c) Clearly, B produces the greatest contribution for each hour of labour used, A is second best, and C produces the lowest contribution per labour hour. The product mix should therefore be as follows.

			Hours	Contribution
				£
B	800 units (max)	10 hours per unit =	8,000	24,000
A	800 units	15 hours per unit =	12,000	12,000
			20,000	36,000

No C can be produced. After using 8,000 hours producing sufficient B to satisfy demand, 12,000 hours remain to produce A. This is enough time to produce 800 units.

2.4   *Example*

Problems of scarce resources are very common in the examination. The above example illustrates a simple solution to enable you to familiarise yourself with the basic form of approach. Now work through the exercise below (without consulting the suggested answer) to test your understanding and ability to be systematic and logical in laying out your answer.

The Ulster Agricultural Co-operative is planning its production for next season and asks you, as a management accountant, to recommend the optimal mix of vegetable production for the coming year. They have given you the following data relating to the current year:

	Potatoes	*Turnips*	*Parsnips*	*Carrots*
Area occupied, in acres	25	20	30	25
Yield per acre, in tonnes	10	8	9	12
	£	£	£	£
Selling price per tonne	100	125	150	135
Variable costs per acre:				
Fertilisers	30	25	45	40
Seeds	15	20	30	25
Pesticides	25	15	20	25
Direct wages	400	450	500	570

Fixed overheads per annum: £54,000

The land which is being used for the production of carrots and parsnips can be used for either crop, but not for potatoes or turnips. The land being used for potatoes and turnips can be used for either crop, but not for carrots or parsnips. Similarly land used for parsnips and carrots is interchangeable. To provide an adequate market service, the co-operative must produce each year at least 40 tonnes each of potatoes and turnips and 36 tonnes each of parsnips and carrots.

Required

(a)   Present a statement to show:

(i)   the profit for the current year;

(ii)   the profit for the production mix which you would recommend.

(b)   Assuming that the land could be cultivated in such a way that any of the above crops could be produced and there was no market commitment, you are required to:

(i)   advise the co-operative on which crop they should concentrate their production;

(ii)   calculate the profit if they were to do so;

(iii)   calculate in sterling the breakeven yield per acre for this crop.

2.5   *Solution*

(a)   **Profit statements**

(i)   *Currently*

	Potatoes	*Turnips*	*Parsnips*	*Carrots*	*Total*
Sales (tonnes)	250	160	270	300	

	£	£	£	£	£
Sales revenue	25,000	20,000	40,500	40,500	126,000
Variable costs	11,750	10,200	17,850	16,500	56,300
Contribution	13,250	9,800	22,650	24,000	69,700
Fixed costs					54,000
Profit					15,700

(ii) *Recommended*

	Potatoes	Turnips	Parsnips	Carrots	Total
Contribution	£13,250	£9,800	£22,650	£24,000	
Acreage	25	20	30	25	
Contribution/ acre	£530	£490	£755	£960	
Required sales (tonnes)		40	36		
Acres required		5	4		
Acres available	40			51	
Sales (tonnes)	400			612	
	£	£	£	£	£
Sales revenue	40,000	5,000	5,400	82,620	133,020
Variable costs	18,800	2,550	2,380	33,660	57,390
Contribution	21,200	2,450	3,020	48,960	75,630
Fixed costs					54,000
Profit					21,630

The recommended production mix has been found by producing the minimum quota of those two crops which cannot be rotated with the lowest contribution per acre. The balance of the land is used to produce the two more profitable crops. Profit has increased by £5,930.

(b) **Advise if no specific market commitment**

(i) *Recommended crop*

As assumed in part (a) above, if land is the limiting factor, then the co-operative should concentrate on that crop which produces the greatest contribution per acre, namely **carrots**, at £960.

(ii) *Profit from carrots*

With all 100 available acres given over to carrots generating a contribution of £960/acre, the profit will be:

	£
Contribution	96,000
Fixed costs	54,000
Profit	42,000

Profit has increased by £20,370 over the previous recommendation and £26,300 over the original budget.

(iii)   *Breakeven yield*

Given that the 100 acres of land is now given to carrots then the acreage costs of 100 × (£40 + £25 + £25 + £570) = £66,000 will be committed to production together with £54,000 of fixed costs making £120,000 to be recovered in total.

Thus each acre must generate carrots with a sales value of

£120,000 ÷ 100 = £1,200

Notes

(1)   This is equivalent to a yield of 8.89 tonnes per acre.

(2)   The original contribution per acre here is of no relevance; a breakeven yield of £54,000 ÷ £960/acre or 56.25 acres or £91,125 presumes that the co-operative would contemplate a year of semi-idleness not putting the remaining 43.75 acres to any use.

2.6   Learning outcome

At this stage of the chapter we have now covered the following Learning Outcome:

Calculate and interpret the profit-maximising sales mix for a company with a single resource constraint and limited freedom of action.

3   Linear programming

3.1   More than one limiting factor

Production decisions involving a single factor which is in limited supply, can be solved using a simple system of ranking by contribution per unit of the limiting factor. In reality, there may be a number of constraints on production, eg. labour hours and machine hours; under such circumstances a different approach to the problem is required, and use is made of linear programming techniques. For examination purposes, you may be required to formulate and solve a problem using the graphical approach, or alternatively interpret a simplex tableau; you would not be asked to formulate *and* solve a problem using the simplex approach.

3.2   Uses of linear programming

Linear programming is used to determine the optimal production plan in the attainment of some objective which is usually of an economic nature (eg. maximisation of profit, minimisation of cost). The most common problem in decision-making to which the technique is applicable is the allocation problem, in which competing resources must be allocated in accordance with certain conflicting demands or constraints in such a way as to optimise the 'return' from the system. Examples of such allocation problems include production scheduling where several products can be made on each of several different machines; farm management problems such as the Ulster Agricultural example; and airline routing, to determine optimal timing and routing of flights to make the best use of crews, fuel and money.

3.3   Formulation of the mathematical model

We shall now consider the formulation of the mathematical model. The relationships in the model may be classified as follows.

(a)   *Constraints* – These are limitations on the availability of the resources, output, etc. If the constraint covers a number of variables it is referred to as being structural, but a constraint on only one item is often termed a limit.

(b)   *The objective function* – This refers to the 'desired result', expressed as an equation. In business this function is usually the maximisation of profit and/or minimisation of cost but in other spheres (particularly in the public sector) other criteria may apply which are difficult to evaluate.

The easiest way to understand the formulation of the required equations is by following through a simple example.

3.4   Example

A distillery produces two qualities of Scotch whisky; these are type A (40% alcohol and in standard bottles) which is intended for the home market and type B (slightly stronger and in larger bottles) which is for export. After maturing in vats, both types require two stages of processing; blending and bottling. The process times for a standard batch of each type of whisky are:

	Process time (hours)	
	Blending	*Bottling*
Type A	1½	1
Type B	2	3

There are 2,400 hours available for each process but because of the steady but limited demand for type A the number of batches of that type must not exceed 1,200; apart from this, all stocks produced can be sold. The contribution per batch is £200 for type A and £300 for type B. Construct the mathematical model for this situation with a view to deciding which product mix will maximise the total contribution to profit.

3.5   Solution

This type of problem should be dealt with by means of three steps – study them very carefully.

Step 1

Assign symbols to the unknown quantities:

Let   x = number of batches of type A produced;
        y = number of batches of type B produced;
        P = total contribution to profit (although Z is often used for the objective function).

Step 2

Express the constraints in terms of inequalities:

(i)   For the blending process 2,400 hours in total are available to provide 1½ hours for each batch of A produced and 2 hours for each batch of B. Since x and y are the number of batches of A and B respectively, this gives the inequality:

1½x + 2y ≤ 2,400

(ii)   For the bottling process, 2,400 hours are available to provide 1 hour for each batch of A and 3 hours for each batch of B.

Therefore: x + 3y ≤ 2,400

(iii)   Production of type A must not exceed 1,200 batches, ie:

x ≤ 1,200

(iv)   Because production cannot be negative:

x ≥ 0, y ≥ 0

Step 3

Formulate the objective function:

The function to be maximised is the total contribution to profit (ie P). Since types A and B contribute £200 and £300 per batch respectively, total contribution:

P = 200x + 300y

The model is thus:

Maximise	P =	200x + 300y
when	1½x + 2y	≤ 2,400
and	x + 3y	≤ 2,400

but subject to the limits 0 ≤ x ≤ 1,200 and y ≥ 0

4   Graphs

4.1   Revision of straight-line graphs

Having formulated the model the result may be obtained by mathematical manipulation in one of several ways. Before attempting to find the solution to a problem, here is a brief revision of graphical representations of straight lines and inequalities.

The equation of a straight line is of the form:

y = mx + c (sometimes quoted as y = a + bx)

where m gives the gradient (or slope) of the line and c gives the point at which it cuts the y-axis. The graphs of two simple examples are shown in Figure 1.

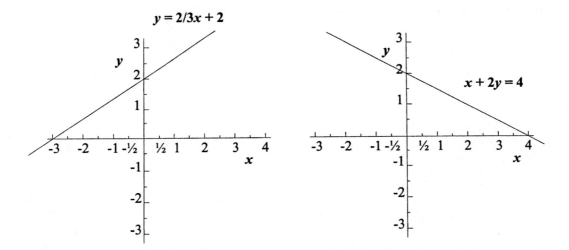

Figure 1

Note: The easiest way to plot a straight line is first to put x = 0 and determine the value for y, thus fixing one point on the line (ie on the y-axis). Secondly put y = 0 and determine the value of x, giving another point on the line (this time on the x-axis). Joining these two points and extending the line as far as is required gives the graph. For example, if the equation is:

x + 2y = 4, then when x = 0, y = 4/2 = 2, and when y = 0, x = 4

Now join the points (0,2) and (4,0) and extend the line as shown.

4.2 Graphical representation of inequalities

We now consider how to depict an inequality on a graph, for instance, $3x + 2y \leq 6$. The solutions of this expression are all those combinations of x and y which satisfy the given condition (ie $3x + 2y \leq 6$).

(a)   The first step is to plot the straight line $3x + 2y = 6$. Obviously all points on this line satisfy the given inequality, which states 'less than or equal to'.

(b)   The remaining solutions are all points on one side of the given line; however, we have to decide which side is appropriate. The easiest test is to see if the origin (ie the point x = 0, y = 0) satisfies the inequality. If it does, then all points on the same side of the line as the origin form the remaining solutions; if it does not, it will be all points on the opposite side of the line from the origin.

4.3 Example

Depict the inequality $3x + 2y \leq 6$ on a graph.

4.4 Solution

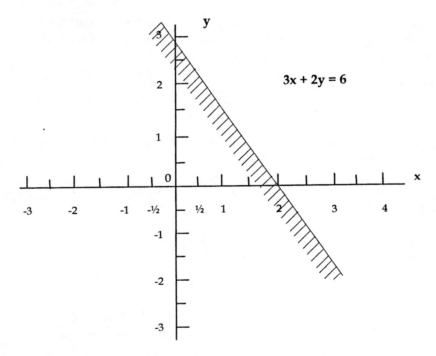

Figure 2

The shaded area (and that area below and to the left of the shading) gives all the solutions of the inequality. Notice that all points on the line $3x + 2y = 6$ are solutions in this case, whereas for the inequality $3x + 2y < 6$, the solutions would be all points in the shaded area but not including any point on the line. This is sometimes shown by drawing a dotted line for the given equation.

Now consider a more complicated example where the required solutions must satisfy more than one inequality.

4.5 Example

Represent graphically the solutions of:

$x + y \geq 1$ and $2x - y \geq 1$

4.6   Solution

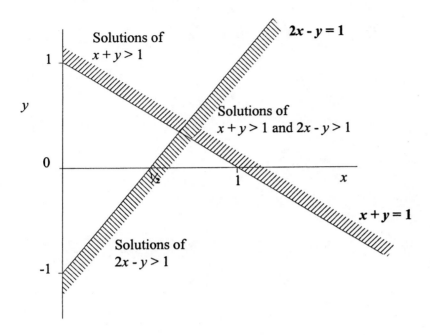

Figure 3

Solutions of x + y ≥ 1 are above and including the line x + y = 1.

Solutions of 2x – y ≥ 1 are below and including the line 2x – y = 1.

Both the inequalities are satisfied where these two regions overlap.

At this point it may be a good idea to practise a few examples, but possibly with three (or even four) inequalities on one graph, until you are completely familiar with the technique. Having mastered this you are in a position to solve linear programming problems by the graphical method.

5   The distillery example – continued

5.1   Graphical representation

Looking back at the data of the distillery example, we had reached the point where we wanted to maximise P = 200x + 300y,

> when 1½x + 2y ≤ 2,400, and x + 3y ≤ 2,400

subject to the limits 0 ≤ x ≤ 1,200 and y ≥ 0.

Ignoring the objective function P for the moment, we can graphically represent all the values of x and y which satisfy the four inequalities as follows.

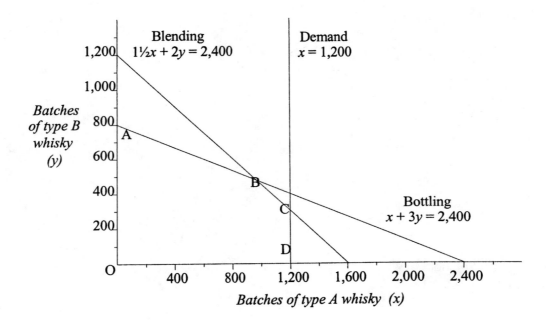

Figure 4

With the given constraints, all feasible values for x and y lie in the area of the graph OABCD (shading has been removed to save time and to keep the graph clear). The point within or on the edge of this area must now be found where the contribution to profit (P) attains its greatest value.

Here we make use of a theorem, the proof of which is not required for your purposes.

In simple terms this states that the maximum value of the objective function (P in this case) occurs on the edge of the area giving all feasible values for the variables (which here are x and y). In fact, this maximum usually occurs at only one corner of the polygon (although it could occur at all points along a line that bounds the region).

Note: The area containing all solutions is sometimes called the feasibility polygon (or feasibility region).

The objective function is P = 200x + 300y. For a given value of P, this can be represented by a straight line, while for several different values of P the graphs form a family of parallel lines, as shown on the next graph.

It can be seen that the value of P increases as the lines become further from the origin (the point x = 0, y = 0). In fact, in the quadrant of the xy-plane which we are considering (where x ≥ 0 and y ≥ 0), P takes its minimum value of zero on the line which passes through the origin.

Referring back to the graph, we now require to find which particular straight line, from the family shown gives the maximum value for P over the polygon OABCD. This maximum is likely to occur at one of the vertices of the polygon (ie A, B, C, D or O) but we can disregard O since we have already decided that the minimum value is attained at this point.

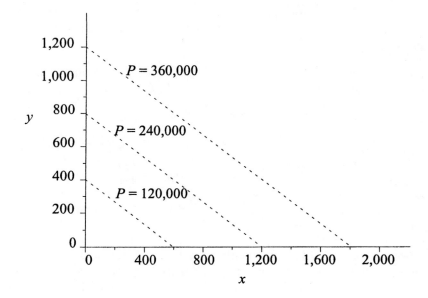

Figure 5

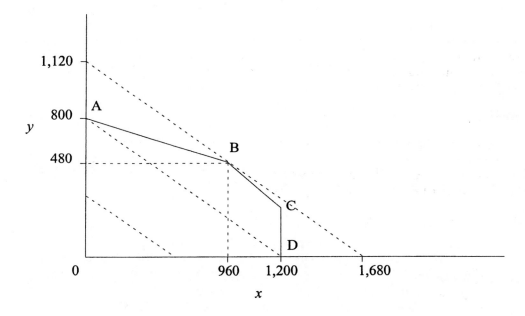

Figure 6

5.2   Final solution

From the final graph, the required line is P = 336,000 which passes through the vertex B of the polygon. This can be determined in one of two ways:

(a)   the correct slope for the family of parallel lines can be found (an objective function, such as P = 120,000, can be drawn), after which the line with that slope can be drawn as far from the origin as possible while still touching just one point of the polygon;

(b)   because we know that the maximum is likely to occur at A, B, C or D, we could evaluate P = 200x + 300y at each of these points – the highest value will be the correct answer.

If the problem has many constraints, the second method may become rather tedious since the values of x and y at the extreme points must be calculated by solving the equations of the two intersecting lines at each point.

The distillery problem asked which processing mix would maximise the contribution to profit (which was shown to be P = 200x + 300y). The maximum value is £336,000, given by the line:

200x + 300y = 336,000

Although there are many possible values of x and y which satisfy this equation, the only feasible solution for this problem is at B where the line touches the polygon. At B, x = 960 and y = 480. This can be read off from the graph, but it is safer to find the values of x and y at B by solving simultaneously the equations of the two lines that intersect at B. The necessary process mix is therefore 960 batches of type A whisky and 480 batches of type B. The contribution to profit will then be £336,000.

 Although the method outlined above is called the graphical method of solution it does not always require an accurate graph to be drawn. The approach adopted here consists of drawing reasonably accurate graphs showing the feasibility polygon and the lines of the objective function, but producing the figures required by solving the equations rather than by reading from the graph. This method is generally more accurate but can be more time-consuming, especially where there are many constraints and awkward figures. If it is decided that the answers are to be read from a graph, then proper graph paper should be used and as large a scale as possible employed on both *x*- and *y*-axes (although not necessarily the same scale on each axis, of course!)

5.3 Advantages and disadvantages of the graphical method

(a)   *Advantages*

(i)   This is a simple pictorial method which is very easy to follow.

(ii)   It is easy to see from the graph how a slight alteration to one or more of the constraints may affect the solution.

(b)   *Disadvantages*

(i)   For a two-dimensional graphical solution, only two variables can be considered. It is theoretically possible to extend this method to three dimensions, in which case a constraint will be represented by a plane instead of a straight line, while the feasible region will be a polyhedron, not a polygon. However, this is not advisable because a three-dimensional model would be required for accurate representation. The graphical method is of no practical value when the number of variables exceeds three.

(ii)   If results are to be read from a graph a small degree of accuracy is lost.

(iii)   As with all methods of solution, the relationships must be strictly linear for the results to be accurate.

(iv)   Too many constraints lead to an overcomplicated graph.

6   Assumptions and limitations of linear programming

6.1 Introduction

The usefulness of linear programming depends upon the extent to which the mathematical model represents an accurate simulation of the actual conditions. Thus, any factors that impinge upon the accuracy of the model will restrict its usefulness.

We can consider the assumptions and limitations under the following headings:

(a)   linearity;
(b)   divisibility;
(c)   product independence;
(d)   certainty; and
(e)   cost classification.

6.2   Linearity

Our linear programming model assumes linear relationships between the variables. This implies that:

 ♦   Any number of items can be sold at the same unit price up to the total quantity demanded. This ignores the usual practical relationship which dictates that demand falls as price increases.

♦   Each unit of output requires the same quantity of input at any volume level, and those inputs have the same unit costs throughout. This again ignores practical effects like the reduction in labour time owing to learning curve effects, or the reduction in unit costs owing to bulk buying discounts.

Obviously if the assumption as to linearity is removed, then a straight line graph will no longer give us the correct decision.

6.3   Divisibility

 Linear programming assumes perfect divisibility of products and resources. Thus a solution may call for the production of fractions of output, where the units are not in fact divisible. This may not be a problem where we are dealing with high volume outputs of small unit value since any fractions can be regarded as immaterial, or else where the problem extends for several periods and work in progress can be accommodated.

The assumption that resources are also perfectly divisible, and so any specified quantity can be obtained, may not be realistic either. It may not be possible to obtain the precise quantity of material for the chosen output mix, owing to the nature of the resources. For example, we may not be able to obtain materials by the kilogram, but rather in steps of 100 kg or one production batch of material.

6.4   Product independence

We have implicitly assumed that the products under review are independent. This assumption is invalidated where:

 ♦   The products are substitutes one for another, such that an increase in demand for one of our products will lead to a reduction in demand for the other.

♦   The products are complementary, such that an increase in demand for one product leads to an increase in demand for the other product. An example here may be sales of television sets and video recorders.

6.5   Certainty

 We have assumed that all of the variables in the model, such as contribution per unit of output or material usage per unit, are known with certainty; however, most will be best estimates of what we think the variables will be.

One way around this problem is to carry out sensitivity analysis (see below).

6.6 Cost classification

Since our objective is to maximise contribution, the model depends upon our ability to separate costs into fixed and variable elements. Any questions over the reliability of estimates will reduce the value of the result obtained.

6.7 Some final considerations

It is worth noting that the answer from a linear programming model is only as accurate as the data used in its formulation. Other possible problems here are the presence of non-quantifiable costs and benefits that cannot be formulated as mathematical constraints. Nevertheless, they must be included in the decision process at some stage.

7 Sensitivity analysis

7.1 Introduction

We stated above that one of the limitations of linear programming was the uncertainty of the parameters included in the formulation.

With sensitivity analysis we will compute by how much the various factors can be changed before our optimum production mix would also change.

We will use the example of the distillery that we formulated and solved in the previous section.

7.2 Changes in constraints

It should be obvious that as one or more of the critical constraints changes, the optimal solution will change. It should be equally obvious that relaxing a non-critical constraint will not change the optimal solution at all, whereas the reverse tightening up of such a constraint – will have an effect on the result if the change is so great that the constraint becomes critical.

For example, in the original solution to the distillery problem, the non-critical constraint on production of type A whisky ($x \leq 1,200$) could be tightened until it read $x \leq 960$ before it became critical. If it were tightened any further the optimal solution would change from the original values of $x = 960$ and $y = 480$. Thus it requires a reduction of 240 batches (from 1,200 batches to 960 batches) in this constraint before the solution is affected.

This change could be expressed as a percentage of the original figure and the result could be quoted as 'a 20% reduction in the constraint is required before the optimal solution is affected'.

This process tests how sensitive the solution is to changes in a constraint, and is called sensitivity analysis.

7.3 Objective function

It is important to note that changes in the objective function could also change the result, since the optimal point of the feasibility region is chosen by considering the slope of the objective function.

Therefore sensitivity analysis can be performed to determine by how much the contribution from one batch of each type of whisky must change before the optimal solution changes. This is most easily effected by holding the contribution from one product constant while changes in the other contribution are investigated.

7.4 Changes of gradient

The optimal solution occurs at the point of the feasibility region which lies on the objective function line with the largest value for P which still touches the feasibility area. However, if the slope of the objective function were to change, the optimal solution could also change.

Referring back to the graph, the optimal solution can be seen to occur at point B, when P = 336,000.

If the slope of the objective function line were steeper (but still negative) you should see that the optimal solution could occur at point C. For this to happen the slope of the objective function must be greater than the slope of the line BC. When the two gradients are equal, the solution is not unique since B and C lie on the same line of constant contribution and either point could be chosen.

The equation of the line BC is $\frac{3}{2}$ x + 2y = 2,400 which can be rewritten as y = - $\frac{3}{4}$ x + 1,200

The slope is therefore - $\frac{3}{4}$. (This can also be seen as the coefficient of x, $\frac{3}{2}$, divided by the coefficient of y, 2, ie $\frac{3}{4}$.)

Thus, if the slope of the objective function line were to change from its original – $\frac{2}{3}$ to become – $\frac{3}{4}$, the optimal solution would not be unique. The points B, C and any point on the line joining them would all give the same maximum value for the contribution.

If the slope were to change still further so that the objective function line became steeper than the line BC, then the optimal solution would occur at C. This would happen if, for example, the objective function had a slope of -1.

7.5 Critical points

With this knowledge it is now possible to investigate how much of a change is required in the contribution, for each of the two products, before the optimal solution to the problem will change. However, a conclusive result can only be produced if the changes are investigated for each product, independently.

For example, if it is assumed that the contribution from a batch of type B whisky remains constant at £300, it is possible to calculate the change necessary in the contribution from a batch of type A whisky to cause the optimal solution to change. This is easily worked as follows.

Let the contribution from a batch of type A whisky be z.

The objective function was P = 200x + 300y with gradient – $\frac{200}{300}$. It is now P = zx + 300y with gradient – $\frac{z}{300}$.

The point at which the optimal solution is just about to change is when the gradients of the objective function line and the line BC are equal. This is when:

$$\frac{z}{300} = \frac{3}{4}$$

ie

$$z = \frac{900}{4} \text{ or } 225$$

Thus the contribution from a batch of type A whisky must increase from £200 to £225 before the optimal solution changes.

7.6 Learning outcome

At this stage of the chapter we have now covered the following Learning Outcome.

> Solve a two-plus constraint/limitation problem for two products using the graphical method and explain the results.

8 Conclusion so far

You have now seen two methods of decision-making when production plans are subject to restrictions (constraints):

♦ key factor analysis – when one resource is in short supply; and
♦ linear programming – when several constraints apply.

The approach to the first method is to identify product contribution, calculate contribution per key factor then rank products accordingly. A neat presentation helps to determine the optimal plan.

To master linear programming you need to be able to draw graphs and solve simultaneous equations (and know what equations to solve simultaneously and why). Remember the steps:

♦ assign symbols to unknowns;
♦ formulate objective functions;
♦ formulate constraints;
♦ represent the problem graphically;
♦ find the optimal point from the graph;
♦ check the optimal mix algebraically.

9 Shadow prices

9.1 Definition   *Learn !*

The shadow price of a scarce resource is the amount by which the objective function changes if one extra unit of the scarce resource becomes available.

They can also be called dual prices or dual values or shadow costs and they are related to ideas of opportunity costs.

9.2 Calculation   *Not on Syllabus*

From the above definition shadow prices only exist for 'scarce' resources, that is critical constraints. Once the critical constraints for a particular problem have been identified, they can be relaxed **in turn** (not simultaneously) by one unit and the new solution found.

Consider the example of the whisky distillery. The two critical constraints at the optimal solution were:

Blending hours: $1\frac{1}{2}x$ + $2y$ = 2,400
Bottling hours: x + $3y$ = 2,400

If either of these are relaxed by one hour (2,401 hours available), the shape of the feasibility region will hardly change since the effect will be for the new constraint lines to lie parallel to the original ones but slightly further from the origin (O). The point B, with slightly different coordinates from the original solution, will still be the optimal point.

Blending constraint

If the blending constraint is relaxed by one hour, the new optimal solution will lie at the intersection of (1) and (2):

$$1\frac{1}{2}x + 2y = 2,401 \quad (1)$$

$$x + 3y = 2,400 \quad (2)$$

Multiply (1) by 2 and (2) by 3:

3x	+	4y	=	4,802	(3)
3x	+	9y	=	7,200	(4)

Subtract (3) from (4): $\qquad$ 5y $\quad$ = $\quad$ 2,398

$\qquad\qquad\qquad\qquad\qquad$ y $\quad$ = $\quad$ 479.6

Substituting in (2): $\qquad$ x $\qquad$ = $\quad$ 2,400 – 1,438.8

$\qquad\qquad\qquad\qquad\qquad\qquad$ = $\quad$ 961.2

Contribution to profit: 200x + 300y = 192,240 + 143,880 = 336,120

This shows an increase of £120 over the original value of the optimal contribution. Thus the shadow price for blending hours is £120 per hour (as per the simplex tableau).

You will also notice that the new coordinates of B have x increased by 1.2 ($\frac{6}{5}$) and y decreased by 0.4 ($\frac{2}{5}$) as before.

Bottling constraint

If the bottling constraint is relaxed by one hour, the new optimal solution will lie at the intersection of:

1½ x	+	2y	=	2,400	(5)
x	+	3y	=	2,401	(6)

Multiply (5) by 2 and (6) by 3:

3x	+	4y	=	4,800	(7)
3x	+	9y	=	7,203	(8)

Subtract (7) from (8) $\qquad$ 5y $\quad$ = $\quad$ 2,403

$\qquad\qquad\qquad\qquad\qquad$ y $\quad$ = $\quad$ 480.6

Substituting in (6): $\qquad$ x $\qquad$ = $\quad$ 2,401 – 1,441.8

$\qquad\qquad\qquad\qquad\qquad\qquad$ = $\quad$ 959.2

Contribution to profit: 200x + 300y = 191,840 + 144,180 = 336,020

This shows an increase of £20 over the original value of the optimal contribution. Thus the shadow price for blending hours is £20 per hour.

9.3   Interpretation

The shadow prices just calculated give an idea of how much **extra** it is worth paying to obtain one extra hour of each scarce resource.

 Since one extra hour on the blending process will yield an extra £120 contribution, it would be worthwhile paying anything up to £120 **in excess of the original price** for this hour. Similarly, if one extra hour on the blending process yields an extra £20 contribution, then this gives the maximum excess premium it is worth paying for the hour.

These results could help management take decisions regarding overtime working, the installation of extra machinery or the hiring of additional staff.

9.4 Limits

Although the previous calculations were based on the assumption that only one extra hour was available, the results hold true for any number of hours up to the point where the constraint has been relaxed so far that the critical constraints change. The point at which this occurs for the bottling constraint is shown by the following graph.

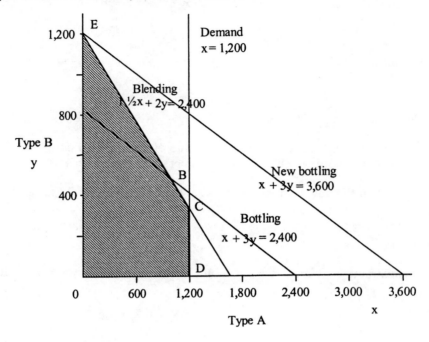

Figure 7

As more bottling hours become available, the line representing this constraint moves further away from the origin. It is only worth doing this up to the point where the number of bottling hours ceases to be a critical constraint. This occurs when the bottling constraint line ($x + 3y = $ constant) passes through the point E ($x = 0$; $y = 1,200$). At this stage the feasibility region is the shaded area OECD and the bottling constraint line is $x + 3y = 3,600$.

Thus it may be worthwhile trying to increase the number of bottling hours available by 1,200, up to a maximum of 3,600, but it is not worth increasing this capacity any further.

With the solution above, the optimal value of contribution occurs at point E where $x = 0$ and $y = 1,200$.

Contribution	=	200x + 300y
	=	£360,000

A similar exercise can be carried out on the blending constraint. Try to prove for yourself that it is only worthwhile increasing the number of blending hours by 200 to 2,600.

Practice question 1 *(The answer is in the final chapter of this book)*

Usine Ltd

Usine Ltd is a company whose objective is to maximise profits. It manufactures two speciality chemical powders, gamma and delta, using three processes: heating, refining and blending. The powders can be produced and sold in infinitely divisible quantities.

The following are the estimated production hours for each process per kg of output for each of the two chemical powders during the period 1 June 20X0 to 31 August 20X0:

	Gamma (hours)	Delta (hours)
Heating	400	120
Refining	100	90
Blending	100	250

During the same period, revenues and costs per kilo of output are budgeted as

	Gamma £ per kg	Delta £ per kg
Selling price	16,000	25,000
Variable costs	12,000	17,000
Contribution	4,000	8,000

It is anticipated that the company will be able to sell all it can produce at the above prices, and that at any level of output, fixed costs for the three-month period will total £36,000.

The company's management accountant is under the impression that there will only be one scarce factor during the budget period, namely blending hours, which cannot exceed a total of 1,050 hours during the period 1 June 20X0 to 31 August 20X0. He therefore correctly draws up an optimum production plan on this basis.

However, when the factory manager sees the figures he points out that over the three-month period there will not only be a restriction on blending hours, but in addition the heating and refining hours cannot exceed 1,200 and 450 respectively during the three-month period.

Required

(a)   Calculate the initial production plan for the period 1 June 20X0 to 31 August 20X0 as prepared by the management accountant, assuming blending hours are the only scarce factor. Indicate the budgeted profit or loss, and explain why the solution is the optimum.

(b)   Calculate the optimum production plan for the period 1 June 20X0 to 31 August 20X0, allowing for both the constraint on blending hours and the additional restrictions identified by the factory manager, and indicate the budgeted profit or loss.

(c)   State the implications of your answer in (b) in terms of the decisions that will have to be made by Usine Ltd with respect to production during the period 1 June 20X0 to 31 August 20X0 after taking into account all relevant costs.

(d)   Under the restrictions identified by the management accountant and the factory manager, the shadow (or dual) price of one extra hour of blending time on the optimum production plan is £27.50. Calculate the shadow (or dual) price of one extra hour of refining time. Explain how such information might be used by management, and in so doing indicate the limitations inherent in the figures. *No longer on Syllabus*

10 Decision making

10.1 Introduction

A decision is a choice among various alternative courses of action for the purpose of achieving some defined goal or objective. Thus a prerequisite of a successful decision is the definition of the objective to be accomplished.

In this chapter we will discuss the criteria to be used in making operational or tactical decisions that have an impact in the short-term.

A fundamental requirement for good decision making will be a careful analysis of costs in order to include only those that are relevant to the analysis. Note however that it will not always be possible to convert all elements of the decision to quantifiable amounts. In many business situations, it is inevitable that qualitative judgements have to be made.

In this chapter we are concerned particularly with quantitative decisions, based on data expressed in monetary values and relating to costs and revenues as measured by the management accountant.

10.2 The role of the management accountant

The role of the management accountant in this decision-making process is particularly concerned with:

♦ recognising the essential structure of a decision problem and posing the right questions for its solution;

♦ identifying what information (or data) is relevant to the solution of the problem; and

♦ providing that data.

In some cases the management accountant will make decision calculations as well as providing data for them; but it is less likely that he will do so when the computations involve the use of quantitative techniques such as probability theory or linear programming.

These fall within the province of specialists such as the operational researcher or the management scientist. The accountant should, however, have some understanding of these techniques otherwise he will find difficulty in providing appropriate data or in interpreting the results obtained.

The remainder of this chapter will be concerned with discussion of the nature of those costs which are relevant for the purpose of decision making. Two general points, however, can be made at this stage:

♦ As all decisions are concerned with what will happen in the future, costs for decision making will be estimates of future costs. Historical data will have importance only to the extent that it provides a basis from which the future can be predicted.

♦ The decision maker will be interested only in costs which will change as a result of adopting a particular alternative, in other words, in those costs which could be avoided (and those revenues which would be foregone) if that particular alternative were not adopted.

We shall be dealing, therefore, with the economist's concept of the nature of costs.

11 Relevant costs for decision making

11.1 Introduction

Although an existing structure of costs, analysed between fixed and activity-variable items, will remain valid over a defined range of existing activities, the purpose of decision making will normally be to alter some aspect of the business. When this is done, then the pre-existing levels of variable cost per unit or relevant fixed costs will cease to be applicable.

It will become necessary, therefore, to define for each decision which items of cost or revenue will be changed as a result of taking the decision.

 Therefore we are moving away from a formal structure of fixed and variable costs, back to the economist's concept of truly 'marginal' changes.

Relevant costs are only those expected future costs that will differ under alternative courses of action.

 The following paragraphs consider the main types of cost that may be given to you in an examination question and how the relevant cost concept applies to them.

11.2 Historical cost

 Every decision deals with the future. The function of the decision maker is to select courses of action for the future and this decision must by its nature be based on predictions. Historical costs in themselves are therefore irrelevant to decisions, though they may be the best available basis for predicting future costs.

11.3 Variable costs

 Costs which have been classified as variable by convention or on the basis of past experience may not in fact vary under the circumstances of a particular volume decision. Accepting a special sales order, for example, may not involve incurring additional selling costs.

11.4 Fixed costs

 Costs which have been classified as fixed by convention or on the basis of past experience may in fact be affected by a particular decision. This may be for two reasons:

♦ The costs are fixed in relation to the levels of activity previously experienced, but a decision may extend the range of activity and thus cause certain fixed costs to be stepped up to a new level.

♦ The costs are fixed in relation to the normal time horizon for forecasting; but if the time span of an action exceeds the normal period, then fixed costs may change.

11.5 Incremental versus common costs

 Incremental costs are the changes in cash costs that arise as a result of the decision, and will therefore be relevant to that decision However costs which will be identical for all alternatives (common costs) are irrelevant and can be ignored for the purpose of decision making.

Examples here include:

♦ Kathryn is about to buy machine Q for her factory. It will cost £15,000. She is offered a contract that will require her to buy a larger machine for £20,000. The incremental cost of the machine that will be charged to the contract will be:

	£
Cost with the contract	20,000
Cost without the contract	15,000
	5,000

♦ The component division of Dick Ltd has been offered a contract to supply ten components at a price of £6,000.

The relevant cost of the contract is £3,500.

Head Office charges all contracts with £2,000 to recognise the fact that fixed costs have to be covered. (Head Office costs are unaltered by the acceptance or rejection of this contract.)

If the contract is accepted, the company will be £2,500 better off.

	£
Revenue	6,000
Costs	3,500
	2,500

Therefore the company should accept it.

Note: The Head Office fixed overheads will be the same whether or not the contract is accepted and thus should be ignored.

Another way of putting this is that they are not incremental costs but common costs.

11.6 Past costs

Costs incurred in the past ('sunk costs') will always be irrelevant. The decision maker has no opportunity to alter what has already happened. Some specific examples of this are:

♦ **Obsolete stock** – the cost of stock already held, and now proved to be obsolete, has no relevance to a decision regarding its disposal or other use; even though the decision may result in a book loss being reported.

♦ **Old equipment** – the cost of new equipment and the disposal value of old equipment are relevant future transactions. The book value of old equipment is irrelevant to any decision making technique.

Practice question 2 *(The answer is in the final chapter of this book)*

Charlotte

Charlotte has been offered a contract to supply 20 fugrands at a price of £100,000. She consults you before deciding whether or not to accept the contract and you determine the following.

Labour

It will take 60 hours to produce a fugrand. This is made up of 40 unskilled labour hours and 20 hours of skilled labour.

Unskilled labour is freely available at £5 per hour.

Skilled labour is in short supply and Charlotte's existing skilled workers are fully occupied and cannot be moved from their current jobs. They earn £10 per hour, but if they have to work overtime a premium of 200% is payable.

Variable overhead

Variable overhead accrues at £3 per hour.

Fixed overhead

Fixed overhead is absorbed at £10 per hour.

Material

Each fugrand requires the following material:

2 kg of Cotassium pyanide
3 litres of Wedrine
1 metre of Clastip

Cotassium pyanide is inherently unstable. Unless Charlotte uses her stock of 30 kg on this contract it will degenerate into a poisonous chemical that will have to be disposed of at a cost of £100 per kilogram.

The current price of Cotassium pyanide is £1,000 per kilogram.

Charlotte has no stock of wedrine but has discovered that UB Limited will supply it at a price of £500 per litre.

Her stock of clastip is embarrassingly large because of a purchasing error. This material is obsolete and so cannot be sold. Its only possible use is as a substitute for a more modern material in another product. Each metre of clastip so used will save the purchase of 1 cm of the new material which costs £10 per metre.

Machinery

The following machines are required to make fugrands

Z200   –   cost £5,000
CBX   –   cost £50,000

It transpires that the CBX will also do the job of the CB500 as well as producing fugrands. Charlotte uses a CB500 in her existing business and it is due to be replaced at a cost of £30,000.

Should Charlotte accept the contract?

12 Summary

Linear programming is an important examination area. You should be very familiar with the graphical and algebraic solutions.

Shadow pricing is also an important examination area. It is a very straightforward extension of the basic techniques and should present few computational difficulties. However, you must ensure that you know how to interpret the concept of a shadow price.

Multiple choice questions (The answers are in the final chapter of this book)

1   A company produces and sells four types of fashion garments: A, B C and D. Selling prices, costs of manufacture and maximum sales demand are given below.

	A £	B £	C £	D £
Selling price	50	42	45	55
Material cost (£5 per unit)	15	5	15	20
Labour cost (£4 per hour)	8	12	4	12
Overhead cost	5	7	6	4
Total variable cost	28	24	25	36
Allocated fixed costs	6	7	5	2
Total cost of manufacture	(34)	(31)	(30)	(38)
Profit per item	16	11	15	17
Maximum sales demand	50,000	40,000	60,000	30,000

Both materials and labour are in short supply. Materials are restricted to 500,000 units and labour is restricted to 300,000 hours.

Which type of fashion garment should be chosen first in production scheduling?

A   Garment A
B   Garment B
C   Garment C
D   Garment D

2   One unit of a certain raw material can be used to make 3 units of the product Z or to make 2 units of V. Manufacture of the product V requires at least an equivalent production of Z. 100 units of the raw material are available.

If V and Z denote the units to be produced, which of the following constraints represents the above restrictions?

A $\dfrac{Z}{3} + \dfrac{V}{2} \le 100, Z \ge V$

B $\dfrac{Z}{3} + \dfrac{V}{2} \le 100, Z \le V$

C $3Z + 2V \ge 100, Z \ge V$

D $3Z + 2V \ge 100, Z \le V$

3   The graph below represents the linear programming problem

Maximise $3X_1 + 2X_2$

Subject to $2X_1 + 3X_2 \geq 12$

$4X_1 + 2X_2 \leq 16$

$X_1 + X_2 \geq 5$

and $X_1 \geq 0, X_2 \geq 0$

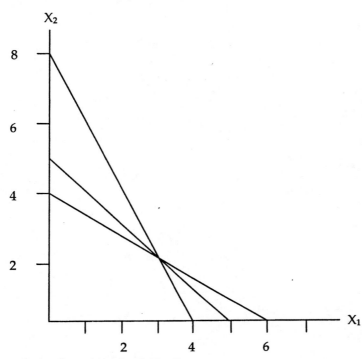

What is the optimal solution?

A $X_1 = 4, X_2 = 0$

B $X_1 = 3, X_2 = 2$

C $X_1 = 0, X_2 = 5$

D $X_1 = 0, X_2 = 8$

CHAPTER 11

Process costing

EXAM FOCUS

Process costing is one of the most complex areas of the syllabus and tends to be the area of cost accounting that most students find hardest to understand. However, it appears on a regular basis in exams, and therefore it is an area worth looking at repeatedly to make sure that you can have a reasonable attempt at any question asked. Apart from computational questions, you may face written questions as well. Developing good examination technique when approaching questions will help you to score maximum marks.

LEARNING OUTCOMES

This chapter covers the following Learning Outcome of the CIMA Syllabus.

> Apply and evaluate the use of activity-based, absorption, marginal and process costing and throughput accounting in the context of planning and decision making

1 Process costing

1.1 Definition

Process costing is defined as:

> "The costing method applicable where goods or services result from a sequence of continuous or repetitive operations or processes. Costs are averaged over the units produced during the period, being initially charged to the operation or process."

Process costing is sometimes referred to as continuous operation costing as the goods produced result from a sequence of continuous or repetitive operations or processes.

Examples include the chemical, cement, oil, paint and textile industries.

1.2 Illustration

Process costing is used when a company is mass producing the same item and the item goes through a number of different stages. Here is an example.

First stage   Input some material valued at £1 per kg

Process (do some work to) the material (which costs money)

Output the material now valued at £2 per kg

Second stage   Input material from the first stage valued at £2 per kg

Process the material in a different way, increasing the cost again

Output the material now valued at £4 per kg

Final stage   Input material from the second stage valued at £4 per kg

Process the material again, increasing the cost

Output the material now valued at £9 per kg. This now goes into finished goods ready to be sold. Cost of sales is £9 per kg.

There are two main complications.

- ♦ What happens if some of the material to the process is lost?
- ♦ What happens if the process is not complete at the end of a period?

1.3 Ledger accounts in process costing

To keep track of the costs we are going to prepare a process account for each process. This resembles a T account with extra columns. The reason for the extra columns is that we have to keep track of how many units we are working on as well as their value.

 The usual costs appearing in such an account are those for materials, labour and overheads. (Labour and overheads are often combined under the heading 'conversion costs'.) In the case of materials we record both units and monetary amount; in the case of conversion costs we record the monetary amount only, because they do not add any units.

1.4 Example

Typically a process account might appear as follows.

Process 2 account

	Kg	£		Kg	£
Input materials from Process 1	2,000	2,950	Output materials to Process 3	2,500	4,544
New materials	500	550			
Labour		564			
Overheads		480			
	2,500	4,544		2,500	4,544

In this simple case, the output to process 3 would be costed at:

$$\frac{£4,544}{2,500} = £1.82 \text{ per unit}$$

2 Normal and abnormal losses

2.1 Normal losses

In many industrial processes, some input is lost or damaged during the production process. The first thing we will look at in process costing is the concept of normal losses and abnormal losses or gains.

 Normal loss represents items that you expect to lose during a process, and its cost is therefore treated as part of the cost of good production.

2.2 Example

At the start of a heating process 1,000kg of material costing £16 per kg is input. During the process, conversion costs of £2,000 are incurred. Normal loss (through evaporation) is expected to be 10% of input. During March 1,000kg were input and output was 900kg.

Prepare the process account for March.

2.3   Solution

To prepare the process account we need to balance the units and then balance the cost.

Firstly, to balance the units we put input units on the left and output units on the right. Normal loss also appears on the right.

The process account will look as follows.

Process account – March (units only)

	Kg	£		Kg	£
Input	1,000		Output	900	
Conversion costs	-		Normal loss	100	
	1,000			1,000	

As you can see the units put in on the left total those on the right; our units balance.

Now we can go on to put in costs and values.

The input was valued at £16 per kg, giving a cost of input of £16,000. Conversion costs are £2,000. Normal loss is valued at zero – its cost will be absorbed into good production. Output is valued at cost divided by expected output (ie cost/(input – normal loss)).

In this example output is valued at £18,000/900kg = £20 per kg

The total value of the output is therefore 900 × £20 = £18,000

The completed process account now looks as follows.

Process account – March

	Kg	£		Kg	£
Input	1,000	16,000	Output	900	18,000
Conversion costs		2,000	Normal loss	100	–
	1,000	18,000		1,000	18,000

Notice that the units and the monetary amounts balance.

2.4   Abnormal loss

Any actual loss in excess of the normal (expected) loss is known as abnormal loss. This is **not** treated as part of normal production cost and is separately identified and costed throughout the process. Its cost is then written off to profit and loss.

2.5   Abnormal loss - example

In April, 1,000kg were input (at £16 per kg) to the same process as above and actual output was 800kg.

Required

Prepare the process account for the month of April.

2.6 Solution

Again look at the units only to start with.

Process account – April (units only)

	Kg	£		Kg	£
Input	1,000		Output	800	
Conversion costs	-		Normal loss	100	
	1,000			900	

As you can see, 1,000kg were input to the process but only 900kg have been accounted for coming out of the process. The extra 100kg is an *abnormal loss*. It represents items that we did not expect to lose. In this example it may have been that the temperature was set too high on the process, causing more of the input to evaporate.

To make the units balance we therefore include 100 units on the right of the process account to represent this abnormal loss.

Process account – April (units only)

	Kg	£		Kg	£
Input	1,000		Output	800	
			Normal loss	100	
Conversion costs	-		Abnormal loss	100	
	1,000			1,000	

Now that the units balance we can examine the costs.

Input, normal loss and output are valued at the same amount as before. The value for abnormal loss is the same as that of output, ie £20 per kg.

Process account – April

	Kg	£		Kg	£
Input	1,000	16,000	Output	800	16,000
			Normal loss	100	–
Conversion costs	-	2,000	Abnormal loss	100	2,000
	1,000	18,000		1,000	18,000

The units and values are now balanced. The £2,000 value of the abnormal loss represents lost output. This output cannot be sold (it has evaporated) and therefore the profits of the company will be reduced. In the accounts, the value of abnormal loss is debited to the profit and loss account.

2.7 Abnormal gain

An abnormal **gain** occurs where losses are **less** than expected. Its treatment is the same as abnormal loss only the debits and credits are reversed.

2.8   *Example*

In May 2,000 kg at £16 per kg were input to the heating process and £4,000 conversion costs incurred. This month output was 1,950 kg.

Required

Prepare the process account for the month of May.

2.9   *Solution*

We begin by looking at the units columns.

Process account – May

	Kg	£		Kg	£
Input	2,000		Output	1,950	
Conversion costs	-		Normal loss	200	
	2,000			2,150	

Again it can be seen that the two sides do not balance. This time the reason is that we have more output than expected. We would have expected to lose 10% of input (ie 200kg) so we expected output to be 1,800kg. In fact it was 1,950kg, an increase of 150kg. This additional output is an *abnormal gain*.

The completed process account is shown below.

Process account – May

	Kg	£		Kg	£
Input	2,000	32,000	Output	1,950	39,000
Conversion costs	-	4,000			
Abnormal gain	150	3,000	Normal loss	200	–
	2,150	39,000		2,150	39,000

Output and abnormal gain are both valued at £36,000/(2,000 – 200)kg = £20 per kg. Since we now have additional units to sell, the abnormal gain is credited to the profit and loss account. We have an additional 150 units to sell at £20 per unit.

3   Scrap value

3.1   Introduction

So far we have assumed that all losses are scrapped (ie they have nil value) but what happens if this is not the case?

3.2   Example

Maine Ltd processes a liquid. When it is produced a residue forms on top of the liquid. This is skimmed off and sold off for 90p/litre. Normal waste is 10% of input. Costs for batch 975D were as follows.

		£
Materials (10,000 litres @ £2 per litre)		20,000
Labour		2,000
Overheads		500
Total		22,500
Actual output		8,500 litres

Required

Prepare the process account.

3.3   Solution

The process account will include normal loss as before but this time it is **valued at its scrap value**. The sales value of the normal loss is then **subtracted** from the costs of the process before calculating value per unit.

In the example we would receive 1,000 litres @ £0.90 = £900 for selling the normal loss. This is entered in the process account. The same amount is then subtracted from the process costs, leading to the following valuation.

$$\text{Value per unit} = \frac{£20,000 + £2,000 + £500 - £900}{10,000 - 1,000} = £2.40 \text{ per litre.}$$

Although we actually have 1,500 loss units to sell (1,000 litres of normal loss plus 500 units of abnormal loss), we only include the sales value of the **normal** loss in this calculation.

Process account

	Ltrs	£		Ltrs	£
Material	10,000	20,000	Output @ £2.40	8,500	20,400
Labour	–	2,000	Normal loss @ £0.90	1,000	900
Overheads		500	Abnormal loss @ £2.40	500	1,200
	10,000	22,500		10,000	22,500

3.4   Normal and abnormal loss accounts

We now require two additional T accounts to show the value of the normal and abnormal loss in this situation. These match the costs of the losses (from the process account) against the scrap proceeds. Here we show separate accounts for each type of loss, sometimes they will be combined into one 'process loss' account.

3.5   Example

Show the normal and abnormal loss accounts for Maine Ltd.

3.6   Solution

Normal loss (scrap)

	Ltrs	£		Ltrs	£
Normal loss from process account	1,000	900	Cash proceeds	1,500	1,350
Abnormal loss	500	450			
	1,500	1,350		1,500	1,350

Note: This account may also be called a "scrap" account.

This T account takes the total sales of 1,500 units and cash proceeds received of £1,350 and divides it between the normal and abnormal loss units.

Abnormal loss

	Ltrs	£		Ltrs	£
Abnormal loss from process = full value of lost units @ £2.40	500	1,200	Cash received for abnormal loss @ £0.90	500	450
			P&L (balancing figure)		750
	500	1,200		500	1,200

If the scrap value of the losses were nil, then we would have written off £1,200 to the profit and loss account. However, in this case we were able to sell the abnormal loss for £0.90 per unit. Since we received £450 for selling the abnormal scrap, we are only £750 worse off than if we sold all the lost units at full value.

In effect we are worse off by (£2.40 – £0.90) = £1.50 per unit lost. Since the abnormal loss was 500 units then we are worse off by 500 × £1.50 = £750 which matches the P&L figure in the abnormal loss account.

In the above, the normal and abnormal loss accounts are being used purely to calculate the debit or credit to the profit and loss account. Remember they are not needed if the losses have no scrap value since the value of abnormal loss may be debited straight to the profit and loss account.

Practice question 1 *(The answer is in the final chapter of this book)*

X plc

X plc processes a chemical. Input to a batch was as follows.

	£
Materials (10,000 litres)	10,000
Labour and overheads	800
Total	10,800

Normal loss is 10% of input.

Actual output = 8,700 litres. The remaining liquid was skimmed off and sold for 36p per litre.

Required

Record this in a process account, a normal loss account and an abnormal loss account.

Practice question 2 *(The answer is in the final chapter of this book)*

Chemical compound

A chemical compound is made by raw material being processed through two processes. The output of Process A is passed to Process B where further material is added to the mix. The details of the process costs for the financial period number 10 were as shown below.

Process A	
Direct materials	2,000 kg @ £5 per kg
Direct labour	£7,200
Process plant time	140 hours @ £60 per hour
Process B	
Input from process A	?
Direct material	1,400 kg @ £12 per kg
Direct labour	£4,200
Process plant time	80 hours @ £72.50 per hour

The departmental overhead for period 10 was £6,840 and is absorbed into the costs of each process on direct labour costs in each process.

	Process A	*Process B*
Expected output	80% of input	90% of input
Actual output	1,400 kg	2,620 kg

Assume no opening or closing work-in-progress.

Normal loss is contaminated material which is sold as scrap for £0.50 per kg from Process A and £1.825 per kg from Process B.

Required

Prepare the following accounts.

(a)   Process A
(b)   Process B
(c)   Normal loss (scrap)
(d)   Abnormal loss/gain
(e)   Finished goods (extract)
(f)   Profit and loss (extract)

---

4   Equivalent units and work in process

4.1   Introduction

We begin with a word of warning. This next section on equivalent units is not easy to assimilate in one go: do not worry if you have to read it through a number of times.

Process costs are used for many products where the process may not be completed at the end of a period (eg manufacturing cars). We need some way of calculating the value of work in process at the beginning and at the end of a period.

To do this we use the concept of **equivalent units**.

Illustration

We have 1,000 units that are 50% complete at the end of a period. How many finished units is this equivalent to?

1,000 × 50% = 500 equivalent units (these are abbreviated to EUs).

In other words, we could have made 500 units and finished them instead of 1,000 half-finished units.

The calculation of equivalent units is quite straightforward.

 Equivalent units = Number of physical units × percentage completion.

4.2   Example

DL Ltd is a manufacturer. In Period 1 the following production occurred.

Opening work in process (abbreviated as OWIP)	=	Nil
Started and finished units	=	1,000
Closing work in progress (abbreviated as CWIP)	=	2,000 units each 25% complete

Required

How many finished units is this equivalent to?

4.3   Solution

		EUs
Started and finished	1,000 × 100%	1,000
Starting closing WIP	2,000 × 25%	500
Total		1,500

 Costs for Period 1 will be spread over 1,500 units. Later in this chapter we will see how this is done. For the moment it is important to consider what we are trying to do. We will spend money in Period 1 making products, of which some will be completed and some will be unfinished (ie in closing stock) at the end of the period.

How much do we charge customers buying the completed products and how much is the closing stock valued at?

4.4   Example

In Period 2 the following production occurred in DL Ltd.

Completed opening WIP (which was 2,000 units 25% complete)
Started and finished 500 units
Closing WIP = 1,000 units 60% complete.

Required

How many EUs were produced?

4.5   Solution

		EUs
Finishing opening WIP	2,000 × 75%	1,500
Started and finished units	500 × 100%	500
Starting closing WIP	1,000 × 60%	600
Total		2,600

One of the most common mistakes in the examination is the incorrect treatment of opening WIP. If the WIP is 25% complete at the start of the period then to finish it (ie to complete it) will require an additional (100% – 25%) = 75% of input.

Notice then that for closing WIP we take how much work has been done and for opening WIP we take how much is *left to do*. Those units that are started and finished within the period are always 100% complete.

4.6 Valuing work in process and finished goods

If we can calculate the cost of an equivalent unit we can calculate the cost of finished goods and closing WIP.

The cost per equivalent unit is simply calculated as total cost divided by the number of EUs produced. Assume that in DL above the costs in Period 1 were £6,000.

Earlier we calculated that 1,500 EUs were produced in Period 1. This was made up as follows.

		EUs
Started and finished	1,000 × 100%	1,000
Starting closing WIP	2,000 × 25%	500
Total		1,500

Cost per EU = £6,000/1,500 = £4 per EU.

This can be used to calculate the value of the finished goods and closing WIP.

Value of goods started and finished = 1,000 × £4 = £4,000.

You can see that the value of finished goods is £4 per unit and the total value of finished goods is £4,000.

Value of closing WIP = 500 × £4 = £2,000.

This will go in the balance sheet for Period 1 and will become the value of opening WIP for Period 2.

 Note that closing WIP is valued using EUs and not physical units. Many students get this wrong in the exam.

Our process account for Period 1 would look as follows.

Process account – Period 1

	£		£
Costs	6,000	Finished goods	4,000
		Closing WIP c/f	2,000
	6,000		6,000

 You can see that if there is no opening WIP the method is quite straightforward.

- Calculate total equivalent units.

- Calculate total costs.

- Calculate cost per equivalent unit.

- Value finished goods and closing WIP as number of EUs × cost per EU.

5   Dealing with opening WIP

5.1   Introduction

Above we calculated the closing WIP as 500 EUs worth £2,000. This will become the opening WIP for Period 2. When we continue production in Period 2, what will we do with the work we have already done and the costs already incurred?

There are two different methods and you must be able to use both.

♦   FIFO
♦   AVCO

FIFO – first in first out

 The idea here is that there are four distinct phases of production.

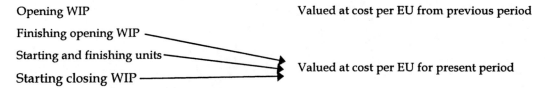

Opening WIP	Valued at cost per EU from previous period
Finishing opening WIP	
Starting and finishing units	Valued at cost per EU for present period
Starting closing WIP	

The value of finished goods will be made up of two parts:

Value of the opening WIP brought forward + units finished at cost per EU for the period.

Value of closing WIP is as before:

Closing WIP EUs × cost per EU.

Notice then that the value of the opening WIP is simply added to the value of finished goods, and the EUs of the opening WIP are ignored. We only use the EUs to *finish* the opening WIP.

AVCO – average cost

Under this second method we imagine that the opening WIP units were produced in Period 2, ie we include costs and production in Period 2.

In other words treat the periods as the same and only calculate one cost per EU for the period. This will be used to value both Period 1 and Period 2.

5.2   Example

Staying with DL Ltd, production in Period 2 was as follows.

		EUs	
Finishing opening WIP	2,000 × 75%	1,500	(£2,000 costs associated with these from period 1)
Started and finished units	500 × 100%	500	
Starting closing WIP	1,000 × 60%	600	
Total		2,600	

Assume that Period 2 production costs were £13,000.

Required

Prepare the process account under both FIFO and AVCO.

5.3   Solution - Method 1 FIFO

For Period 2, cost per unit = £13,000/2,600 = £5 per EU. This is made up as follows.

		£
Finishing opening WIP	1,500 × £5	7,500
Started and finished goods	500 × 100% × £5	2,500
Closing WIP	1,000 × 60% × £5	3,000
		13,000

Value of closing WIP = £3,000

This is for period 2 only. We must also include the £2,000 spent in Period 1. This will be included in the value of finished goods.

Value of finished goods	£
Costs of Period 1 brought forward	2,000
Finishing opening WIP	7,500
Started and finished goods	2,500
Total	12,000

Process account – Period 2

	£		£
Costs from Period 1 b/f	2,000	Finished goods	12,000
Costs in Period 2	13,000	Closing WIP	3,000
	15,000		15,000

5.4   Solution - Method 2 AVCO

Imagine that opening WIP was also produced in Period 2, ie include it as started and finished (100% completed in Period 2). In other words, include all 2,000 physical units and £2,000 costs.

The EUs for period 2 will be as follows:

		EUs	
Opening WIP		2,000	(£2,000 costs associated with these from period 1)
Started and finished units	500 × 100%	500	
Starting closing WIP	1,000 × 60%	600	
Total		3,100	

Total costs = £13,000 + £2,000 = £15,000 (including costs brought forward as though they had occurred in Period 2).

Cost per EU = £15,000/3,100 = £4.839 per EU.

		£
Started and finished	2,500 × 100% × £4.839	12,097
Closing WIP	1,000 × 60% × £4.839	2,903

No adjustment is needed for Period 1 costs as they have already been included.

Process account – Period 2

	£		£
Costs from Period 1 b/f	2,000	Finished goods	12,097
Costs in Period 2	13,000	Closing WIP	2,903
	15,000		15,000

Practice question 3 *(The answer is in the final chapter of this book)*

Process WIP

On 1 March 20X0 a process contained 50 units, each 20% complete. During March work started on another 300 units and at the end of the month there were still 75 units in the process, each 60% complete.

The total cost of materials input during March was £3,596 and the opening work in progress had a value of £100.

Required

Calculate the value of both finished goods and closing WIP under the following methods.

(a)   The FIFO method.

(b)   The average method.

6   Treatment of materials and other costs

6.1   Different degrees of completion

So far we have talked about 'production costs' in general. In most questions, however, these will be split between various types of cost.

Assume that a process involves some direct materials and some direct labour and overheads.

Labour and overhead costs added together are often called **conversion costs**.

Usually, all the material is put in at the beginning of the process, whereas the conversion is 'added' as the product advances through the process. This means there may be a **different amount of equivalent units for conversion and materials.**

A good example is making a cake. All the materials (cake mix, fruit etc) are put in at the beginning, whereas cooking the cake advances through the process over time. So if the cake takes two hours to cook, after one hour the cake is 50% complete as regards the heating but is 100% complete with regard to materials.

Because of this, we have to keep track of the equivalent units for materials and for conversion separately.

For example, imagine we have a process in which all the materials are input at the beginning and that at the end of November there are 200 units 75% complete.

For conversion there are 200 × 75% = 150 EUs.

For materials all 200 units are complete (since all material went in at the beginning), ie 200 EUs.

6.2 Example

Blue Ridge Ltd specialises in making disinfectants. Production requires several successive processes and the production details of the first process are as follows.

Opening work in process	200 units
Degree of completion:	
Materials (valued at £6,060)	75%
Conversion (valued at £2,940)	25%
Units started in period	1,200 units
Closing work in process	400 units
Degree of completion:	
Materials	100%
Conversion	50%
Costs incurred in April:	
Materials	£75,000
Conversion	£69,000

Required

Calculate the value of closing work in process and completed units.

6.3 Solution

First start, as always, with a physical flow of units:

Opening WIP	+	Units started	=	Units completed	+	Closing WIP
200	+	1,200	=	1,000	+	4000

The 1,000 units completed is a balancing figure and includes the 200 units b/f in OWIP.

The effective units, costs and costs per unit are most clearly set out in a table as follows:

Input	Effective units			Costs			Costs per EU (£)
	Completed in period	c/f in CWIP	Total EU	b/f in OWIP	In period	Total costs (£)	
Materials	1,000	400 (100%)	1,400	6,060	75,000	81,060	57.90
Conversion	1,000	200 (50%)	1,200	2,940	69,000	71,940	59.95
						153,000	117.85

Work carefully through the table to ensure you are quite happy about where all the figures have come from.

Note that for the 'completed in period column', effective units = physical units, as the opening WIP units are being treated as being wholly processed in this period. These units are then added to the effective units for the CWIP, to arrive at the total EU units treated as having been processed in the period.

The costs associated with the OWIP are added in, line-by-line, to the costs incurred in the period, to give total costs. These are then divided by the total EU to get a cost per EU for each type of input cost, and a total cost for each completed unit.

The costs may now be attributed to the categories of output as follows:

			£	£
Completed units:	1,000 × £117.85			117,850
Closing WIP:	Materials	400 × £57.90	23,160	
	Conversion	200 × £59.95	11,990	
				35,150
				153,000

The process account would appear as follows. Note that if any units are entered in here, they would be *physical* units, not EU, as this would get too confusing!

Process account

	£		£
Materials b/f	6,060	Completed goods	117,850
Conversion b/f	2,940	Closing work in progress	35,150
Materials	75,000		
Conversion	69,000		
	153,000		153,000

7   Equivalent units and losses

7.1   Introduction

So far we have looked at examples with either equivalent units, OR with losses. The example below covers both in one question.

7.2   Example

MR Ltd produces its product using two processes. The following data relates to process 2 in April:

Opening Work-in-Progress:	2,400 Kg		
Materials	100% complete	value	£8,232 (incl process 1 costs)
Conversion	50% complete	value	£954
Transfers from process 1	224,000 Kg	value	£670,880
Transfers to finished goods	210,800 Kg		
Closing Work-in-Progress:	3,200 Kg		
Materials	100% complete		
Conversion	75% complete		

Costs incurred in the period:

Additional Materials	£63,466
Conversion	£170,598

Normal loss is 5% of total units completed and occurs on inspection, at the end of the process. Losses have no scrap value.

You are required to prepare the process 2 account for April.

7.3 Solution

First start, as always, with a physical flow of units, this time including the losses:

Opening WIP	+	Units started	=	Good units completed	+	Normal loss	+	Abnormal loss (bal)	+	Closing WIP
2,400	+	224,000	=	210,800	+	11,160 (W)	+	1,240	+	3,200

Working

The normal loss is 5% of total units completed – ie both good and loss units. This must be total input units – CWIP units, ie 2,400 + 224,000 – 3,200 = 223,200. Thus normal loss is 5% × 223,200 = 11,160 units.

Normal loss percentages can be computed on a number of different bases – read the question carefully!

The effective units, costs and costs per unit are set out in the following table. Note that you do not need a separate column for normal loss as its cost is absorbed into the cost of other units:

Input	Effective units				Costs			Costs per EU (£)
	Completed in period	AL	c/f in CWIP	Total EU	b/f in OWIP	In period	Total costs (£)	
Process 1/ materials	210,800	1,240	3,200 (100%)	215,240	8,232	670,880 + 63,466	742,578	3.45
Conversion	210,800	1,240	2,400 (75%)	214,440	954	170,598	171,552	0.80
							914,130	4.25

The costs may now be attributed to the categories of output as follows:

			£	£
Completed units:	210,800 × £4.25			895,900
Abnormal loss units:	1,240 × £4.25			5,270
Closing WIP:	Process 1/mats	3,200 × £3.45	11,040	
	Conversion	2,400 × £0.80	1,920	
				12,960
				914,130

The process account would thus appear as follows:

Process 2 Account

	Kg	£		Kg	£
Opening WIP	2,400	9,186	Finished Goods	210,800	895,900
Process 1	224,000	670,880	Closing WIP	3,200	12,960
Added materials		63,466	Normal Loss (earlier working)	11,160	0
Conversion		170,598	Abnormal Loss	1,240	5,270
	226,400	914,130		226,400	914,130

Note the treatment of abnormal loss. It is treated in the same way as before, in that the units are the balancing figure of the account, and they are valued the same as goods output.

Do not ignore the abnormal loss in the calculation of cost per equivalent unit because the unit (Kg) would have been worked on.

Practice question 4 *(The answer is in the final chapter of this book)*

Process X

A company operates Process X. All material is introduced at the start of Process X.

Details for Process X are as follows.

Opening work in process is 6,000 units 60% complete.

Costs contained in opening WIP

Materials	£24,000
Conversion	£15,300
Units started during period	16,000
Material costs in period	£64,000
Conversion costs in period	£75,000

Closing WIP is 4,000 units 75% complete.

Required

Prepare the process account.

8 Joint products and by-products

8.1 Introduction

It is typical of many manufacturing operations that a process may yield not only the main product desired but also one or more secondary products. This poses the question of how to apportion the process costs to the various products.

The objective of this section is to consider the most commonly used methods of costing joint products and to consider the effect of the presence of a by-product.

The process output will not be separately identifiable until a certain stage of processing is reached. This is sometimes referred to as the **split-off point**; and the undifferentiated costs incurred up to that point are known as **joint-product costs** or **pre-separation costs**. It is not possible to determine positively what proportion of the pre-separation costs relates to each of the products emerging. It is therefore necessary to use **arbitrary** methods of apportioning pre-separation costs over the different products; and this introduces, to a greater or lesser extent, an element of unreliability as to the accuracy of the costs of each product.

8.2 By-products

If the saleable value of both products is relatively significant, the outputs are usually called **joint products**. If the secondary product has a small market value relative to that of the principal product, that secondary item is referred to as a **by-product** of the principal item of output; and in such cases a decision may be taken not to cost it separately.

8.3 Joint products

Joint products are those resulting from the same process and having substantially equal importance (in value) to the company. After the different products have been separated they may be sold in their (then) existing state or further processed in order to give them a higher sales value. Whereas post-separation costs are usually identifiable with the particular product to which they relate, pre-separation costs can only be apportioned in accordance with one of the recognised bases outlined as follows:

♦ According to sales value, which may be:

  – the market value at the point of separation;

  – the market value after further processing has been carried out, ie the final sales value;

  – the net realisable value or notional sales value method, ie the final sales value less the post-separation costs;

♦ According to physical measurement, which may be:

  – actual, where there is a common unit of measurement for all products;

  – weighted in accordance with some technical estimation which reduces all output to a common basis.

8.4 Example

The following details relate to a company producing three items (A, B and C) which result from a joint process and which can be further processed individually in order that they can be sold at higher prices:

Product	Sales value after further processing £	Sales value at point of separation £	Post separation costs £	Output units	Technical weighting
A	12,000	9,500	2,000	6,000	5
B	48,000	30,500	14,000	16,000	8
C	40,000	10,000	24,000	4,000	3

The process costs to the point of separation totalled £40,000.

Calculate the profit (per product and in total) that would be shown under each of the bases of pre-separation cost apportionment referred to above.

8.5 Solution

Market value at separation

Product	Final sales value £	Sales value at point of separation £	Joint costs* £	Post separation costs £	Total costs £	Profit £
A	12,000	9,500	7,600	2,000	9,600	2,400
B	48,000	30,500	24,400	14,000	38,400	9,600
C	40,000	10,000	8,000	24,000	32,000	8,000
	100,000	50,000	40,000	40,000	80,000	20,000

*Joint costs are apportioned in the ratio:

$$\frac{£40,000}{£50,000} \times 100 = 80\% \text{ of sales value at point of separation.}$$

Thus, for A, joint costs are 80% of £9,500 = £7,600, etc.

Final sales value

Product	Final sales value	Joint* costs	Post separation costs	Total costs	Profit
	£	£	£	£	£
A	12,000	4,800	2,000	6,800	5,200
B	48,000	19,200	14,000	33,200	14,800
C	40,000	16,000	24,000	40,000	Nil
	100,000	40,000	40,000	80,000	20,000

*Joint costs are apportioned in the ratio: $\dfrac{£40,000}{£100,000} \times 100 = 40\%$ of final sales value.

Thus, for A, joint costs are 40% of £12,000 = £4,800, etc.

Net realisable value

Product	Final sales value	Post separation costs	Net realisable value	Joint costs*	Profit
	£	£	£	£	£
A	12,000	2,000	10,000	6,667	3,333
B	48,000	14,000	34,000	22,667	11,333
C	40,000	24,000	16,000	10,666	5,334
	100,000	40,000	60,000	40,000	20,000

*Joint costs are apportioned in the ratio: $\dfrac{£40,000}{£60,000} \times 100 = 66\frac{2}{3}\%$ of net realisable

value.

Thus, for A, joint costs are $66\frac{2}{3}\%$ of £10,000 = £6,667, etc.

Physical measurement

Product	Final sales value	Output units	Joint costs*	Post separation costs	Total costs	Profit
	£	£	£	£	£	£
A	12,000	6,000	9,231	2,000	11,231	769
B	48,000	16,000	24,615	14,000	38,615	9,385
C	40,000	4,000	6,154	24,000	30,154	9,846
	100,000	26,000	40,000	40,000	80,000	20,000

*Joint costs are apportioned in the ratio: $\dfrac{£40,000}{26,000} = £1.5385$ per unit.

Thus, A's joint costs are 6,000 × 1.5385 = £9,231, etc.

Weighted units

Product	Final sales value	Output units	Weighting	Weighted united	Joint costs*	Post separation costs	Total costs	Profit
	£	£		£	£	£	£	£
A	12,000	6,000	5	30,000	7,059	2,000	9,059	2,941
B	48,000	16,000	8	128,000	30,118	14,000	44,118	3,882
C	40,000	4,000	3	12,000	2,823	24,000	26,823	13,177
	100,000	26,000		170,000	40,000	40,000	80,000	20,000

*The joint costs are apportioned in the ratio: $\dfrac{£40,000}{170,000} = 23.529\text{p}$ per weighted unit.

Thus, for A, joint costs are 30,000 × £0.23529 = £7,059, etc.

 Note that all these methods give the same profit overall, it is just split between the products in different proportions.

9 By-products

9.1 Introduction

By-products are items of relatively low market value that are produced in conjunction with a main product having a significant value. As with joint products, by-products may be sold either in their existing state or after further processing.

Pre-separation costs are not charged to the by-products, but any revenue obtained from the sale of those products is either:

♦ Method 1

Credited to the process account, thereby reducing the pre-separation charge to the main product; or

♦ Method 2

Credited directly to profit and loss account.

Method 1 would be used if the by-product revenue is a normal occurrence. Method 2 would be used if the revenue were unusual or exceptional.

9.2 Illustration

Referring back to the example in Section 8.4, suppose that the joint process that produces A, B and C also produces 5,000 units of by-product X. X can be sold, as it is, for 20p/unit

♦ None of the joint process costs of £40,000 would be attributed to X

♦ The sales revenue from X, 5,000 × 20p = £1,000

would either be

- deducted from the joint process costs, leaving £39,000 to be split between A, B and C by whichever method is chosen; or

- credited directly to the Profit and Loss account for the period as sundry sales income.

Practice question 5 *(The answer is in the final chapter of this book)*

Product X

(a) Distinguish between the cost accounting treatment of joint products and of by-products. **(3 marks)**

(b) A company operates a manufacturing process which produces joint products A and B, and by-product C.

Manufacturing costs for a period total £272,926, incurred in the manufacture of:

Product A	16,000 kgs (selling price £6.10 per kg)
Product B	53,200 kgs (selling price £7.50 per kg)
Product C	2,770 kgs (selling price £0.80 per kg)

Required

Calculate the cost per kg (to 3 decimal places of a £) of products A and B in the period, using market values to apportion joint costs. **(5 marks)**

(c)   In another of the company's processes, Product X is manufactured using raw materials P and T which are mixed in the proportions 1:2.

Material purchase prices are:

P   £5.00 per kilo
T   £1.60 per kilo

Normal weight loss of 5% is expected during the process.

In the period just ended 9,130 kilos of Product X were manufactured from 9,660 kilos of raw materials. Conversion costs in the period were £23,796. There was no work in process at the beginning or end of the period.

Required

Prepare the Product X process account for the period.   **(6 marks)**

(Total - 14 marks)

10   Summary

You should now be able to:

♦   Explain continuous operation/process costing

♦   Demonstrate how costs are collected in the ledger account (process account)

♦   Consider the type of losses experienced in process costing and their effects

♦   Consider the treatment of abnormal gain ie where the normal loss is less than expected

♦   Identify the effect of scrap values/disposal costs for losses

♦   Prepare the accounting entries for the process account, normal loss account (aka the scrap account); and abnormal loss and gain account

♦   Discuss the implication of opening and closing work in progress

♦   Prepare the accounting entries for the process account, normal loss account; and abnormal loss and gain account using the weighted average method of valuing work-in-progress

♦   Explain joint products and by-products

Multiple choice questions *(The answers are in the final chapter of this book)*

1   In process costing, the value attributed to any abnormal gain units is:

A   debited to the process account and credited to the abnormal gain account

B   debited to the abnormal gain account and credited to the normal loss account

C   debited to the normal loss account and credited to the abnormal gain account

D   debited to the abnormal gain account and credited to the process account

2   In process costing an equivalent unit is:

A   a notional whole unit representing incomplete work

B   a unit made at standard performance

C   a unit being currently made which is the same as previously manufactured

D   a unit made in more than one process cost centre

3   Process B had no opening stock. 13,500 units of raw material were transferred in at £4.50 per unit. Additional material at £1.25 per unit was added in process. Labour and overheads were £6.25 per completed unit and £2.50 per unit incomplete.

If 11,750 completed units were transferred out, what was the closing stock in Process B?

A   £77,625.00

B   £14,437.50

C   £141,000.00

D   £21,000.00

4   The following details relate to the main process of X Ltd, a chemical manufacturer:

Opening work-in-progress	2,000 litres, fully complete as to materials and 40% complete as to conversion
Material input	24,000 litres
Normal loss is 10% of input	
Output to process 2	19,500 litres
Closing work-in-progress	3,000 litres, fully complete as to materials and 45% complete as to conversion

The numbers of equivalent units to be included in X Ltd's calculation of the cost per equivalent unit, using a *weighted average basis* of valuation, are:

	Materials	*Conversion*
A	21,400	20,850
B	22,500	21,950
C	22,500	20,850
D	23,600	21,950

CHAPTER 12

Answers

Chapter 1 solutions

1   Hearn Ltd

To: Mrs Mason

From: An Accountant

Date: 14th December 20X9

Subject: Main features of your cost-benefit analysis and further information that you
             will require.

The purpose of the cost-benefit analysis that you require is to support your belief in retaining
the existing computer-based management accounts. For this analysis to be persuasive it should
include the following features.

Benefits of existing systems

This can be further broken down into the separate components making up the present system:

Benefits of standard costing and variance analysis

A properly run standard costing system which involves sound budgeting techniques and
relevant variance analysis, followed up by the appropriate action, should provide the
following benefits:

(a)   accurate forecasting and planning;

(b)   the control needed to ensure the best use of the company's assets;

(c)   employees would be responsible and accountable in setting and achieving targets;

(d)   variance analysis should highlight areas that are out of control;

(e)   a framework for performance evaluation;

(f)   motivation.

Benefits of existing monthly reports

At present these reports highlight monthly and cumulative variances. The benefits of this type
of report are:

(a)   it is produced promptly and at frequent intervals which allows time for remedial
         action to be taken;

(b)   it highlights cumulative figures thereby showing whether corrective action is being
         taken and its effectiveness;

(c)   it shows the overall position taking all variances into account;

(d)   it focuses attention on the need to be profitable.

Benefits of computer-based systems

These are more implied but would be helpful in presenting your case. Production of data should be:

(a)   fast;
(b)   timely;
(c)   cost-effective.

The disadvantages of not having the existing system in place could be:

(a)   no focus on profit;
(b)   inefficient usage of resources may go unnoticed;
(c)   incorrect emphasis on full order books at the expense of profit;
(d)   lack of reporting could easily erode the contribution of products.

Plus there would also be lost all the advantages which accrue with standard costing and variance analysis. One major disadvantage would be the total lack of management information.

Costs

If the contents of the report have so far highlighted the benefits then reference would certainly have to be made to the cost aspects. Specific points to consider here could include:

Disadvantage   –   Cost of two members of staff.

Advantage   –   Cost savings accruing from information provided by the management accounting systems.

There will have to be tangible benefits in cost terms otherwise there will be no obvious advantage in maintaining the system. These will be quite hard to quantify but include:

(a)   the cost of wasted material;
(b)   the waste due to bad planning, ie not having a standard usage in the first place;
(c)   lost production possibly due to lack of motivation;
(d)   loss of profitability.

If these aspects could be quantified then it should be possible to present a case showing that the benefits of the present systems (in strictly financial terms) outweigh the costs.

Information required

This then leads on to the second aspect of this report ie, what further information is necessary. Most additional information that is not yet already available will focus on the need to evaluate the benefits. Therefore you should ascertain as far as possible the answers to the following questions.

(a)   What sort of variances is the present system reporting?

(i)   Are they large?
(ii)   Are they controllable?
(iii)   Are they planning or operational type variances?
(iv)   What is the cost of control?
(v)   What is the overall picture?
(vi)   Who is responsible for them?

This could be one of the easier benefits to evaluate.

(b)   Can savings be made if targets were introduced?   Are lack of standards producing slack usage?

(c)   Is it possible to identify the sort of projects that Mr MacGeorge would accept to the detriment of the company if there was no management reporting system?

(d)   Can the present systems be streamlined in any way ie, save costs but maintain the function?

I hope this report has been helpful but please contact me again should you require further assistance.

Answers to multiple choice questions

1   A

First item takes 10 minutes

Average time for 2 units = 10 minutes $\times$ 90% = 9 minutes

$\therefore$ Total time for 2 units = 2 $\times$ 9 = 18 minutes

$\therefore$ Marginal time for 2nd unit = 18 – 10 = 8 minutes

2   B

Although it depends on the psychology of the individual person, most employees are best motivated by attainable standards.

3   D

There will be some additional costs necessary in setting up and running a standard cost system.

Chapter 2 solutions

1 **(a)**

	kg	£
Actual materials purchased at actual price per kg	3,000	6,200
Actual materials purchased at standard price per kg	3,000	6,000
Materials price variance	–	200 A

	kg	£
Actual materials used at standard price per kg	2,900	5,800
Standard materials for production achieved at standard price per kg	3,200	6,400
Materials usage variance	300	600 F

(b)

	kg	£
Actual materials purchased at actual price per kg	6,000	2,400
Actual materials purchased at standard price per kg	6,000	3,000
Materials price variance	–	600 F

	kg	£
Actual materials used at standard price per kg	5,600	2,800
Standard materials for production achieved at standard price per kg	6,000	3,000
Materials usage variance	400	200 F

2 **D**

	£
Actual usage at standard price	
3,758.4 × £17	63,892.8
Standard usage at standard price	
1,392 × 2.5 × £17	59,160.0
Usage variance (adverse)	4,732.8

3 **A**

	£
Actual purchases at actual price	62,013.6
Actual purchases at standard price	
3,758.4 × £17	63,892.8
Price variance (favourable)	1,879.2

4   C

	£
Standard cost of actual production	
1,500 × £5	7,500
Actual cost (valuing closing stock at standard)	
£8,000–£1,000	7,000
Variance (favourable)	500

(Note that this computes the price variance over quantity purchased, not quantity used.)

5   A

Usage variance compares actual quantity with standard quantity, and values the difference at the standard price.

	kg
Actual usage = 120,000 + 5,000	125,000
Standard usage = 40,000 × 2.5 kg	100,000
Adverse usage variance	25,000

$$\therefore \text{Standard price} = \frac{£32,500}{25,000} = £1.30 \text{ per kg}$$

$$\therefore \text{Price variance} = \quad 120,000 \times (1.30 - 1.20) = £12,000 \text{ favourable}$$

6   D

	kg	£
Actual quantity purchased at actual price	1,800	1,170
Actual quantity purchased at standard price	1,800	1,350
Price variance (F)		180

7   (a)

	Hours	£
Actual hours paid at actual rate per hour	5,000	14,000
Actual hours paid at standard rate per hour	5,000	15,000
Direct labour rate variance	–	1,000 F
Actual hours worked at standard rate per hour	5,000	15,000
Standard hours for production achieved at standard rate per hour	5,600	16,800
Direct labour efficiency variance	600	1,800 F

(b)

	Hours	£
Actual hours paid at actual rate per hour	50,000	210,000
Actual hours paid at standard rate per hour	50,000	200,000
Direct labour rate variance	–	10,000 A
Actual hours paid at standard rate per hour	50,000	200,000
Actual hours worked at standard rate per hour	48,000	192,000
Direct labour idle time variance	2,000	8,000 A
Actual hours worked at standard rate per hour	48,000	192,000
Standard hours for production achieved at standard rate per hour	54,000	216,000
Direct labour efficiency variance	6,000	24,000 F

(c)

	Hours	£
Actual hours worked at actual rate per hour	6,300	3,000
Actual hours worked at standard rate per hour	6,300	3,150
Variable overhead expenditure variance	–	150 F
Actual hours worked at standard rate per hour	6,300	3,150
Standard hours for production achieved at standard rate per hour	6,000	3,000
Variable overhead efficiency variance	300	150 A

(d)

	Hours	£
Actual hours worked at actual rate per hour	4,700	2,000
Actual hours worked at standard rate per hour	4,700	1,880
Variable overhead expenditure variance	–	120 A
Actual hours worked at standard rate per hour	4,700	1,880
Standard hours for production achieved at standard rate per hour	5,400	2,160
Variable overhead efficiency variance	700	280 F

8   (a)   Although standard costing has, as one of its purposes, the allocation of responsibility for cost variances, it is often found in practice that the analysis of variances is merely the beginning of a further task of investigation before ultimate responsibility can be equitably assigned.

We may find, for example, that our analysis discloses a favourable materials price variance and an adverse usage variance. Theoretically this should indicate that the buyer is operating efficiently and the production manager inefficiently. This need not necessarily be true, however. The buyer could have taken advantage of a special offer of material at less than standard price, not appreciating that the material was slightly below standard quality. It is very likely that the inferior material would give rise to production problems of machining, handling and possibly others which could well result in excess usage; hence the adverse usage variance.

(b)   As regards labour, the payment of higher than standard rates (suggested by an adverse rate of pay variance) may well have the effect of providing greater motivation, and hence cause speedier work, which would be reflected in a favourable efficiency variance.

There may well be interdependence between the material and labour cost variances; for instance, the speedier work suggested by the favourable labour efficiency variance may have been accomplished by disregarding material usage standards.

From the foregoing it will be seen that not only is there possibly interdependence between the variances of each element of cost, but also cross-interdependence between the elements of cost.

9   B

	Hours	*£*
Actual hours worked at actual rate	9,300	66,960
Actual hours worked at standard rate	9,300	60,450
Standard hours at standard rate	10,000	65,000

rate variance £6,510 A

efficiency variance £4,550 F

10   C   (See working above.)

11   D

	£
Standard cost of production = 1,000 × £25	25,000
Total cost variance	250 (F)
Actual expenditure	24,750
Actual hours worked $= \dfrac{£24,750}{£5.50}$	4,500
Standard hours to produce 1,000 units	5,000
Favourable efficiency variance	500

At the standard rate of £5/hour = £2,500 favourable

12   B

13   (a)

	Hours	*£*
Budgeted hours at actual total cost	8,000	4,150
Budgeted hours at standard cost	8,000	4,000
Fixed overhead expenditure variance	–	150 A

Budgeted hours at standard cost	8,000	4,000
Actual hours worked at standard rate	7,800	3,900
Fixed overhead capacity variance	200	100 A
Actual hours worked at standard rate	7,800	3,900
Standard hours for production achieved at standard rate	7,600	3,800
Fixed overhead efficiency variance	200	100 A

(b)

	Hours	£
Budgeted hours at actual total cost	4,000	2,800
Budgeted hours at standard cost	4,000	3,000
Fixed overhead expenditure variance	–	200 F
Budgeted hours at standard rate	4,000	3,000
Actual hours worked at standard rate	3,900	2,925
Fixed overhead capacity variance	100	75 A
Actual hours worked at standard rate	3,900	2,925
Standard hours for production achieved at standard rate	4,400	3,300
Fixed overhead efficiency variance	500	375 F

14   A   Standard absorption rate (SAR) = $\dfrac{£9,000}{500}$ = £18/hour

	£
Standard hours for actual production at SAR = $185 \times 2.5 \times 18$	8,325
Budgeted hours at SAR	9,000
Volume variance	675 A

15   C

Actual hours at SAR	10,800
Budgeted hours at SAR	9,000
Capacity variance	1,800 F

16   D

Standard hours at SAR	8,325
Actual hours at SAR	10,800
Efficiency variance	2,475 A

17   **D**

18   **C**

The volume variance is a measure of under-or-over-absorption. It is therefore a comparison of the budgeted hours that would exactly absorb the budgeted fixed cost, with the standard hours for actual production over which the fixed cost has been absorbed through the costing system.

19   **A**

Stock at actual cost

	£	£
Sales (9,500 × 30)		285,000
Production cost	230,000	
Stock at actual cost		
(500/10,000 × 230,000)	11,500	
		218,500
Profit		66,500

With adverse cost variances of £16,000

Standard cost of production =

230,000 – 16,000 = £214,000

∴ Valuing closing stock at standard gives

500/10,000 × 214,000 = £10,700

	£	£
Thus: Sales		285,000
Actual production cost	230,000	
Stock at standard cost	10,700	
		219,300
Profit		65,700

20   **(a)**

Sales variances

	Units
Budgeted sales	14,400
Actual sales	13,200
Reduction in sales (units)	1,200
Volume variance (margin) 1,200 × £0.24	£288 A

Materials variances

			£
(i)	*Price variance*		
	Actual cost of purchasing 560 kg		3,494.40
	Standard cost of purchasing 560 kg		3,360.00
	Price variance		134.40 A

			kg
(ii)	*Usage variance*		
	Actual usage for producing 13,200 units		560
	Standard usage for producing 13,200 units		528
	Excess used		32
	Usage variance = 32 × £6		£192 A

Labour variances

			£
(i)	*Rate variance*		
	Actual cost of labour hours paid		
	(40 × 30 × 4 = 4,800 hours)		7,296
	Standard cost of labour (4,800 × £1.44)		6,912
	Rate variance		384 A

			Hours
(ii)	*Idle time*		
	Hours paid		4,800
	Hours worked (36 × 30 × 4)		4,320
			480
	Idle time variance (480 × £1.44)		£691.20 A

			Hours
(iii)	*Efficiency variance*		
	Hours worked		4,320
	Standard hours for actual production		4,400
			80
	Efficiency variance (80 × £1.44)		£115.20 F

Variable expenses

			£
(i)	*Expenditure variance*		
	Actual cost of variable expenses (4,320 hours)		2,400.00
	Standard cost of variable expenses (4,320 × £0.54)		2,332.80
	Expenditure variance		67.20 A

(ii)	*Efficiency variance*	Hours
	Hours worked	4,320
	Standard hours for actual production	4,400
		80
	Efficiency variance (80 × £0.54)	£43.20 F

Fixed overhead expenses

(i)	*Expenditure variance*	£
	Actual overhead	3,840
	Budgeted overhead	3,456
	Expenditure variance	384 A

(ii)	*Volume variance*	Hours
	Budgeted hours (40 × 30 × 4)	4,800
	Standard hours for actual production	4,400
		400
	Volume variance (400 × £0.72)	£288 A

Analysed into:

Capacity variance	Hours
Budgeted hours	4,800
Hours worked	4,320
	480
Capacity variance (480 × £0.72)	£345.60 A

Efficiency variance	Hours
Hours worked	4,320
Standard hours for actual production	4,400
	80
Efficiency variance (80 × £0.72)	£57.60 F

(b) **Operating statement**

	£
Budgeted profit	3,456
Sales margin volume variance	(288)
	3,168

Cost variances	Favourable £	Adverse £	
Materials			
Price		134.40	
Usage		192.00	
Labour			
Rate		384.00	
Idle time		691.20	
Efficiency	115.20		
Variable expenses			
Expenditure		67.20	
Efficiency	43.20		
Fixed expenses			
Expenditure		384.00	
Capacity		345.60	
Efficiency	57.60		
	216.00	2,198.40	(1,982.40)
Actual profit			1,185.60

21 Joachim Joiners

(a) **Operating statement for the year ended 31.12.X3**

	Favourable £	Adverse £	£
Budgeted profit			16,000
Sales margin variances:			
Price (£150,000 – 4,400 × £30)	18,000		
Volume (400 × £4)	1,600		
			19,600
			35,600
Cost variances:			
Materials:			
Price: 12,500 × (£2.5 – £2)	6,250		
Usage: (4,800 × 2 – 12,500) × £2.5		7,250	
Labour, etc.:			
Rate: (5,500 × £7) – £39,000		500	
Efficiency: (4,800 – 5,500) × £7		4,900	
	6,250	12,650	
Fixed production overhead			
Expenditure: £40,000 – £21,000	19,000		
Efficiency: (4,800 – 5,500) × £8		5,600	
Capacity: (5,500 – 5,000) × £8	4,000		
	29,250	18,250	

Variable selling overhead
      Expenditure: (£4 × 4,400) – £20,000   2,400

Fixed selling overhead
      Expenditure: £8,000 – £9,000   1,000
      Volume: (4,400 – 4,000) × £2   800

                                        30,050   21,650

                                                            8,400

Actual profit   44,000

Note: This profit is with stock valued at standard total absorption cost.

(b)   Alternative stock and profit figures

     (i)   **Standard direct costing**

           Stock 400 units @ £12 per unit   =   £4,800
           Profit £44,000 – 400 × £8   =   £40,800

           (adjusting for fixed cost included in stock)

     (ii)   **Total absorption costing – stock at actual cost**

           Stock $\dfrac{400}{4,800}$ × £85,000   =   £7,083

           Profit £44,000 – $\dfrac{400}{4,800}$ × £(29,250 – 18,250) = £43,083

           (total net production variances).

     (iii)   **Direct costing – stock at actual cost**

           Stock £(25,000 + 39,000) × $\dfrac{400}{4,800}$ = £5,333

           Profit £40,800 + £(12,650 – 6,250) × $\dfrac{400}{4,800}$ = £41,333

(c)   SSAP 9 stock valuation

A possible alternative stock valuation in line with SSAP 9 would be actual marginal cost of £5,333 plus production overheads 'based on the normal level of activity'. It could be argued that this figure is the standard fixed overhead absorption rate of £8 per unit or actual fixed overheads spread over budgeted production, ie., £21,000 ÷ 5,000 = £4.20 per unit.

The second of these would produce a stock figure of £7,013, though it is not obvious that this is the required figure.

22   D

	£
Budgeted sales (21,000 × £100)	2,100,000
Budgeted variable costs (21,000 × £60)	1,260,000
Budgeted contribution	840,000
Budgeted fixed cost (580,000 + 20,000)	600,000
Budgeted profit	240,000

23   D   The sales margin variance is the volume difference @ the standard profit margin.

24   A

	£
Budgeted sales at standard profit margin 5,000 × £2	10,000
Actual sales at standard profit margin 4,800 × £2	9,600
Sales margin volume variance (adverse)	400

25   B

	£
Actual sales at standard price 4,800 × £8	38,400
Actual sales at actual price 4,800 × £8.50	40,800
Sales margin price variance (favourable)	2,400

26   B

	Type 1 £	Type 2 £	Type 3 £
Standard selling price/unit	£1,000	£2,000	£1,500
Actual selling price/unit	£1,050	£2,200	£1,400
	£50	£200	£(100)
Actual sales (units)	900	1,100	2,000
Price variances	£45,000 (F)	£220,000 (F)	£(200,000) (A)

∴ Net variance = £65,000 favourable

27   **D**

	£
Actual gross profit	137,000
Add adverse cost variance	2,000
	139,000
Add adverse sales margin volume variance	5,500
	144,500
Less: Favourable sales price variance	4,000
Budgeted gross profit	140,500

(You will be more accustomed to working the other way – that is starting with budgeted profit and working back to actual profit.)

28   **B**

If production exceeds sales, then stocks will always increase.

Consider the following:

Sales	10 units at £10 each
Production	12 units at £8 each
Variable cost per unit	£5
Fixed overhead per unit	£3

	Marginal costing		Absorption costing	
	£	£	£	£
Sales (10 × 10)		100		100
Cost of production	96		96	
Closing stock	10		16	
		86		80
Reported profit		14		20

Thus, if stocks are increasing marginal costing will always produce less profit, as more overheads are written off in the period.

29   C

The higher the closing stock value, then the higher will be the reported profit (because cost of sales is lower).

Thus Foxtrot should include fixed overheads in the stock valuation.

	Actual £	Standard £
Costs per unit:		
Variable	7	6
Fixed	3	5
	10	11

Since standard TAC gives the highest unit cost, this should be the basis for valuing stock.

30   C

Standard cost (ie. standard quantity in standard mix at standard prices) = £270

Since the standard mix is 7D:3E

$$70D + 30E = 270 ----------- (1)$$

With a mix variance of £10 adverse, the actual mix must have cost £280.

Since we need 10 gallons of D more than expected, and there is no yield variance then

$$80D + 20E = 280 ------------ (2)$$

$(1) \times 2$ gives: $140D + 60E = 540$

$(2) \times 3$ gives: $240D + 60E = 840$

$$\therefore D = \frac{300}{100} = £3$$

31   C

Chapter 3 solutions

1   **Tungach**

(a)   *Material variances*

Revision usage variance	=	20% × 1.5kg × £8 × 4,000 units
	=	£9,600 (A)

Revision price variance	=	1.5kg × 1.2 × (£8 - £7.50) × 4,000 units
	=	£3,600 (F)

Material usage variance	=	standard cost of production - actual material used at standard price
	=	(4,400 × 1.8kg × £7.50) - (7,800 × £7.50)
	=	£59,400 - £58,500
	=	£900 (F)

Material price variance	=	actual material used at standard price - actual material used at actual price
	=	(7,800 × £7.50) - (7,800 × £7.90)
	=	£58,500 - £61,620
	=	£3,120 (A)

Labour variances

Revision rate variance	=	20p × 2 hours × 4,000 units
	=	£1,600 (F)

Labour efficiency variance	=	standard cost of production - actual useful hours at standard rate
	=	(4,400 × 2 hours × £4.30) - (9,050 × £4.30)
	=	£37,840 - £38,915
	=	£1,075 (A)

Labour idle time variance	=	idle hours at standard rate
	=	150 × £4.30
	=	£645 (A)

Labour rate variance	=	hours paid at standard rate - hours paid at actual rate
	=	(9,200 × £4.30) - (9,200 × £4.60)
	=	£39,560 - £42,320
	=	£2,760 (A)

(b)   First we must calculate the revised contribution per unit.

	£	£
Selling price		30.00
Direct material (1.8kg @ £7.50)	13.50	
Direct labour (2 hours @ £4.30)	8.60	
		(22.10)

Contribution 7.90
_____

Extra capacity variance $= \left(\dfrac{9,200}{2} - 4,000\right) \times £7.90$

$= 600 \times £7.90$

$= £4,740$ (F)

Productivity drop variance $= \left(4,400 - \dfrac{9,050}{2}\right) \times £7.90$

$= 125 \times £7.90$

$= £987.5$ (A)

Idle time variance $= \dfrac{150}{2} \times £7.90 = £592.5$ (A)

Stock increase variance $= (4,400 - 4,100) \times £7.90$
$= 300 \times £7.90$
$= £2,370$ (A)

(c) **Report**

To: The management of Tungach Ltd

From: The Management Accountant

Date: X January 20X0

Subject: Operating statement for period 9

This report explains the meaning and relevance of the figures given in the operating statement for period 9. You will see that the statement explains the reasons for the difference between our original budgeted contribution of £36,000 for the period and the actual contribution outturn of £25,690.

The revision variances first reflect the fact that a number of permanent changes have occurred since the standard costs and revenues were first set. In particular the permanent change implemented in the product specification with effect from period 7 requires an extra 20% material per unit, so more material will be used than originally budgeted for. Our original prices taken for resources in the standard were also inaccurate: material costs 50p per kg less than originally thought, while labour costs 20p per hour less. Both these factors produce favourable revision variances.

Let us now consider the idle time and stock increase sales volume variances. Total labour hours of 9,200 hours have been paid for, of which 150 hours are idle time. This means the employees were paid while being unproductive for 150 hours. Possible reasons could be machine breakdown, or tooling up. Possible corrective action could be a more active machine maintenance programme. During the period we see that finished stock increased by 300 units. This is bad news since stock items deteriorate rapidly so could become unsaleable. The sales director should be called to account rapidly to ensure that these goods can be sold in period 10 before they deteriorate.

Finally, we consider the material usage and material price operating variances. The usage variance tells us that the amount of actual material used was slightly less than the amount expected for the actual production level achieved. The production manager should be able to comment on this situation. Perhaps the estimate of requiring 20% more material per product unit was inaccurate. The price variance reflects the bad news in having paid £7.90 per kilo of material during the period, when £7.50 had been agreed as the current efficient price. The purchasing manager is responsible for this matter and must be advised to seek lower prices in future periods, perhaps by changing suppliers.

2   Newstyle Furniture Ltd

Operating statement for Period 1

	Favourable £	Adverse £	£
Budgeted profit (W1)		10,500	
Sales margin variances: (W2)			
price		700	
quantity	420		280
			10,220
Cost variances			
Materials (W3)			
price	270		
usage		400	
Labour: (W4)			
rate of pay		1,412	
efficiency 512			
Variable overhead: (W5)			
expenditure	102		
efficiency 192			
Fixed overhead: (W6)			
expenditure	50		
efficiency 80			
volume	20		
	1,074	1,964	890
Actual profit			9,330

Workings

(1)   Budgeted profit per unit

		£	£
Sales			10.00
Costs:	materials	3.00	
	labour	3.20	
	variable overhead	1.20	
	fixed overhead $\dfrac{£30,000}{60,000}$	0.50	
			7.90
Profit per chair			£2.10

Budgeted production in 20 days $\dfrac{60,000}{240} \times 20$ 5,000 chairs

Budgeted profit 5,000 chairs × £2.10   £10,500

(2)   **Sales margin variances**

		£
Price		
	Standard revenue on actual sales	52,000
	Actual revenue	51,300
		700 (A)
Quantity		
	200 chairs @ £2.10	420 (F)

(3)   **Materials**

			£
(i)	Price variance		
		actual cost of 32,000 kg	15,730
		standard cost	16,000
			270 (F)

			kg
(ii)	Usage variance		
		expected usage for 5,200 chairs	31,200
		actual usage	32,000
		excessive usage	800
		@ 50p per kg	£400 (A)

(4)   Labour

    (i)   Rate of pay

	£
actual cost of 2,520 hrs	17,540
standard cost (2,520 × £6.4)	16,128
	1,412 (A)

    (ii)   Efficiency

	Hrs
standard time for 5,200 chairs	2,600
actual time taken	2,520
hours gained through efficiency	80
@ £6.40 per hour	512 (F)

(5)   Variable overhead

    (i)   Expenditure variance

	£
actual cost of 2,520 hours	6,150
standard cost (2,520 × £2.40)	6,048
	102 (A)

    (ii)   Efficiency variance

80 hours @ £2.40	192 (F)

(6)   Fixed overhead

    (i)   Expenditure variance

	£
budgeted cost (£30,000 × $^{20}/_{240}$)	2,500
actual cost	2,550
	50 (A)

    (ii)   Efficiency variance

80 hours @ £1	80 (F)

(The absorption rate is calculated by dividing the budgeted cost by the budgeted number of hours to be worked: £30,000 / (60,000 × ½ hrs) = £1.)

    (iii) Volume variance

	hrs
actual hours worked	2,520
budgeted 60,000 × ½ × $^{20}/_{240}$	2,500
	20
@ £1 per hour	£20 (F)

	£	£
Actual profit statement		
Sales		51,300
Materials	15,730	
Labour	17,540	
Variable overhead	6,150	
Fixed overhead	2,550	
		41,970
Profit		9,330

Answers to multiple choice questions

1   D

Expected cost of not investigating	$= 0.6 \times £1,500$
	$= £900$
Expected cost of investigating	$= £300 + 0.6 \times 0.25 \times £1,500$
	$= £525$
Expected net benefit	$= £375$

2   D

Usage of materials is likely to be unfavourable as the materials are substandard, thus there will be more wastage and rejects.

Time spent by labour on rejected items that will not become output leads to higher than standard time spent per unit of output.

3   C

The flexed budget is obtained by adjusting actual usage for standard cost.

Chapter 4 solutions

1   A manager's attitude towards budget preparation will be influenced by the manner in which subsequent control will be exercised. Some senior officers, bearing in mind that the master budget will be a commitment to the achievement of a certain level of profit, treat every item of detail in budgets as similarly firm commitments. A £20 overspending in period 6 on stationery, say, is treated as a management failure equal in culpability to a 50% shortfall in profit. Under such a regime, managers will obviously attempt to ensure that their budgets are capable of achievement even under the most adverse circumstances; in other words, they will set 'loose' budgets as described in the question. Where senior officers are prepared to judge variances from budget in the light of actual circumstances (which will almost certainly differ from those prevailing when the budget was set), there is less need for managers to protect themselves by falsifying their budget expectations and more effective control should result.

It must be borne in mind that all budgets are subject to review, either by the managing director or the budget controller or by a budget committee, before they are finally approved and, as the reviewer should have a good understanding of the business, many inadequacies in the original budget submissions will be eliminated.

Having regard to the above comments, it would seem unnecessary to remove the preparation of budgets from managers, whose participation will ensure their acceptance of subsequent control, to the accounts department who will not be answerable for the achievement of the budget and whose knowledge of departmental operations, however good, cannot be as comprehensive as that of the managers on the spot.

Whatever the degree of participation by the accounts department in budget preparation, the idea that budgets can be set by extrapolation from previous periods' results is highly dangerous in times when external circumstances are subject to frequent and significant change.

2   The capital expenditure budget comprises the acquisition of land and buildings and the purchase and/or installation of plant and machinery and other fixed assets. It is concerned partly with relatively short-term and small-value items like motor vehicles, but in many businesses (and for all businesses from time to time) preponderantly with high-cost items which will be retained for use over a long period of time. The capital expenditure budget incorporates the specific results of policy decisions with which the business will have to live for some time and of which it could not divest itself without significant loss.

Budgets for operating revenue and costs, on the other hand, are part of a long-term plan only in the sense that at the time the budget is prepared these represent the best possible short-term actions which will assist the business towards its long-term objectives. It is conceivable, and happens frequently, that changes in tactics will be made during the course of the budget year and the operating budget will then be revised in the light of changed circumstances. Since such changes do not involve disinvestment, they can be made without a change in overall policy and without significant loss.

3   What are the actions that have to be organised in implementing a budgetary control system?

     (a)   The management organisation structure of the business must be clearly defined because budget responsibilities and 'budget centres' will depend on this.

(b) The budget period and its subdivision into control periods must be decided.

(c) The major constraint on the scale of the activities of the business (the principal budget factor) must be identified. All sub-budgets will be derived from this.

(d) Having regard to that constraint, the business objectives for the budget period and the longer-term objectives of which they form part must be decided by the board and communicated to the managers concerned with budgetary control.

(e) Instructions must be issued about the way in which budgets are to be prepared, the forms to be used, the accounts codes (if these are not already in issue) and the timetable for the completion of the various stages of budget preparation. Such instructions are often incorporated into a 'budget manual'.

(f) The preparation of sub-budgets must be coordinated, both as to timing and as to their compatibility with each other.

(g) The sub-budgets must be consolidated into a master budget for approval, probably at board level. The approach must be communicated to the managers who will be responsible for implementing budgets.

(h) There must be regular feedback of actual results through the accounts department, and the reporting and analysis of variances from budget.

(i) Variances must be investigated by the managers responsible and there must be periodic review at a senior level of the reasons for variances and the actions taken or proposed in consequence.

Who is responsible for organising these actions?

(a) The board must initiate the chain of actions by issuing a statement of objectives, approving the final master budget and reviewing progress against the major objectives.

(b) The channel of communication between functional managers and the board may be the managing director or a budget committee (of which he will probably be the chairman).

(c) The issue of budget instructions and the coordination of budget preparation may be the responsibility of the budget committee or of a budget controller (who in small companies may be the management accountant).

(d) The consolidation of budgets may be the responsibility of the accounts department or of the budget controller.

(e) The issue of control reports is the accounts department's responsibility.

(f) The overall review of performance will be the responsibility of the managing director or of a managing committee or local board (which may have the same constitution as the budget committee).

(g) The actual preparation of budgets, and the responsibility for explaining variances and initiating corrective action where necessary ought to rest with the functional and departmental managers. In other words, there must be participation in budgetary control.

Answers to multiple choice questions

1   C

		£
Debtors = £80,000 × 60% × 1.2		57,600
Creditors = £80,000 × 70%		56,000
Stock = £80,000 × 70% × $\frac{12}{10}$		67,200

$$\text{Current ratio} = \frac{\text{debtors} + \text{stock}}{\text{creditor} + \text{overdraft}} = 2$$

So $\dfrac{£57,600 + £67,200}{£56,000 + \text{overdraft}} = 2$

Therefore 2 (£56,000 + overdraft) = £124,800 and 2 x overdraft = £12,800, so overdraft = £6,400.

2   B

Sales forecast	= £96,000
Net profits	= 0.25 × £96,000
	= £24,000
Capital employed	= 10 × £24,000
	= £240,000
Working capital	= 0.5 × £240,000
	= £120,000
Current assets – Current liabilities	= £120,000
$\dfrac{\text{Current assets}}{\text{Current liabilities}}$	= 2
Current liabilities	= £120,000

3   B

Cash collected

	£
July's sales £25,000 × 20%	5,000
June's sales £20,000 × 60%	12,000
May's sales £30,000 × 10%	3,000
	20,000

Chapter 5 solutions

1   (a)   There are many examples which you could choose. Here are three:

    (i)   the relationship between cost and amount of raw material purchased will be linear between limits but at a certain level a quantity discount may be introduced which destroys the linearity;

    (ii)   in agriculture, as rainfall increases, many items of food (eg. grain and fruit) will have better crops, but if there is too much rain the crops will be damaged;

    (iii)   the theory of marginal costing assumes that fixed costs are constant irrespective of the quantities produced, but if sales rise drastically, the total of fixed costs will increase respectively, as extra equipment is acquired.

(b)

x	y	xy	x^2
5	11.8	59.0	25
7	14.7	102.9	49
9	18.5	166.5	81
11	24.0	264.0	121
13	26.2	340.6	169
15	30.1	451.5	225
60	125.3	1,384.5	670

$$b = \frac{n\sum xy - \sum x \sum y}{n\sum x^2 - (\sum x)^2}$$

$$= \frac{6 \times 1,384.5 - 60 \times 125.3}{6 \times 670 - 60 \times 60}$$

$$= \frac{789}{420} = 1.88$$

$$a = \frac{\sum y}{n} - b\frac{\sum x}{n} = \frac{125.3}{6} - 1.88 \times \frac{60}{6}$$

$$= 2.08$$

Regression line is:

y   =   1.88x + 2.08

Thus fixed cost   =   £2,080

and variable cost   =   £1,880 per 1,000 units

2

x	y	xy	x²
1	-6	-6	1
21	-4	-84	441
41	+2	82	1,681
61	+3	183	3,721
81	+7	567	6,561
101	+11	1,111	10,201
306	13	1,853	22,606

b
$$= \frac{n\sum xy - \sum x \sum y}{n\sum x^2 - (\sum x)^2}$$

$$= \frac{6 \times 1,853 - 306 \times 13}{6 \times 22,606 - 306 \times 306}$$

$$= \frac{7,140}{42,000} = 0.17$$

a
$$= \frac{\sum y}{n} - b\frac{\sum x}{n} = \frac{13}{6} - 0.17 \times \frac{306}{6}$$

$$= -6.5$$

Regression line is: $y = 0.17x - 6.5$

From this it can be seen that the dimension of the components starts at 6.5×0.0001 cms below the nominal measurement and gradually increases.

The gradient of the line (ie. 0.17) gives the rate of increase or 'drift' of the machine setting per piece. Therefore the 'drift' is 0.17×0.0001 cms per component produced.

If the process continues to 'drift' in this way the regression line will indicate to the quality controller when a quality control limit will be exceeded.

3 **B** (Note: Seasonal variations do not have to repeat themselves over a period of a year. In this case it is over a day.)

4 **A** The linear regression method is only appropriate if the underlying trend is approximately linear.

5 **B** 4 qtr moving totals:

(100 + 104 + 110 + 109)	=	423
(423 – 100 (March yr 1) + 102 (March yr 2))	=	425
(425 – 104 + 108)	=	429
(429 – 110 + 112)	=	431
(431 – 109 + 108)	=	430

Trend = (moving totals (order 2) of above)/8

= (423 + 425)/8, (425 + 429)/8, (429 + 431)/8, (431 + 430)/8

= 106, 106.75, 107.5, 107.625

6   The quarterly sales of alcoholic drinks in off-licences and supermarkets in the UK is an example of a time series.

The trend would probably be a gradual but steady increase due to increased standards of living.

Seasonal variations would appear as a dramatic increase in sales just before Christmas.

Cyclical variations would not be apparent over a short period of time but if the figures could be scrutinised over many years there should be some evidence that the sales of alcohol were linked with the economic situation. In a period of economic depression people do not have as much money to spend on luxuries such as alcohol.

Random variations could occur because of a budget decision to raise the duty on alcoholic drinks sharply.

7   (a)

			Values (£million)		
Year	Qtr	Actual	4–qtr–total	4–qtr average	Average (trend)
1	1	173			
	2	206			
			795	199	
	3	198			204
			838	209	
	4	218			212
			855	214	
2	1	216			216
			876	219	
	2	223			220
			879	220	
	3	219			219
			876	219	
	4	221			218
			865	216	
3	1	213			217
			871	218	
	2	212			215
			849	212	
	3	225			
	4	199			

Expenditure by distributive trades

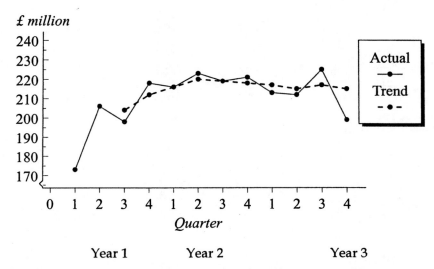

(b)   The method of least squares would be used in preference to the method of moving averages only in cases where the trend follows a regular increasing or decreasing path which appears on the graph as almost a straight line. In the present case the trend path is a curved line in the graph; therefore the method of moving averages will produce a more useful trend line.

8

Year	Qtr	Value	4–qtr total	4–qtr average	Centred average (trend)	Seasonal variations
20X7	1	134				
	2	153				
			601	150.25		
	3	163			150.4	+12.6
			602	150.5		
	4	151			150.6	+0.4
			603	150.75		
20X8	1	135			150.3	–15.3
			599	149.75		
	2	154			150.3	+3.7
			603	150.75		
	3	159			150.4	+8.6
			600	150.00		
	4	155			150.6	+4.4
			605	151.25		
20X9	1	132			153.5	–21.5
			623	155.75		
	2	159			156.3	+2.7
			627	156.75		
	3	177				
	4	159				

	Qtr 1	Qtr 2	Qtr 3	Qtr 4
20X7			+12.6	+0.4
20X8	–15.3	+3.7	+8.6	+4.4
20X9	–21.5	+2.7		
Sum	–36.8	+6.4	+21.2	+4.8
Average	–18.4	+3.2	+10.6	+2.4

Deseasonalisation

Year	Qtr	Value	Variations	Deseasonalised data
20X7	1	134	–18.4	152.4
	2	153	+3.2	149.8
	3	163	+10.6	152.4
	4	151	+2.4	148.6
20X8	1	135	–18.4	153.4
	2	154	+3.2	150.8
	3	159	+10.6	148.4
	4	155	+2.4	152.6
20X9	1	132	–18.4	150.4
	2	159	+3.2	155.8
	3	177	+10.6	166.4
	4	159	+2.4	156.6

Chapter 6 solutions

1   Planning

(a)   Strategic planning requires an understanding of the long-term goals or objectives of an organisation.   Every organisation should be able to state its long-term goals or objectives.   For example, the organisation's long-term goals may be expressed as "to sustain our competitive advantage with minimum operating costs compatible with delivering a quality product/service to our customers and seeking continuous performance improvement."

Strategic management must be dynamic in nature.   Basic elements which it should incorporate are that it should: agree and communicate to all concerned the chosen business direction embracing the principles of its main goals; involve development in the management of plans; be action orientated and seek to 'manage change'; and require commitment from all parties.

The operational planning requirements are

♦   action plans

♦   organisation structure consideration (to facilitate the implementation of plans)

♦   financial plans and budgets.

(b)   To achieve a strategic planning goal of sustaining competitive advantage at minimum cost through speedy delivery of quality products to customers, there are two possible solutions which operational planning may suggest.

1   Build up finished goods stock levels to ensure availability (for speedy delivery) of products.

2   Increase inspection of various points in the production cycle to help detect faults and allow re-work, thus ensuring only quality products reach the customer.

The above solutions illustrate the problems of not linking strategic and operational planning.   These problems are as follows.

♦   *Unrealistic plans* — the building up of finished goods stock levels may be neither feasible, because of space, nor desirable, because of cost and changing customer demand patterns.

♦   *Inconsistent goals* — it may increase the likelihood of quality products reaching the customer, but it is unlikely to be a minimum cost option.

♦   *Poor communication* — it indicates a lack of discussion to determine the most appropriate strategy required to minimise the customer complaints problem whilst pursuing the aim of a minimum cost strategy.

♦   *Inadequate performance measurement* — increased stock levels may be seen as a 'good' performance indicator because of the current operational planning decision. However, they do not measure changes in other factors such as customer complaints and tend to lead to increased costs for the company rather than increasing profits.

2 Total quality

(a) Standard costing is a technique used to monitor performance. To do this, agreed levels of price and performance are set as standards, which are then measured against actual levels and analysed accordingly.

For standard costing to work, one must assume that the standards set apply over the time period required in order that they may be compared against actual events.

The philosophy adopted in a total quality environment is different:

- ◆ 'It aims towards an environment of zero defects at minimum cost'. The idea of standard costing conflicts with this, as, for example, a normal loss may be built into the standards at an agreed level.

- ◆ 'It aims towards the elimination of waste where waste is defined as anything other than the minimum essential amount of equipment, materials, space and workers' time.' Again, this conflicts with the idea of standard costing as the standards may be set with an acceptable level of waste built-in.

- ◆ 'It requires an awareness by all personnel of the quality requirements compatible with supplying the customer with products of the agreed design specification.'

(b) The setting of standards is usually the responsibility of specific members of the workforce or departmental management. This approach can lead to conflicting decisions as to the optimum improvement strategy.

In a standard costing system, labour efficiency is measured in terms of the ratio of output achieved to standard input. This approach does not focus on other issues of effectiveness, only on quality.

High quality with a focus on value-added activities and support services is implied by the term effectiveness within a total quality environment. If efficiency is achieved at a cost to the organisation, it will be measured as internal or external cost within a total quality environment. In the standard cost variance measure, these costs will not be identified.

The basis for efficiency measurement in a standard cost system is individual labour task situations. It is more likely, within a total quality environment, that labour will be considered in multi-task teams. The completion of each part of the production process will be the responsibility of one of the teams.

Output will not be the only consideration when measuring effectiveness. In a total quality environment other aspects are considered including defect levels at the various stages of production and the incidence of re-work.

3 Calton

(a) **Calculation summaries**

(i) *Total production units*

	Before implementation		After implementation
First quality output	5,000		5,000
Specification losses (5%)	250	(2.5%)	125
	5,250		5,125

Downgrading at inspection

(12.5% of production)	750	(7.5%)	416
	6,000		5,541

(ii)   *Material purchases (m²)*

	Before implementation		*After implementation*
Pre-inspection material required (6,000 × 8m²)	48,000	(5,541 × 8)	44,328
Process waste (4% of material input)	2,000	(2.50%)	1,137
Material input	50,000		45,465
Scrapped incoming material (5%)	2,632	(3%)	1,406
Purchases (m²)	52,632		46,871

(iii)   *Gross machine hours*

	Before implementation		*After implementation*
First quality (6,000 × 0.6hrs)	3,600	(5,541 × 0.5hrs)	2,771
Unit rectification (200 × 0.2hrs)	40	(100 × 0.2hrs)	20
	3,640		2,791
Idle time	910		399
Gross hours required	4,550		3,190

(b)   **Calton Ltd Profit & Loss Account for the period**

	Before implementation £	£		*After implementation* £	£
Sales (W1)		562,750			534,245
Costs:					
Material (52,632 × £4)	210,528		(46,871 × £4)	187,484	
Machine costs (4,550 × £40)	182,000		(3,190 × £40)	127,600	
Inspection/storage (52,632 × £0.10)	5,263		(46,871 × £0.10)	4,687	
Replacement delivery (250 × £8)	2,000		(125 × £8)	1,000	
Inspection/other	25,000			15,000	
Product liability (3% × £500,000)	15,000		(1% × 500,000)	5,000	
Sundry costs	60,000			54,000	
Prevention costs	20,000			60,000	
		519,791			454,771
Net profit		42,959			79,474

(c)   In assessing the overall effectiveness of the management of quality, analysis of quality costs is a significant management tool. A means of determining action priorities and problem areas is also provided by the analysis of quality costs.

Internal failure costs If work falls short of the quality standards but the failure is discovered before the product is transferred to the customer, it is known as an internal failure cost. Examples of these costs include the machine processing losses, downgrading of products, and materials which are scrapped due to poor receipt and storage.

External failure costs These are similar to internal failure costs, but the failure is only discovered after the product has been transferred to the customer. Examples of these costs include product liability claims and the costs of making free replacements, including delivery costs.

Appraisal costs The costs of evaluating purchased materials, processes and services to ensure they conform to the desired specification are called appraisal costs. Examples of these include inspection during the production process, inspection of materials in storage, calibration checks, and vendor rating.

Prevention costs Costs associated with implementing quality management programmes are known as prevention costs. Some of the most important prevention costs, and the most common in practice, are training costs.

Workings

(W1)   Sales

	Before implementation £		After implementation £
First quality (5,000 × £100)	500,000	(5,000 × £100)	500,000
Second quality (750 × £70)	52,500	(416 × £70)	29,120
Third quality (200 × £50)	10,000	(100 × £50)	5,000
Scrap (50 × £5)	250	(25 × £5)	125
	562,750		534,245

4   Snecas

(a)

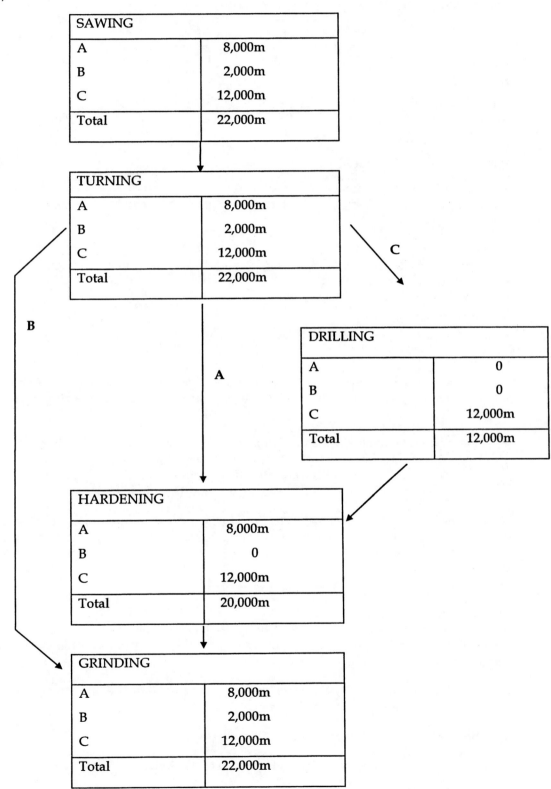

(b) *STATEMENT OF BUDGETED PROFIT FOR YEAR ENDED….*

	A		B		C	
Sales quantity	Per metre £	8,000m Total £000	Per metre £	2,000m Total £000	Per metre £	12,000m Total £000
Sales revenue (W1)	252	2,016	210	420	252	3,024
Less variable costs:						
Direct materials (W2)	(74.2)	(593.6)	(74.2)	(148.4)	(74.2)	(890.4)
Sawing	(36)	(288)	(36)	(72)	(36)	(432)
Turning	(14)	(112)	(14)	(28)	(14)	(168)
Drilling	0	0	0	0	(40)	(480)
Hardening	(26)	(208)	0	0	(26)	(312)
Grinding	(25)	(200)	(25)	(50)	(25)	(300)
Contribution	76.8	614.4	60.8	121.6	36.8	441.6
Fixed costs (W3)						
Sawing	(4)	(32)	(4)	(8)	(4)	(48)
Turning	(5)	(40)	(5)	(10)	(5)	(60)
Drilling	0	0	0	0	(9)	(108)
Hardening	(16)	(128)	0	0	(16)	(192)
Grinding	(7)	(56)	(7)	(14)	(7)	(84)
Net profit (loss)	44.8	358.4	44.8	89.6	(4.2)	(50.4)

(c) The amended machine layout has a significant increase in profitability to £44.80 per metre for both product A and B, from £12.50 per metre and a loss of £27.50 per metre respectively.

♦ This increase is due to the amended absorption of fixed costs. Previously products A and B were attributed part of the drilling fixed costs, when neither one used this machine type. Thus A and B were subsidising product C. Similarly product B did not use hardening, but was still attributed a proportion of the cost.

♦ Depending on the elasticity of the products, (ie the proportionate change in demand caused by a change in price), it may be possible to change the prices of A, B and/or C and increase overall profit.

For example:

The sales volume for product C is 12,000m. This could be an indication that the price is too low. An increase in price may lead to fall in demand, leading to a fall in variable costs. The change in sales revenue will depend on the new price and the change in sale; it could rise or fall.

If the reduction in variable costs is greater than the fall/rise in revenue, then contribution (and thus profit), will increase.

♦ The product mix will depend on the following two factors:

(1) The production capacities of each cell of machines.

If there was a reduction in product C there would be unused capacity in drilling, but the spare capacity in sawing, turning, hardening and grinding would be used by A.

If there is a spare capacity in hardening, a reduction in B would be effective by creating spare capacity in the other machines for product A.

Any spare capacity yielded in sawing, turning and grinding from a reduction in A could be used by B. However, this would also yield spare capacity in hardening which could only be used by C, the least profitable product.

(2) Whether the three products are entirely independent of each other, or complements, or independents.

If the products are not independent, a change in sales of say A may affect the demand for, say, C.

(d) A cellular layout should reduce costs in the following ways.

(1) Avoiding the costs of moving work in progress and machine utilisation management costs.

(2) Reducing the likelihood of bottlenecks in production. This makes production more efficient and able to respond more rapidly to changes in demand.

(3) By controlling the conversion process more closely which will reduce material scrap.

(4) By reducing the level of investment in working capital stock due to more efficient production.

(5) By improving production planning and thus reducing stock costs.

Workings

(W1) *Selling price per metre*

	A £	B £	C £
Direct material	70	70	70
Labour and overheads (£70.00 × 225%)	157.5	157.5	157.5
Add/(less) current profit/(loss)	12.5	(27.5)	12.5
Current selling price	240	200	240
Add: 5% increase	12	10	12
Budgeted selling price	252	210	252

(W2) *Direct material costs*

	£
Current price per metre	70
Add: 6% increase	4.2
Budgeted price per metre	74.2

(W3) *Fixed costs*

Machine operation	Fixed labour and overhead (total)	Aggregate quantity passing through (metres) (part a)	Absorbed overhead cost per metre (£)
Saw	88,000	22,000	4
Turn	110,000	22,000	5
Drill	108,000	12,000	9
Harden	320,000	20,000	16
Grind	154,000	22,000	7
Drill	108,000	12,000	9
Harden	320,000	20,000	16
Grind	154,000	22,000	7

5   Repak

(a)   (i)   Using basic budgeted information only

The average cost per cubic metre will be the same for each customer as no information is available regarding the apportionment of labour and overhead costs to each customer.

Average cost per cubic metre = total cost/total cubic metres handled

= (£350,000 + £30,000 + £500,000 + £60,000)/100,000 = £9.40 per cubic metre

The number of packaging units required is calculated as follows.

Paul Ltd	25,000 × 3	=	75,000 units
George Ltd	45,000 × 2	=	90,000 units
John Ltd	30,000 × 1	=	30,000 units
			195,000 units

Packaging material cost per unit of packaging = total cost/number of packaging units

= £1,950,000/195,000 = £10 per unit.

Product cost per cubic metre:

	John Ltd £	George Ltd £	Paul Ltd £
Packaging material	10	20	30
Labour and overheads	9.4	9.4	9.4
	19.4	29.4	39.4

(ii)   Using additional information

Cost allocation:

	Ratio	Receipt and inspection £000	Storage £000	Packing £000	Total £000
Labour: basic	(15:10:75)	52.5	35.0	262.5	350.0
Labour: overtime	(50:15:35)	15.0	4.5	10.5	30.0
Occupancy	(20:60:20)	100.0	300.0	100.0	500.0
Admin & management	(40:10:50)	24.0	6.0	30.0	60.0
		191.5	345.5	403.0	940.0

Requirements in each activity:

	Receipt & inspection) (hours)	Storage (sq metres)	Packing (hours)
John Ltd	2,500	9,000	18,000
George Ltd	6,750	13,500	33,750
Paul Ltd	6,250	5,000	25,000
Total	15,500	27,500	76,750

Cost per hour   (£191,500/15,000)   £12.355
Cost per square metre (£345,000/27,500)   £12.564
Cost per hour   (£403,000/76,750)   £5.251

Using ABC: Cost per product unit

	John Ltd £	George Ltd £	Paul Ltd £
Packaging material	10.00	20.00	30.00
Receipt and inspection	1.03	1.85	3.09
Storage	3.77	3.77	2.51
Packing	3.15	3.94	5.25
Total per unit	17.95	29.56	40.85

Examples of above workings:

John Ltd: Receipt and inspection = £12.355 × 5/60 = £1.03
George Ltd: Storage = £12.564 × 0.3 sq metres = £3.77
Paul Ltd: Packing = £5.251 × 1 hour = £5.25

(b)   The three activities which have been identified for Repak Ltd in part (a) are receipt and inspection, storage and packaging.

Cost drivers are the factors which cause costs to occur at a given level.

The cost drivers for the activities are as follows.

Activity	Cost driver
Receipt and inspection	Relative fragility
Storage	Size of incoming package
Packing	Complexity of packing

An activity-based costing (ABC) approach results in a more accurate product cost per unit. By linking costs to the activities and the cost drivers which cause the relative use of each activity, ABC improves product costing.

Below is a comparison of the labour and overheads charged to each cubic metre, using an ABC system and the existing system.

	ABC system	Existing system
John Ltd	£7.95	£9.40
George Ltd	£9.56	£9.40
Paul Ltd	£10.85	£9.40

A better focus for cost control is achieved using ABC, enabling Repak Ltd to concentrate on cost drivers and on ways in which the use of each may be reduced.

For example, to reduce unit costs, a change in procedure may be implemented which will reduce the time required in receipt and inspection, both in overall terms and in respect of the more fragile products.

6 Sapu

(i) Absorption costing approach

	Product A £		Product B £
Direct material (80/5)	16	(300/10)	30
Direct labour (40/5)	8	(100/10)	10
	24		40
Variable overheads:			
Material related (W1)	4		7.5
Labour related (W2)	9		11.25
Total variable cost	37		58.75

Workings

(W1) Material related overheads

Overhead	=	£1,500,000 × 40% = £600,000
Overhead absorption rate	=	Overhead/total direct material cost of all products
	=	£600,000/£2,400,000
	=	25% on direct material cost.

Absorbed material related overhead per unit:

	A £	B £
25% × £16/£30	4.00	7.50

(W2)   Labour related overheads

Overheads	=	£1,500,000 × 60% = £900,000
Overhead absorption rate =		Overhead/total direct labour cost for all products
	=	£900,000/£800,000
	=	112.5% on direct labour cost.

Absorbed labour related overhead per unit:

	A £	B £
112.5% × £8/£10	9.00	11.25

(ii)   ABC approach

	A £	B £
Direct material cost	16	30
Direct labour cost	8	10
	24	40
Variable overheads:		
Material related (W3)	26.67	6.67
Labour related (W4)	45	7.5
Total variable costs	95.67	54.17

WORKINGS

(W3)   Material related

Bulk is the cost driver for material related overheads.

		Bulk
Product A:	4 × 5,000	20,000
Product B:	1 × 10,000	10,000
Other products:	1.5 × 40,000	60,000
	Total Bulk	90,000

Material related overhead per unit of bulk = Overhead/total bulk

= £600,000/90,000

= £6.67 per unit of bulk

Overhead cost per unit of production:

	A £	B £
£6.67 × 4/1	26.67	6.67

(W4) **Labour related**

The number of labour operations is the cost driver for labour related overheads.

		Labour operations
Product A:	6 × 5,000	30,000
Product B:	1 × 10,000	10,000
Other products:	2 × 40,000	80,000
Total labour operations		120,000

Labour related overhead	=	Overhead/total labour operations
	=	£900,000/120,000
	=	£7.50 per labour operation

Labour related overhead cost per unit of production:

	A £	B £
£7.50 × 6/1	45.00	7.50

(b) **Report**

To: Management

From: Management Accountant

Subject: Production and Sales Strategy for Products A and B

Date: xx/xx/xx

Products A and B have market prices of £75 and £95 per unit respectively. These prices result in 5,000 units of A and 10,000 units of B being the obtainable market share in the forthcoming period.

Two methods of calculating unit product cost and contribution can be used: the absorption method which is currently in use or the activity-based costing (ABC) method.

The unit product information for both methods is as follows.

	Product A		Product B	
	Absorption method £	*ABC method* £	*Absorption method* £	*ABC method* £
Selling price	75.00	75.00	95.00	95.00
Direct material	(16.00)	(16.00)	(30.00)	(30.00)
Direct labour	(8.00)	(8.00)	(10.00)	(10.00)
Variable overheads:				
Material related	(4.00)	(26.67)	(7.50)	(6.67)
Labour related	(9.00)	(45.00)	(11.25)	(7.50)
Contribution	38.00	(20.67)	36.25	40.83
Contribution: sales (%)	51	–	38	43

Company policy stipulates that before proceeding with the production/sale of any product the product must have an estimated contribution sales ratio (C/S ratio) of at least 40%.

Using the existing absorption approach the production of Product A would be accepted with a C/S ratio of 51%, but Product B would be rejected as it only has a C/S ratio of 38%.

However, using an ABC approach, which recognises the cost drivers for overheads, product A would be rejected as it has a negative contribution. Product B would be accepted instead as it has a C/S ratio of 43%.

As ABC gives a fairer representation of costs, I recommend that the ABC approach be adopted and therefore based on the above calculations, the production of Product A should cease and production of Product B should continue.

(c)   Target costing could be applied to the environment in which Sapu plc finds itself.

♦   For the given selling prices of Products A and B a market has been identified.

♦   The production costs for Product A must be considerably reduced if it is to comply to the C/S ratio of 40%.

It may be possible to reduce the direct material and labour costs by, for example, changing to a cheaper supplier or changing the design specification.

Also, it may be possible to reduce unit overhead costs due to the high cost driver incidence in both material bulk and labour operations.

♦   In order to ensure that Product B does not fall below the target of C/S ratio of 40% due to a fall in selling price or an increase in cost, Sapu plc may wish to attempt to reduce cost now.

(d)   Where spare capacity exists, it is acceptable to produce any product which has a positive contribution (even if it is below the target of 40% C/S ratio.) This will provide a cash inflow to the company, and help towards fixed costs, and therefore should be adopted unless there is a more profitable way to utilise the spare capacity. However, if this action is likely to affect orders for products where the C/S radio of 40% is being applied, the marginal cost pricing policy should not be adopted.

7   Energy costs

(a)   *Zero-based budgeting*

Zero-based budgeting (ZBB) requires that the budget for each cost centre should be made from scratch (a zero-base), and therefore all expenditure must be justified.

For each department or component of a business, decision-packages will be created, which are ranked and will compete with each other for available resources.

Incremental budgeting, on the other hand, uses as its base the previous year's budget. This will usually lead to a 'plus a percentage for inflation' approach to budgeting. As this approach does not examine in a critical way the activities which cause costs, it will not lead to cost reduction but may instead perpetuate inefficiencies.

ZBB is particularly appropriate for 'discretionary' costs such as research and development and training and can also be applied to *energy costs*.

♦ Some costs, such as power costs per unit of output, will vary with the level of output and therefore can only be significantly reduced if the output level is reduced. However, the power costs incurred in moving raw materials and work in progress depend on the degree of movement which is required. Focusing on these costs and on ways to reduce them will be made easier with ZBB.

♦ There are certain costs where an organisation is committed to expenditure. For example, the operating of the specially humidified materials store or maintaining a statutory temperature range in the work place. ZBB will examine these costs and ways of reducing them whilst still meeting requirements.

♦ ZBB will examine any expenditure required to reduce energy costs. Insulation of the steam pipes would reduce heat loss, and steam loss from the valves could be reduced through increased maintenance. A cost/benefit analysis could be performed to determine any net saving which these procedures would produce.

(b)   *Total quality management*

Total quality management (TQM) is a business philosophy which has the following features.

♦ A zero defect environment at minimum cost

♦ All employees must be aware of ways in which products of agreed specification can reach the customer at minimum cost

♦ Waste of all types is eradicated

♦ All aspects of the business operation are embraced

♦ The need to minimise non-value added activities is recognised

TQM can be applied to the energy costs highlighted in the question.

♦ A TQM philosophy will examine the ways in which the statutory temperature range can be maintained as efficiently as possible.

♦ Instead of operating a specially humidified material store, it may be more cost effective to introduce a 'just-in-time' stock delivery system.

♦ All improvements in quality will eliminate the need for re-work and minimise defective units and thus reduce the power costs per unit of output.

♦ A TQM approach will seek to eliminate losses from steam pipelines and steam valves and heat losses through windows, which are both types of waste.

♦ An example of a non-value added activity is the movement of raw materials and work in progress. A TQM approach would seek to eliminate these movements, and thus reduce the energy costs associated with them, possibly by the introduction of a just in time system which will deliver direct to the factory line, or the introduction of dedicated cells.

Answers to multiple choice questions

1   C

Let x = the mark-up on a 7-day holiday

Remembering that   Revenue – Cost   = Profit

76,000 (1+x) + 66,000 (1 + 2x) – 200,000   = 50,000

142,000 + 208,000x   = 250,000

$$x = \frac{108,000}{208,000}$$

= 0.519

Price of a 14-day holiday $= \frac{£66,000}{120} \times (1 + (2 \times 0.519))$

= £1,120.90

2   D

Let x = the mark-up on a 7-day holiday

Remembering that   Revenue – Cost   = Profit

and noting that total expenses $= \frac{£(50,000 + 40,000)}{0.6}$

= £150,000

then

50,000 (1 + x) + 40,000 (1 + 1.5x) – 150,000   = 40,000

90,000 + 110,000x   = 190,000

$$x = \frac{100,000}{110,000}$$

= 0.909

Price for a 7-day holiday $= \frac{£50,000}{200} \times (1 + 0.909)$

= £477

3   B

Standard cost card

	£	£
Direct costs	100	100
Indirect costs	40	
	140	
Mark-up	(50%) 70	(110%) 110
Selling price	210	210

Chapter 7 solutions

1   Critical success factors

(a)   Critical success factors are those areas of a business and its environment which are critical to the achievement of its goals and objectives. A company may, for example, express its main goal as being a world class business in its chosen areas of operation. Management should identify critical success factors since failure in any one such factor may prevent or inhibit the advancement of the company and the achievement of its goals. Lewis (1980) outlines as critical success factors profitability, market position (ie market share), productivity, product leadership, personnel development, employee attitudes, public responsibility, balance between short-range and long-range goals.

(Other relevant comment and examples would be accepted.)

(b)   Where productivity is seen as a critical success factor it is necessary to maintain tight control over its measurement and interpretation. The main focus is likely to be on the results, ie the output measure and its use. The results may also be influenced, however, by control of the actions of those involved in tasks which influence the productivity measure.

Relevant checks that adequate control is being exercised over productivity measurement and use are as follows.

♦   Is the productivity measurement congruent with the desired result? For example, a higher productivity measure may be obtained in one department which simply leads to higher levels of work in progress with consequent additional costs.

♦   Is the productivity measurement sufficiently accurate? It is important that the actual result is determined by and measured against well tested and agreed standards and not some crude measure. The productivity measure can only be used as a useful control base if it is an accurate measure of the desired goal or objective.

♦   Is the productivity measure objective and free from bias? For example, bias may occur where there is the capacity to make value judgements as to the inclusion of certain classes of idle time or rework in the productivity measure. Lack of control in this context could lead to action which will not result in a relevant strategy for the future. In addition, control must be implemented in order to ensure that the data is not manipulated in order to give measures which are acceptable to management, but which do not reflect what has actually occurred.

♦   Is the measure available at the appropriate time? If the productivity measure is to be used as a signal for control action it must be available quickly and at regular intervals. Where the technology permits, this could be available as part of an on-line information analysis in a computer integrated manufacturing system.

♦   Is the measure understandable? It is important that the users of the measure are conversant with its uses and limitations. The trend should be viewed as well as individual measures in order to monitor where an 'out of control' situation is indicated.

♦   Are the rewards (and punishments) associated with good (or bad) results significant and clearly defined? The behaviour of individuals in the provision of information and the acceptance of its use is likely to be influenced by the way in which the control process is implemented.

2   BS

(a)   (i) and (ii)

		Hours	
	Budget	Actual	
Gross hours	120,000	132,000	
Non-chargeable hours			
Standard (16%)	(19,200)	(21,120)	
Excess		(18,480)	see analysis below
Chargeable hours	100,800	92,400	

		Hours		(ii)
				Client income gains/losses at £75/hour
	Standard	Actual	Variance	£
Gross hours	132,000	132,000		
Non-chargeable hours				
Contract negot (std 4%)	5,280	9,240	(3,960)	(297,000)
Remedial advice (std 2%)	2,640	7,920	(5,280)	(396,000)
Other (std 10%)	13,200	22,440	(9,240)	(693,000)
Chargeable hours	110,880	92,400	(18,480)	
Budget chargeable hours	100,800			
Capacity gain over budget	10,080		10,080	756,000
Net fall in chargeable hours			(8,400)	(630,000)

Adverse variances in the workings are denoted as ( ).

(b)   (i)

*BS LTD SUMMARY PROFIT AND LOSS ACCOUNT FOR THE
YEAR ENDED 30 APRIL 20X5*

	Budget £000	Actual £000
Revenue from client contracts (chargeable hours × £75)	7,560	6,930
Costs		
Consultant salaries	1,800	1,980
Sundry operating costs	3,500	4,100
	5,300	6,080
Net profit	2,260	850
Capital employed	6,500	6,500

Financial ratios

Net profit: Turnover	29.9%	12.3%
Turnover: Capital employed	1.16 times	1.07 times
Net profit: Capital employed	34.8%	13.1%

The above figures show that BS Ltd has a poor financial performance during the year to 30 April 20X5 compared to that budgeted. Client income is down and operating costs have increased. It would be useful, however, to have a more detailed analysis which attempts, where possible, to link the fall in profit to quality, flexibility, resource utilisation and innovation factors. In addition, it would be useful to have a longer-term trend of financial results in order to see whether the current year figures are representative of a continuing decline or are due to specific short-term conditions.

The financial performance may be examined in more detail by establishing reasons for the fall in chargeable hours. The information in part (a) of the answer analyses the £630,000 fall in revenue and attempts to link it to specific factors such as increased time on remedial advice to clients.

(ii)   *Competitiveness* may be measured in terms of market share or sales growth. BS Ltd's turnover for the year to 30 April 20X5 is lower than budgeted. The trend for the past five years may show a steady growth, however, indicating a high level of competitiveness in the longer term. The 20X5 failure to achieve budgeted profit may be due to efforts to improve longer-term competitiveness, eg through the retention of 60 consultants and the offer of 'free' remedial advice to clients.

Competitiveness may also be measured in terms of the relative success or failure in obtaining business from clients. Table 1 data shows that the budgeted uptake from client enquiries is 40% for new systems and 75% for existing systems advice. The actual percentages are 35% and 80% respectively. For new systems business the percentage has fallen, but the number of new systems worked on has increased from budget (210 from 180). For existing systems advice, although the percentage uptake is higher than budget, the total number of clients is down (288/300) on budget.

(iii)   *Quality* is the totality of features of a service package which bear upon its ability to satisfy customer needs. Key quality factors must be identified and monitored in quantitative and/or qualitative ways. To some extent the increased level of remedial advice, an extra 5,280 hours compared to flexed budget, may indicate a quality problem. The question does indicate, however, that this is an innovation on the part of BS Ltd with a view to future demand improvement. The information in Table 1 indicates that client complaints were four times the budgeted level (20 compared with 5). Also, the number of clients requiring remedial advice was 75 compared to a budget level of 48. BS Ltd should investigate the reasons for the increases in order to identify and eliminate quality problems.

(iv)   *Flexibility* may relate to the company being able to cope with flexibility of volume, delivery speed or job specification. We are told that BS Ltd retains 60 consultants in order that it has increased flexibility in meeting demand. The mix of consultants available will be another indicator of flexibility. Table 1 shows a change in mix from that budgeted which may indicate a high level of awareness of market changes and the need to provide for such changes. Delivery speed should be aided by the policy of retaining consultants and the mix of staff available. The ability to cope with a range of job specifications may be linked to the mix of consultants available. BS Ltd has moved to a work ratio of existing systems advice: new systems of 40%: 60% compared to a budget ratio of 30%: 70% which may indicate an ability to be flexible in response to market demands. Flexibility will be achieved at a cost. The analysis in part (a) of the answer shows the level of excess non-chargeable consultant hours. This may reflect the policy of retention of the consultancy team at 60 consultants.

(v)   *Resource utilisation* may be measured in terms of output to input consultant hours. In the budget the hours charged to clients represents 84% of gross hours. The actual percentage for the year to 30 April 20X5 was 70% of gross hours (92,400/132,000). There is a trade-off between resource utilisation, flexibility and innovation. The strategy implemented must be viewed not only in terms of the results for the current year, but also in terms of the likely impact on future levels of client demand. The increased level of remedial advice (6% of gross hours compared to 2% in the budget) may be viewed as a longer-term investment.

(vi) *Innovation* should be viewed in terms of its impact on financial performance, competitiveness, quality, flexibility and resource utilisation in both the short and long term.

BS Ltd has an innovative feature in allowing 'free' remedial advice after the completion of a contract. In the short term this is adversely affecting financial performance. The answer to part (a) of the question shows that remedial advice hours are 5,280 hours in excess of the standard allowance of 2% of gross hours. This may have resulted in loss of fee income from contracts forgone. The excess hours may also indicate that the process of remedial advice needs to be reviewed. It may be necessary to limit the level of such advice on any one contract. This sort of decision is very much a value judgement which must balance potential future benefits against current financial costs.

Answers to multiple choice questions

1   **C**

Cost is a financial indicator.

2   **A**

The balanced scorecard looks at the financial perspective, the customer perspective, the business process perspective and the organisational learning perspective.

3   **B**

The output of service industries is intangible so, for example, it cannot be assembled in stock to be used later. This makes performance measurement more difficult.

Chapter 8 solutions

1   **Luda**

(a)   **Overhead absorption rate**

		Machine shop £	*Finishing shop* £
Fixed overhead		100,800	94,500
		Hrs	Hrs
(i) **Labour hours**			
P 6,000 units	× 2/× 1.5	12,000	9,000
Q 8,000 units	× 1/× 1	8,000	8,000
R 2,000 units	× 2/× 2	4,000	4,000
		24,000	21,000
Rate per labour hour		£4.20	£4.50
(ii) **Machine hours**			
P 6,000	× 4/ × 0.5	24,000	3,000
Q 8,000	× 1.5/× 0.5	12,000	4,000
R 2,000	× 3/ × 1	6,000	2,000
		42,000	9,000
Rate per machine hour		£2.40	£10.50

(b)   **Product costs**

	P £	*Q* £	*R* £
Materials	18.50	15.00	22.50
Wages	16.00	9.00	18.00
Prime cost	34.50	24.00	40.50

(i)   **Labour hour rate absorption**

	P £	*Q* £	*R* £
Machine shop £4.20 × 2, 1, 2	8.40	4.20	8.40
Finishing shop £4.50 × 1.5, 1, 2	6.75	4.50	9.00
	49.65	32.70	57.90

(ii)   **Machine hour rate absorption**

	P £	*Q* £	*R* £
Prime costs as above	34.50	24.00	40.50
Machine shop £2.40 × 4, 1.5, 3	9.60	3.60	7.20
Finishing shop £10.50 × 0.5, 0.5, 1	5.25	5.25	10.50
	49.35	32.85	58.20

(c)   **Comments**

The alternatives shown in (b) above produce very similar results. If a labour hour rate were used, in total the rate to be applied would be (£195,300/45,000) = £4.34 per hour — not greatly different from either of the two rates calculated separately. However, the same cannot be said of the machine hour rate which in total would be (£195,300/51,000) = £3.83 per hour as compared with rates of £2.40 and £10.50 calculated separately.

2   Cross-services

Calculation of budgeted overhead absorption rates

Overhead item	Basis of apportion-ment	Machine Shop A	Machine Shop B	Assembly	Canteen	Mainten-ance
		£	£	£	£	£
Indirect wages	Given	8,586	9,190	15,674	29,650	15,460
Consumable materials	Given	6,400	8,700	1,200	600	–
Rent and rates Buildings insurance Heat and light	Area	5,000	6,000	7,500	3,000	1,000
Power	Technical estimate	4,730	3,440	258		172
Depreciation	Value of machinery	20,100	17,900	2,200		–
		44,816	45,230	26,832	33,250	16,632
Canteen	Labour hours	7,600	5,890	19,760	(33,250)	–
Maintenance	Machine usage hours	4,752	11,880	–		(16,632)
		57,168	63,000	46,592		

Overhead absorption rate = $\dfrac{\text{Budgeted overhead}}{\text{Budgeted units of base}}$

= $\dfrac{57,168}{7,200}$ $\dfrac{63,000}{18,000}$ $\dfrac{46,592}{20,800}$

= £7.94 per machine hour   £3.50 per machine hour   £2.24 per labour hour

3   Reciprocal services

(a)   Calculation of overhead absorbed and under/over absorption

      (1)   **Overhead absorption rates**

	Filling	*Sealing*
$\dfrac{\text{Budgeted overhead}}{\text{Budgeted direct labour hours}}$	$\dfrac{110{,}040}{13{,}100}$	$\dfrac{53{,}300}{10{,}250}$
	= £8.40	= £5.20
	per labour hour	per labour hour

      (2)   **Amount incurred**

	Filling £	*Sealing* £	*Maintenance* £	*Canteen* £
Per question	74,260	38,115	25,050	24,375
Maintenance (70 : 27 : 3)	17,535	6,764	(25,050)	751
				25,126
Canteen (60 : 32 : 8)	15,076	8,040	2,010	(25,126)
Maintenance (70 : 27 : 3)	1,407	543	(2,010)	60
Canteen (60 : 32)	39	21		(60)
	108,317	53,483		

(b)   The principal aims of overhead apportionment and absorption are as follows.

      (i)   *To obtain the budgeted overhead of each cost centre.* This is needed to enable costs to be controlled and can be used as a basis for assessing the performance of managers and departments. Ideally managers of departments should participate in preparing the budget so that they are motivated to try to keep costs within the budget. A potential problem can arise when selecting the basis of apportionment. Certain costs incurred centrally may either be non-controllable, ie the manager is unable to influence the amount incurred, or appear to be non-controllable from the viewpoint of the manager.

            Taking as an example rent, the rate per square metre is not controllable by individual managers but the area occupied by a department may be. Therefore, if rent is charged to departments at a rate per square metre for the area they intend to occupy, managers have the opportunity to reduce the charge to their cost centre. Space could therefore be saved and used for other purposes. In some cases it may not be practicable to establish an accurate basis for apportioning an overhead between cost centres.

      (ii)   *To obtain the overhead recovery rate.* This rate forms the basis for charging the costs of a department to the 'users' of that department. In the case of a service department (eg maintenance) a recovery rate could be used as a basis for charging maintenance costs to other cost centres. This would enable the maintenance department to be viewed as a profit centre — which should increase the motivation of the manager and would enable the maintenance department's efficiency to be assessed. It should also encourage user departments to control the extent to which they use the maintenance department.

(iii) *To obtain a predetermined overhead cost per unit.* This is needed:

(1) to value stock in the financial accounts which must be on an absorption costing basis, including fixed and variable overheads. Because fixed overheads are included, the accuracy of the rate is dependent on predicting correctly the volume of production;

(2) as a basis for calculating a cost-plus selling price. Here it is necessary also to include non-production overheads. In practice other factors (eg demand conditions) must be considered before a price is finalised;

(3) as a basis for decision-making, eg make or buy, utilisation of scarce resources. For this purpose it will usually be necessary to determine the variable overhead cost per unit. Practical difficulties may arise when trying to split overheads into the fixed and variable elements.

(iv) *To calculate the actual overhead cost of each cost centre.* This figure can be compared with budget (flexed as appropriate) in order to calculate variances.

4   Hensau

(a) The existing overhead absorption rate is:

$$\frac{£15,600 + £19,500 + £13,650}{(2,000 \times \frac{24}{60}) + (1,500 \times \frac{40}{60}) + (800 \times \frac{60}{60})} \quad = \quad \frac{£48,750}{2,600} = £18.75 \text{ per hour}$$

Unit cost

| | | *Product* | |
	X	Y	Z
Direct material	5.00	3.00	6.00
Direct labour	1.60	2.67	4.00
Production overhead	7.50	12.50	18.75
	£14.10	£18.17	£28.75

(b) Cost driver rates

Material receipt and inspection $= \dfrac{£15,600}{10 + 5 + 16}$ $= £503.23$ per batch

Process power $= \dfrac{£19,500}{(2,000 \times 6) + (1,500 \times 3) + (800 \times 2)}$

$= £1.0773$ per power drill operation

Material handling $= \dfrac{£13,650}{(2,000 \times 4) + (1,500 \times 6) + (800 \times 3)}$

$= £0.70361$ per sq metre handled

		Product	
	X	Y	Z
Direct material	5.00	3.00	6.00
Direct labour	1.60	2.67	4.00
Production overhead			
Material receipt/inspection (W1)	2.52	1.68	10.06
Process power (W2)	6.46	3.23	2.15
Material handling (W3)	2.81	4.22	2.11
Cost per unit	£18.39	£14.80	£24.32

Workings

(W1)   Material receipt/inspection

Cost per unit

Product X	£503.23/batch × 10 batches/2,000 units	=	£2.52 per unit
Product Y	£503.23/batch × 5 batches/1,500 units	=	£1.68 per unit
Product Z	£503.23/batch × 16 batches/800 units	=	£10.06 per unit

(W2)   Process power

Cost per unit

Product X	£1.0773/operation × 6 operations	=	£6.46
Product Y	£1.0773/operation × 3 operations	=	£3.23
Product Z	£1.0773/operation × 2 operations	=	£2.15

(W3)   Material handling

Cost per unit

Product X	£0.70361/m² of material × 4m²	=	£2.81
Product Y	£0.70361/m² of material × 6m²	=	£4.22
Product Z	£0.70361/m² of material × 3m²	=	£2.11

5   Experiment

(a)   Machine hour absorption rate $= \dfrac{£10,430 + £5,250 + £3,600 + £2,100 + £4,620}{(120 \times 4) + (100 \times 3) + (80 \times 2) + (120 \times 3)}$

$= \dfrac{£26,000}{1,300} = $ £20 per machine hour.

The total costs for each product are thus:

	A £	B £	C £	D £
Direct materials	40	50	30	60
Direct labour	28	21	14	21
Production overhead	80	60	40	60
Per unit	£148	£131	£84	£141
Total (W4)	£17,760	£13,100	£6,720	£16,920

(b)   Cost driver rates

Machine dept costs (m/c hour basis)	=	£10,430/1,300	=	£8.023 per hr
Set-up costs	=	£5,250/21 (W1)	=	£250 per run
Stores receiving	=	£3,600/80 (W2)	=	£45 per requisition
Inspection/quality control	=	£2,100/21 (W1)	=	£100 per run
Material handling despatch	=	£4,620/42	=	£110 per order

Total costs	A £	B £	C £	D £
Direct materials	4,800	5,000	2,400	7,200
Direct labour	3,360	2,100	1,120	2,520
Machine dep costs	3,851	2,407	1,284	2,888
Set-up costs	1,500	1,250	1,000	1,500
Stores receiving	900	900	900	900
Inspection/quality control	600	500	400	600
Materials handling despatch	1,320	1,100	880	1,320
	£16,331	£13,257	£7,984	£16,928

(c)   Per unit costs

Product	A £	B £	C £	D £
Traditional machine hour method	148.00	131.00	84.00	141.00
ABC method (W3)	136.09	132.57	99.80	141.07
Difference	11.91	(1.57)	(15.80)	(0.07)

The most significant differences concern products A and C. The ABC approach, in theory, attributes the cost of resources to each product which uses those resources on a more appropriate basis than the traditional method. The implication is that product A is more profitable than the traditional approach implies whereas C is less profitable. Alternatively the price of C should be increased whereas that of A could be reduced.

Workings

(W1)   (120 + 100 + 80 + 120)/20 = 21

(W2)   4 × 20 = 80

(W3)   Cost/quantity of each product.

(W4)   Unit cost × quantity of each product.

6 Brunti

(a) (i) Absorption costing profit statement

	XYI 000		YZT 000		ABW 000	
			Products			
Sales/production(units)	50		40		30	
	£000	£000	£000	£000	£000	£000
Sales		2,250.00		3,800		2,190.0
Prime cost	1,600.00		3,360		1,950.0	
Overheads						
Machine dept	120.00		240		144.0	
Assembly dept	288.75		99		49.5	
		2,008.75		3,699		2,143.5
Profit		241.25		101		46.5

Total £388,750

	Machining services	Assembly services	Cost pools Set-ups	Order processing	Purchasing
(£000)	357	318	26	156	84
Cost drivers	420,000 machine hours	530,000 direct labour hours	520 set-ups	32,000 customer orders	11,200 suppliers' orders
	£0.85 per machine hour	£0.60 per direct labour hour	£50 per set-up	£4.875 per customer order	£7.50 per suppliers' order

(ii) Activity-based costing profit statement

	XYI 000		YZT 000		ABW 000	
Sales/production(units)	50		40		30	
	£000	£000	£000	£000	£000	£000
Sales		2,250.0		3,800		2,190.0
Prime cost	1,600.0		3,360		1,950.0	
Cost pools						
Machine dept at £0.85	85.0		170		102.0	
Assembly dept at £0.60	210.0		72		36.0	
Set-up costs at £50	6.0		10		10.0	
Order processing at £4.875	39.0		39		78.0	
Purchasing at £7.50	22.5		30		31.5	
		1,962.5		3,681		2,207.5
Profit/(loss)		287.5		119		(17.5)

Total £389,000

(b)   Activity-based costing (ABC) is considered to present a fairer valuation of the product cost per unit for the following reasons.

It overcomes some of the problems which are associated with conventional absorption costing. In part (a) (i) all of the production overheads and some other overheads had to be allocated or apportioned to the two production cost centres and to service cost centres. Those overheads which could be identified with a particular cost centre would have had to be shared between cost centres using some arbitrary basis such as floor area or the number of employees. In addition, the service department costs would have been apportioned to production cost centres using an arbitrary basis or technical estimates. The total overheads for each production cost centre would then be divided by the estimated number of machine hours or direct labour hours, as appropriate. This meant that costs which could have been more accurately related to the product were not. For example, set-up costs vary more with the number of set-ups than with the number of machine hours or direct labour hours.

In (a) (ii) it can be observed that by having a number of 'cost pools' and dividing them by their 'cost driver' (ie the activity which causes the cost), a more accurate and realistic assessment can be produced. The information so produced using ABC can be significantly different from that which is generated by traditional absorption costing. The differing levels of activity incurred on behalf of each product in terms of the 'cost drivers' (eg the number of set-ups, customer orders, etc) can, and do, have quite a significant impact on the product cost per unit.

7   Sunshine

(a)   **Profit statement**

(i)   **Marginal costing basis**

	Month 1		Month 2		Month 3	
	£	£	£	£	£	£
Sales (£30 per unit)		150,000		255,000		285,000
Variable costs (£23 per unit)	149,500		207,000		230,000	
Add Opening stock	—		34,500		46,000	
	149,500		241,500		276,000	
Less Closing stock	(34,500)		(46,000)		(57,500)	
		(115,000)		(195,500)		(218,500)
Contribution		35,000		59,500		66,500
Fixed costs		(27,000)		(27,000)		(27,000)
Profit		8,000		32,500		39,500

(ii)   Absorption costing basis

	Month 1		Month 2		Month 3	
	£	£	£	£	£	£
Sales		150,000		255,000		285,000
Cost of production						
Variable costs (£23 per unit)	149,500		207,000		230,000	
Fixed costs	27,000		27,000		27,000	
	176,500		234,000		257,000	
Add Opening stock	–		39,000		52,000	
	176,500		273,000		309,000	
Less Closing stock	(39,000)		(52,000)		(65,000)	
Cost of sales		(137,500)		(221,000)		(244,000)
Profit		12,500		34,000		41,000

(b)   Reconciliation of profits

	Month 1 £	Month 2 £	Month 3 £
Absorption costing profit	12,500	34,000	41,000
Increase in stock @ Fixed cost per unit (£3)	(4,500)	(1,500)	(1,500)
Marginal costing profit	8,000	32,500	39,500

8   Ladenis

Standard cost cards	Absorption £	Marginal £
Variable manufacturing cost	8	8
Fixed manufacturing cost	12	–
Production cost	20	8
Variable selling cost	6	6
Fixed selling cost	10	–
Cost of sales	36	14
Profit/contribution	4	26
Selling price	40	40

(a)   **Absorption costing profit statements**

	Jan £000	Feb £000	Mar £000	Total £000
Sales revenue	12.0	16.0	16.0	44.0
Opening stock	—	4.0	4.0	—
Manufacturing costs				
Variable	4.0	3.2	2.4	9.6
Fixed	6.0	6.0	6.0	18.0
	10.0	13.2	12.4	27.6
Closing stock	(4.0)	(4.0)	(2.0)	(2.0)
Production cost of sales	6.0	9.2	10.4	25.6
Selling costs				
Variable	1.8	2.4	2.4	6.6
Fixed	5.0	5.0	5.0	15.0
Cost of sales	12.8	16.6	17.8	47.2
Profit	(0.8)	(0.6)	(1.8)	(3.2)

(b)   **Marginal costing profit statements**

	Jan £000	Feb £000	Mar £000	Total £000
Sales revenue	12.0	16.0	16.0	44.0
Opening stock	—	1.6	1.6	—
Variable manufacturing costs	4.0	3.2	2.4	9.6
	4.0	4.8	4.0	9.6
Closing stock	(1.6)	(1.6)	(0.8)	(0.8)
Production cost of sales	2.4	3.2	3.2	8.8
Variable selling costs	1.8	2.4	2.4	6.6
Cost of sales	4.2	5.6	5.6	15.4
Contribution	7.8	10.4	10.4	28.6
Fixed costs				
Manufacturing	6.0	6.0	6.0	18.0
Selling	5.0	5.0	5.0	15.0
	11.0	11.0	11.0	33.0
Profit	(3.2)	(0.6)	(0.6)	(4.4)

(c)   **Reconciliation**

	Jan	Feb	Mar	Total
Production (units)	500	400	300	1,200
Sales	300	400	400	1,100
Increase/(decrease) in stock	200	–	(100)	100
Amount by which absorption profit should exceed marginal (£12/unit)	£2,400	–	£(1,200)	£1,200

The differences shown in this table correspond to the difference between the profits in (a) and (b).

(Tutorial note - The difference in profit is due to the different treatment of fixed overheads reflected in different stock valuations. Under absorption costing stock is valued at £20 per unit, under marginal costing at £8 per unit, a difference of £12 per unit (the fixed overhead cost per unit). If stock levels rise over a period, absorption costing will show a higher profit; if they fall, marginal costing will show a higher profit. In this case it is more a question of showing lower losses rather than higher profits.)

(d)   **Relative merits of absorption and marginal costing**

Stock valuations

An absorption costing system produces a stock valuation consistent with that required by SSAP 9 *Stocks and Long-Term Contracts* for published accounts. While marginal costing values stock at an amount equal to the additional costs incurred by a firm in producing that stock (some would say a more prudent valuation), adjustments would need to be made to internally used valuations for external reporting.

Profit

As parts (a) and (b) show, under marginal costing profit depends primarily on the level of sales (profit changes from January to February but not from February to March). This is not the case under absorption costing, where profit depends upon both sales and production (hence three different profit figures). With absorption costing it is possible to manipulate profits by over or under-stocking.

Costing procedures

In order to operate an absorption costing system one needs to find a fixed overhead cost per unit figure. This might require complicated allocation, apportionment and absorption calculations. These are not necessary under marginal costing, although it is essential to have an accurate split of costs into their fixed and variable elements. This may involve the use of regression analysis.

Decision-making

Marginal costing information, which clearly distinguishes between fixed and variable costs, is of most use for management decision-making. The one exception to this is with pricing decisions, where many firms base selling prices on absorption costing information.

Answers to multiple choice questions

1   **B**

Closing stock = 5,000 units

Under absorption costing a proportion of the fixed manufacturing overhead will be carried forward in this stock

$$\frac{5,000}{75,000} \times £90,000 = £6,000$$

This is the difference in annual net income.

2   **B**

Cost card

	£
Variable production	60
Fixed production	40
Variable selling	10
Fixed selling	50
Profit	20
Selling price	180

Fixed overheads in stock = 250 × £40 = £10,000

3   **D**

	£
Profit based on standard cost card 600 × £20	12,000
Over-absorption of fixed selling overhead 100 × £50	5,000
Under-absorption of fixed production overhead 50 × £40	(2,000)
	15,000

Chapter 9 solutions

1   C   **Note:** The lines in the graph cannot relate to the same production since if they did, point 3 would be immediately below point 2.

2   B

3   D

4   A

5   B

Total variable costs

		£
Direct materials		8,000
Direct wages		10,000
Overheads		36,000
		54,000

Contribution   =   £102,000 – £54,000 = £48,000

∴ P/V ratio   = $\dfrac{£48,000}{£102,000}$

=   47%

6   (a)   To obtain a cost per unit for fixed overhead Roger divided his fixed overhead by the number of units he expected to produce, ie.

$$\frac{\text{Fixed overhead}}{10,000} = £4$$

In other words his fixed overheads were £40,000.

Note that we are **not** saying that for every unit produced fixed overheads will go up by £4. They cannot (fixed overheads are fixed).

(b)

	£	£
Selling price		75
Variable cost		
Material	12	
Labour	24	
Variable overhead	10	
		46
Contribution		29

(c)   2,000 × £75 = £150,000

(d)

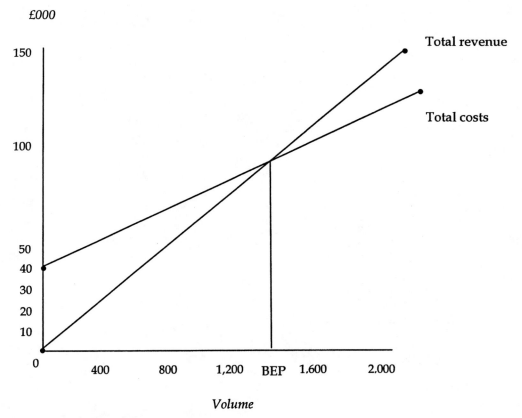

£000

Estimated BEP = 1,400 units

(e) $\quad \text{BEP} = \dfrac{\text{Fixed cost}}{\text{Contribution/unit}} = \dfrac{£40,000}{£29} = 1,379 \text{ units}$

(f) However many extra units Roger makes, his fixed costs will remain constant. The only items that will change are his revenue (total) and variable costs (total).

Accordingly the extra can be found by multiplying the increase in sales by the contribution per unit.

$1,000 \times £29 = £29,000$

7   (a)   Breakeven chart

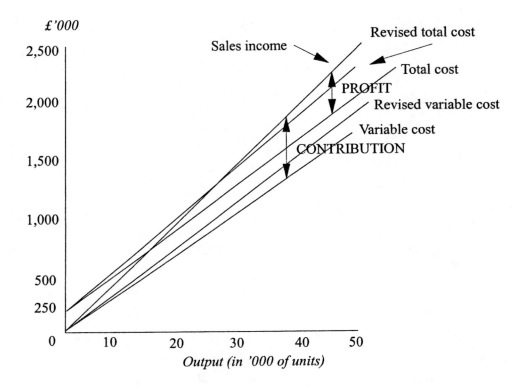

(b)

		£
Annual profit:	50,000 × £15	750,000
Fixed overhead:	50,000 × £5	250,000
Required contribution		1,000,000

Original unit contribution = £(50 – 25 – 3 – 2) = £20

Revised unit contribution £(20 – 1.25*)
        £18.75

Production/sales to yield required contribution   £1,000,000 ÷ £18.75

        = 53,333 units

This means that an increase of 3,333 units is required.

*(ie. 5% of £25)

(c)   The assumptions inherent in breakeven charts are:

(i)   fixed costs remain fixed throughout the range charted;
(ii)   variable costs fluctuate proportionally with volume;
(iii)   selling prices do not change;
(iv)   efficiency and productivity do not change;
(v)   a single product or static mix of products is dealt with;
(vi)   volume is the only factor affecting cost; and
(vii)   linearity is appropriate.

In practice, the required segregation of overheads into 'fixed' and 'variable' is difficult except in those few cases where the category is obvious. Nevertheless, if the exercise is undertaken with care (particularly if each item is looked at separately) a reasonable approximation can usually be obtained.

Although linearity of cost and income behaviour is usually assumed (hence the straight lines on the chart) this is not necessarily so, and a more realistic picture may be obtained by careful study of behaviour at different levels of activity. For example, in the following diagram sales prices have had to be reduced towards the end of the scale, the unit variable cost has also reduced (possibly owing to higher trade discounts after a certain purchasing level has been reached), and fixed costs increase at the point indicated owing to the higher charge for depreciation consequent upon the need to use more machines.

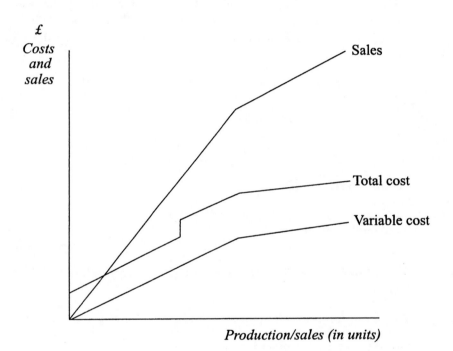

Production/sales (in units)

Chapter 10 solutions

1   Usine Ltd

(a)   **Production plan for the period 1 June 20X0 to 31 August 20X0 assuming that blending hours are the only scarce factor**

	Gamma	*Delta*
Contribution per kg	£4,000	£8,000
Blending hours per kg	100	250
Contribution per blending hour	£40	£32

Usine Ltd should produce and sell Gamma exclusively, because it has the highest contribution per hour of the only scarce resource, blending time. Since the company can sell everything it can produce, all of the scarce resource should be devoted to produce Gamma. This will result in the highest possible contribution towards fixed costs, which will achieve Usine's objective of maximising profits.

Since there are 1,050 blending hours available, Usine Ltd will produce

$$\frac{1,050}{100} = 10.5 \text{ kgs of Gamma}$$

	£
Contribution (10.5 × 4,000)	42,000
Fixed costs	36,000
Profit for the period	6,000

(b)   **Optimum production plan assuming that constraints exist on blending, heating, and refining**

The optimum production mix is found using linear programming.

Let   x = kg of Gamma produced and sold

           y = kg of Delta produced and sold

Constraints:

Heating	400x	+	120y	≤	1,200
Refining	100x	+	90y	≤	450
Blending	100x	+	250y	≤	1,050
Non-negativity			x	≥	0
			y	≥	0

Objective:

Maximise the contribution, C, where C = 4,000x + 8,000y.

From the graph, the feasible region is OABCD.

Graph of quantities of Gamma and Delta produced and sold

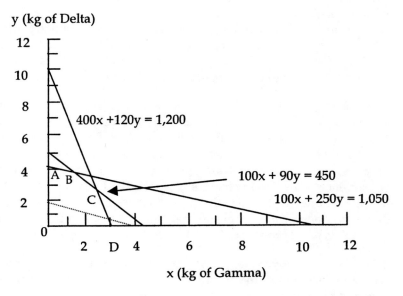

By comparing the slopes of the constraint lines with the slope of the objective line (a specimen line of C = 16,000 has been plotted), the optimum production mix is at point B.

This is the intersection of the blending and refining constraints. Since at this point both of these resources are fully utilised, the optimum production mix can be found by solving the equations for these two lines.

100x	+	250y	=	1,050	(1)
100x	+	90y	=	450	(2)

(1) – (2)

160y	=	600
y	=	3.75

Substituting back into (1)

100x	=	1,050 – (250 × 3.75)
100x	=	112.5
x	=	1.125

Budgeted loss

	£
Contribution from Gamma (1.125 × 4,000)	4,500
Contribution from Delta (3.75 × 8,000)	30,000
	34,500
Fixed costs	36,000
Budgeted loss	(1,500)

(c)   Part (b) shows that the optimum production plan produces a net loss of £1,500 for the three months to 31 August 20X0. Usine Ltd must therefore decide whether to produce at all in the period.

In part this decision will depend upon whether all or part of the £36,000 of fixed costs can be avoided. It is likely that some of the costs will have to be paid even if the production plant is idle: for example insurance costs, equipment rental and maintenance expenses. Additionally we are not told whether the variable costs per kg include any labour costs. If they do, it is unlikely that such costs are truly variable, since workers cannot usually be dismissed for a three month period whilst the plant is shut down.

Management would also have to consider very carefully the accuracy of their estimates of costs, revenues, and resource restrictions. For example, an increase of £400 per kg in the selling price of Delta (assuming that 3.75 kg could still be sold) would result in break-even. This represents an increase of only 1.6% on the existing selling price, and so the production decision would be extremely sensitive to changes in any of the budgeted data. Finally, Usine Ltd should not consider this three month period in isolation. If it were to close down production now there may be an adverse effect on future periods if goodwill is damaged through existing customers going elsewhere.

It may also be advisable to consider future expected demand. If demand cannot be satisfied in the future, consideration should be given to producing now and placing the output in stock for future sale.

In summary, it may be advisable for Usine Ltd to proceed with the production plan identified in part (b).

(d)   **Shadow price of refining time**

If one extra hour of refining time is available, the optimum solution will still occur at the intersection of the refining and blending constraints.

$$100x + 90y = 451 \quad (1)$$
$$100x + 250y = 1,050 \quad (2)$$

$(2) - (1)$

$$160y = 599$$
$$y = 3.74375$$

Substituting into (1)

$$100x = 451 - (90 \times 3.74375)$$
$$100x = 114.0625$$
$$x = 1.140625$$

	£
Revised maximum contribution	
$(1.140625 \times 4,000) + (3.74375 \times 8,000)$	34,512.50
Original contribution	34,500.00
	———
Increase in contribution per hour	
(The shadow price of refining time)	12.50
	———

The shadow prices of £27.50 and £12.50 for blending and refining time respectively represent the increase in contribution that would result from one extra hour of that scarce resource being available.

Consequently they represent the maximum premiums on top of the existing prices that management should be prepared to pay to obtain extra resources. Shadow prices are therefore essential information for management when trying to obtain additional resources to relax critical constraints.

It should also be noted that the shadow price represents the fall in contribution if one less hour of time is available. Hence, if Usine received an offer to sell some of its processing time, the selling price would have to exceed (or at the least equal) the variable cost plus the contribution forgone. In effect, then, the shadow price is an opportunity cost. Similarly the shadow prices could be useful to Usine in a preliminary appraisal of new products. Any new products that utilised blending or refining time should be charged with the full opportunity cost of those resources (variable cost plus shadow price) at the budgeting stage.

The limitations inherent in the figures are largely those of the linear programming technique from which the shadow prices were derived.

The assumptions of divisibility and linearity may be questionable. If we had one extra hour of refining time available could we really modify our production plan by such fine amounts? Also, is the selling price per kg and the variable production cost constant over the entire output range? There is also an assumption that there is independence between the two products, both in terms of production mix and sales quantities.

A particular limitation of the dual price is that it relates to marginal changes in the resource's availability. We would pay a premium of up to £12.50 for one extra hour of refining time, but beyond a certain level other constraints would prevent the use of further amounts. (The maximum amount of refining time Usine could utilise without relaxing **other** constraints could be found by solving the constraints for blending and heating time). It may be impossible for Usine to obtain the additional processing time in small amounts, since it may have to build additional plant or sub-contract.

2   **Charlotte**

Calculation of the cost/benefit of accepting the contract for 20 fugrands

	Note	£
Revenue		100,000
Unskilled labour	1	(4,000)
Skilled labour	1	(12,000)
Variable overhead	2	(3,600)
Cotassium pyanide	4	(7,000)
Wedrine	5	(30,000)
Clastip	6	(2)
Z 200		(5,000)
CBX	7	(20,000)
Net benefit		18,398

As there is a net benefit, Charlotte should accept the contract.

Note 1: Labour

	Unskilled	Skilled
Number of units	20	20
Hours per unit	×	×
	40	20
	800	400
	×	×
Rate per hour	£5	£30*
	£4,000	£12,000

		£
*	Rate	10
	Premium (200% × £10)	20
		30

Note 2: Variable overhead

Number of units	20
Hours per unit	×
	60
	1,200
	×
Rate per hour	£3
	£3,600

Note 3: Fixed overhead

Fixed costs do not vary with the decision and therefore should be ignored.

Note 4: Cotassium pyanide

Requirement: 20 × 2 kg = 40 kg

	£
Saving of disposal costs on stock, 30 kg × £100	(3,000)
Purchase of 10 kg extra, 10 kg × £1,000	10,000
	7,000

Note 5: Wedrine

20 × 3 litres × £500 = £30,000

Note 6: Clastip

Requirement: 20 × 1 m =	20 m
Amount foregone per metre	£0.10 $(\frac{1}{100} \times £10)$
Total foregone	£2

Note 7: CBX

	£
Cost with contract	
One CBX	50,000
Cost without contract	
One CB 500	30,000
	———
Cost of contract	20,000
	———

Answers to multiple choice questions

1   C

Material is not a binding constraint. (Usage in units at maximum sales demand is < 500,000 units).

Product	A	B	C	D
Contribution (£)	22	18	20	19
Labour hours	2	3	1	3
Contribution/key factor	£11	£6	£20	£6.33

2   A

Only pair that satisfy requirements.

3   D

Feasible region (somewhat sneakily) is (0,8), (3,2), (0,5); by considering gradients, optimal = (0,8).

Chapter 11 solutions

1   **X plc**

Process account

	11.1 trs	£		11.1. trs	£
Input material	10,000	10,000	Output	8,700	10,092
Labour and overheads	–	800	Normal loss	1,000	360
			Abnormal loss	300	348
	10,000	10,800		10,000	10,800

Output valued at (£10,800 – £360)/9,000 = £1.16 per litre

Normal loss

	11.1 trs	£		11.1. trs	£
Process	1,000	360	Cash	1,300	468
Bal b/f to abnormal loss	300	108			
	1,300	468		1,300	468

Abnormal loss

	11.1 trs	£		11.1. trs	£
Process	300	348	Normal loss	300	108
			P&L		240
	300	348		300	348

2   **Chemical compound**

  11.1.1.6.1.1 *(a)*   *Process A*

		£		1. g	£ per kg	£
Direct material	2,000	10,000	Normal loss (W2)	400	0.500	200
Direct labour		7,200	To Process B (W3)	1,400	18.575	26,005
Process costs		8,400	Abnormal loss	200	18.575	3,715
Overhead (W1)		4,320				
	2,000	29,920		2,000		29,920

W1   £6,840 × 7,200/(7,200 + 4,200)

W2   Normal loss = 20% of input = 2,000 × 20% = 400 kg

W3   Value of output = £(29,920 – 200)/(2,000 – 400) = £18.575 per kg

11.1.1.6.1.2 (b)   Process B

	kg	£		kg	£ per kg	£
From Process A	1,400	26,005	Finished goods (W6)	2,620	21.7516	56,989
Direct material	1,400	16,800	Normal loss (W4)	280	1.825	511
Direct labour		4,200				
Overhead		2,520				
Process costs		5,800				
		———				
Total costs		55,325				
Abnormal gain (W5, W6)	100	2,175				
	——	———		——		———
	2,900	57,500		2,900		57,500

W4   Normal loss = 10% × (1,400 + 1,400) = 280

W5   Expected output = 2,800 – 280 = 2,520 units; actual output 2,620; 100 units abnormal gain

W6   Cost per unit = £(55,325 – 511) / (2,800 – 280) = £21.7516 (kept this accurate to avoid rounding errors)

11.1.1.6.1.2.3 (c)   Normal loss (scrap) account

	kg	£		kg	£
Process A	400	200	Cash – process A	600	300.00
Process B	280	511	Cash – process B	180	328.50
			Balance – transfer		82.50
	——	——	to abnormal loss	——	———
	680	711		680	711.00

11.1.1.6.1.2.4

11.1.1.6.1.2.5 (d)   Abnormal loss / gain account

	£		£
From normal loss a/c	82.50	Process B	2,175.00
Process A	3,715.00	P & L	1,622.50
	———		———
	3,797.50		3,797.50

11.1.1.6.1.2.6

11.1.1.6.1.2.7 (e)			**Finished goods**	
	kg	£	*kg*	£
Process B	2,620	56,989		

11.1.1.6.1.2.8 (f)		**P & L**	
	£		£
Abnormal loss/gain	1,622.50		

3 Process WIP

Physical flow of units

Opening WIP	+	Units started	=	Units completed	+	Closing WIP
50	+	300	=	275 (bal fig)	+	75

Units started and finished = 275 – 50 = 225

(a)   *FIFO method*

11.1.1.6.1.3 Equivalent units of production

Completing opening WIP (50 × 80%)	40
Units started and finished	225
Closing WIP (75 × 60%)	45
	——
Equivalent units in the period	310
	——

Cost for March = £3,596

$$\therefore \text{Cost per unit} = \frac{£3,596}{310} = £11.60$$

	£
11.1.1.6.1.4 Value of finished goods	
Units started and finished in March (225 × £11.60)	2,610
B/f value of opening WIP	100
Cost to complete opening WIP (40 × £11.60)	464
	——
	3,174
	——
Value of closing WIP (45 × £11.60)	522

(b)   *Average method*

11.1.1.6.1.5 Equivalent units of production

Units completed	275
Closing WIP (60%)	45
	——
	320
	——

11.1.1.6.1.6 Total cost

For March	3,596
B/f	100
	——
	3,696
	——

∴ Cost per unit	=	$\dfrac{£3,696}{320}$	=	£11.55
Value of finished goods	=	275 × £11.55	=	£3,176.25
Value of closing WIP	=	45 × £11.55	=	£519.75

4   Process X

The physical flow of units:

Opening WIP	+	Units started	=	Units completed	+	Closing WIP
6,000	+	16,000	=	18,000 (bal)	+	4,000

The effective units, costs and costs per unit are set out in a table as follows. Note that since 'all the material is introduced at the start of Process X', the CWIP must be 100% complete with respect to materials:

Input	Effective units			Costs			Costs per EU (£)
	Completed in period	c/f in CWIP	Total EU	b/f in OWIP	In period	Total costs (£)	
Materials	18,000	4,000 (100%)	22,000	24,000	64,000	88,000	4.00
Conversion	18,000	3,000 (75%)	21,000	15,300	75,000	90,300	4.30
						178,300	8.30

The costs may now be attributed to the categories of output as follows:

			£	£
				149,400
Completed units:	18,000 × £8.30			
Closing WIP:	Materials	4,000 × £4	16,000	
	Conversion	3,000 × £4.30	12,900	
				28,900
				178,300

The process account will thus appear as follows:

11.1.1.6.1.6.1   Process X account

	£		£
Material b/f	24,000	Closing WIP	28,900
Conversion b/f	15,300	Completed	149,400
Materials in period	64,000		
Conversion in period	75,000		
	178,300		178,300

5   Product X

(a)   A joint product is a product acknowledged in its own right as a main product by virtue of its saleable value. The joint costs need to be apportioned between the joint products at the split-off point to obtain the cost of each of the products in order to value closing stocks and cost of sales.

A by-product is a product that arises incidentally to the main product and therefore will not have a sufficiently high saleable value in order for it to be treated as a main product. The costs incurred in the process are shared between the joint products alone. The by-products do not pick up a share of the costs. The sales value of the by-product at the split-off point is treated as a *reduction in costs* instead of an income.

(b)   Costs to apportion   =   Joint process costs - Revenue from product C

   =   £272,926 - (2770 × £0.80)

   =   £270,710

Market value of output:

Product A - 16,000 × £6.10	=	£97,600
Product B - 53,200 × £7.50	=	£399,000
		£496,600

Apportionment of joint process costs:

Product A = $270,710 \times \dfrac{97,600}{496,600}$ =   £53,204

Product B = $270,710 \times \dfrac{399,000}{496,600}$ =   £217,506

Cost per kg:

Product A = $\dfrac{53,204}{16,000}$ = £3.325 per kg

Product B = $\dfrac{217,506}{53,200}$ = £4.088 per kg

(c)   Production costs:

	kilos	£
Material P	3,220	16,100
Material T	6,440	10,304
	9,660	26,404
Conversion costs		23,796
		50,200

Cost per kg of output = $\dfrac{50,200}{9,660 - 0.05 \times 9,660}$ = £5.47 per kg

Process Account

	kgs	£		kgs	£
Raw Materials	3,220	26,404	Normal loss	483	0
Conversion costs	6,440	23,796	Finished Goods	9,130	49,943
			Abnormal Loss	47	257
	9,660	50,200		9,660	50,200

Answers to multiple choice questions

1   Abnormal loss or gain is the balancing figure in the process account. Any gain will be a debit entry in the account.

The corresponding credit is in the abnormal gain account.

∴ **Correct answer: A**

2   Equivalent units are 'Notional whole units representing uncompleted work'.

∴ **Correct answer: A**

3

	Units
Total input	13,500
Output complete	11,750
Closing work-in-progress	1,750

Valuation:

			£
Materials	:	1,750 × (£4.50 + £1.25)	10,062.50
Labour and overheads	:	1,750 × £2.50	4,375.00
			14,437.50

∴ **Correct answer: B**

4   The physical flow of units:

Opening WIP	+	Units started	=	Units completed	+	Losses	+	Closing WIP
2,000	+	24,000	=	19,500	+	3,500 (bal)	+	3,000

Normal loss   =   10% × 24,000   =   2,400
⇒ Abnormal loss   1,100
                                                  3,500

	Completed in period	*CWIP*	*AL*	*Total*
Materials	19,500	3,000	1,100	23,600
Conversion	19,500	1,350 (45%)	1,100	21,950

∴ **Correct answer: D**

Index

Exam Text Review Form

CIMA PAPER 8 – MANAGEMENT ACCOUNTING – PERFORMANCE MANAGEMENT

We hope that you have found this Text stimulating and useful and that you now feel confident and well-prepared for your examinations.

We would be grateful if you could take a few moments to complete the questionnaire below, so we can assess how well our material meets your needs. There's a prize for four lucky students who fill in one of these forms from across the Syllabus range and are lucky enough to be selected!

	Excellent	*Adequate*	*Poor*
Depth and breadth of technical coverage			
Appropriateness of coverage to examination			
Presentation			
Level of accuracy			

Did you spot any errors or ambiguities? Please let us have the details below.

Page	Error

Thank you for your feedback.

Please return this form to:

The Financial Training Company Limited
Unit 2, Block 2, Wincombe Conference Centre
Wincombe Business Park
Shaftesbury
Dorset SP7 9QJ

Student's name: ....

Address: ....

....

....

CIMA Publications Student Order Form

THE
FINANCIAL TRAINING
COMPANY
PUBLICATIONS DIVISION

To order your books, please indicate quantity required in the relevant order box, calculate the amount(s) in the column provided, and add postage to determine the amount due. Please then clearly fill in your details plus method of payment in the boxes provided and return your completed form with payment attached to:

THE FINANCIAL TRAINING COMPANY, 22J WINCOMBE BUSINESS PARK, SHAFTESBURY, DORSET SP7 9QJ

OR FAX YOUR ORDER TO 01747 858821 OR TELEPHONE 01747 854302

For examinations in Nov 03 ☐ May 04 ☐ Nov 04 ☐ (please tick)

FOUNDATION

PAPER	TITLE	TEXT ORDER	PRICE £	EXAM KIT ORDER	PRICE £	FOCUS NOTES ORDER	PRICE £	AMOUNT £
1	Financial Accounting Fundamentals		21.00		11.00		6.00	
2	Management Accounting Fundamentals		21.00		11.00		6.00	
3a	Economics for Business		21.00		11.00		6.00	
3b	Business Law		21.00		11.00		6.00	
3c	Business Mathematics		21.00		11.00		6.00	

INTERMEDIATE

PAPER	TITLE	TEXT ORDER	PRICE £	EXAM KIT ORDER	PRICE £	FOCUS NOTES ORDER	PRICE £	AMOUNT £
4	Finance		21.00		11.00		6.00	
5	Business Taxation [FA 2002] (May & Nov 2003)		21.00		11.00		6.00	
	Business Taxation [FA 2003] (May & Nov 2004)		21.00	Available Feb 04	11.00	Available Feb 04	6.00	
6a	Financial Accounting (UK Standards)		21.00		11.00		6.00	
7a	Financial Reporting (UK Standards)		21.00		11.00		6.00	
8	Management Accounting - Performance Management		21.00		11.00		6.00	
9	Management Accounting - Decision Making		21.00		11.00		6.00	
10	Systems & Project Management		21.00		11.00		6.00	
11	Organisational Management		21.00		11.00		6.00	

FINAL

PAPER	TITLE	TEXT ORDER	PRICE £	EXAM KIT ORDER	PRICE £	FOCUS NOTES ORDER	PRICE £	AMOUNT £
12	Management Accounting - Business Strategy		21.00		11.00		6.00	
13	Management Accounting - Financial Strategy		21.00		11.00		6.00	
14	Management Accounting - Information Strategy		21.00		11.00		6.00	
15	Management Accounting - Case Study		21.00					

Sub Total	£	

Postage and packing – please note a signature is required on delivery

UK & NI	£5 for up to 10 books		
	If only Focus Notes are ordered, £1 each (max £5)	£	
	First book	**Each additional book**	
Europe	£25	£3	
Rest of World	£40	£4	

TOTAL PAYMENT	£	

The following section **must be filled in clearly** so that your order can be despatched without delay.

TO PAY FOR YOUR ORDER TICK AN OPTION BELOW

A. I WISH TO PAY BY   MASTERCARD ☐   VISA ☐   DELTA ☐   SWITCH ☐

CARD NO. ☐☐☐☐ ☐☐☐☐ ☐☐☐☐ ☐☐☐☐ (Some cards don't need all boxes)

EXPIRY DATE ☐☐☐☐   ISSUE No. ☐☐☐ (Switch only)   All cards - last 3 digits on signature strip ☐☐☐

Cardholder's Signature _____

Cardholder's Name & Address: _____

Cardholder's Tel. No. (Day): _____

B. I WISH TO PAY BY CHEQUE ☐   Cheques should be made payable to *The Financial Training Company Ltd* and must be attached to your order form. **Personal cheques cannot be accepted without a valid Banker's Card number written on the back of the cheque.**

STUDENT NAME:

DELIVERY ADDRESS: (Must be the same as cardholder's address. Please contact us if you wish to discuss an alternative delivery address).

POST CODE: | TEL. NO. (Day):

April 2003 (This order form replaces any previous order forms.)